Steve Michel's SuperCard
Handbook

Steve Michel's SuperCard Handbook

Steve Michel

Osborne **McGraw-Hill**

Berkeley New York St. Louis San Francisco
Auckland Bogotá Hamburg London Madrid
Mexico City Milan Montreal New Delhi Panama City
Paris São Paulo Singapore Sydney
Tokyo Toronto

Osborne **McGraw-Hill**
2600 Tenth Street
Berkeley, California 94710
U.S.A.

For information on translations and book distributors outside of the U.S.A., please write to Osborne **McGraw-Hill** at the above address.

A complete list of trademarks appears on page 385.
Screens produced with Capture from Mainstay Software.

Steve Michel's SuperCard Handbook

1234567890 DOC 89

ISBN 0-07-881540-1

As always, I dedicate this book to my family, Margaret, Lyal, Richard, and Genevieve Michel, without whom none of it would be worth it.

CONTENTS

FOREWORD

SuperCard is on the cutting edge of a new family of programs whose uses cross all categories and professions. What sets SuperCard apart from other programs is that instead of being a single tool that most people need, it is a group of programs that allows individuals to build their own tools.

Desktop publishing contributed to the industry by lowering the cost and effort required to produce professional results. This meant that it became financially reasonable to publish works that, despite their excellence, might sell to only a small audience. It also meant that a lot of great work that would have been lost will continue to exist, and that is a truly important benefit. The flip side is that it is equally easy to produce garbage cheaply and easily.

We've also made software readily available. The Mac's ease of use was built on the bent backs of programmers who had to memorize the contents of technical documents to actually produce software that worked with that simple user interface. Our intention with SuperCard was to lower the "cost" of producing custom and personal software tools. That cost is now measured in weeks and months, as opposed to the months and years of traditional Macintosh software.

One of SuperCard's best features is that, as you become familiar with the program, it will take less time to become productive with it. The reason for this is twofold. First, SuperCard has the ability to create tools that people can use to build more tools that people can use to build more tools. And second, resources such as Steve Michel and this book are available to help you.

Steve was one of my KBTs (Killer Beta Testers), and his touches and suggestions permeate the program. He is extremely qualified to write this book, and his humor makes it enjoyable to read. If you're standing in a bookstore reading this to see if you want the book, buy it! If it's already yours, enjoy it. And enjoy SuperCard—you'll find that you can do remarkable things with it.

—Ben Calica

Books are generally written by one person, but they almost always require the help of others. In this book, I have been helped by a number of people. At Osborne/McGraw-Hill, Jeff Pepper and Judith Brown kept me working, insisted on the stupid title, and made sure the book got out. At Silicon Beach Software, Ben Calica and Stuart Henigson kept me supplied with beta copies of the program and documentation. Bill Appleton wrote a great piece of software and deserves recognition for it. Ric Ford, of MacWEEK, and Greg Merriman read through the chapters and tried to keep me from putting my foot in my mouth. (If they were not always successful, that's not their fault.) Support—moral and otherwise—was provided by Eric Alderman, Dale Coleman, Charles Greiner, Bob Kermish, Dennis Klatzkin, Xavier Raya, and Roger Strukhoff.

ACKNOWLEDGMENTS

When Apple Computer introduced HyperCard in the summer of 1987, reaction was mixed among developers and users. A great many users flocked to the program, embracing it and taking advantage of its unique combination of features. Part database, part graphics program, and part programming language, HyperCard has certainly had a more profound effect on Macintosh users than any other program released.

However, the euphoria over HyperCard predictably gave way to a more sober evaluation of its capabilities. This reevaluation focused on two areas. First, though considerably easier to use than most other programming languages, HyperTalk still requires a fair degree of expertise and learning time to master: it is not for everyone. Second, with all the power of HyperCard and HyperTalk, there are a number of aspects of the Macintosh user interface that HyperCard ignores. While there was not much most developers could do about the first problem, there were a number of things that could be done about the second. Developers prepared numerous HyperCard add-ons to bring to it features that it lacked, such as color and menus.

Bill Appleton and Silicon Beach Software took another approach. They decided to not fix HyperCard piecemeal, but to create another program that offered everything HyperCard offered, and more. That program is SuperCard.

I first saw SuperCard in November, 1987 at a demonstration for the editors of MacWEEK in San Francisco. I was immediately taken with the program. Even though the computer I was using at the time (a Mac SE) could not take advantage of many of SuperCard's features, I knew I wanted those features, and felt that many other stackheads, as well as developers of in-house applications and multimedia presentations, would want them, too.

About This Book

When I approached Osborne/McGraw-Hill about a SuperCard handbook, the question was what to cover in the book? Should we create a complete reference to SuperCard, including everything in the program or the language? Based on the size of existing HyperCard books, it seemed that such a book would inevitably be very large--probably close to 1000 pages. A better idea was to write a book that expressly discussed the features SuperCard offered that HyperCard did not (assuming that most users of SuperCard would already be familiar with HyperCard.)

And that is the book you are holding in your hands. In writing this book, I have assumed that you know HyperCard, that you have probably already more or less memorized the scripting portion of Apple's Hyper-Card Help stack, and that you have read at least some of the 657 (at last count) books dealing with the program. If this doesn't describe you, then this book probably isn't for you. (Though Chapter 5 does cover the basics of scripting, it does so with the focus of explaining how scripting is different in SuperCard from HyperCard.) You should probably spend more time learning HyperCard before going on to SuperCard, or at least make sure you understand the fundamentals of SuperTalk programming as explained in Chapter 5 of the SuperCard manual. For the most part, if you don't find some aspect of the language mentioned in this book, you can assume that it works the same way in SuperCard that it does in HyperCard.

Why This Book Is for You

This book is written by an experienced HyperCard developer for other experienced HyperCard developers who want to quickly learn to master the enhanced features of SuperCard to produce polished, professional applications using SuperCard.

While SuperCard is based on HyperCard—indeed it contains virtually all the capability of HyperCard—the two programs are really quite different. SuperCard sports a number of features that are not available in HyperCard, such as the abilities to use multiple windows, create your own menus, work with graphics objects, and use color. Using these features means more than just adding scripts to work with the new features in your existing stacks. It may mean making significant changes in the way you approach application design.

SuperCard Explained

The Strengths of HyperCard
Why SuperCard?
Changing Your Way of Thinking
The Elements of SuperCard
The SuperCard Environment
The Future

O
N
E

At one time, if you wanted to program a Macintosh, you had to do a great deal of work before putting your program together. Not only did you have to master a complex programming language such as C or Pascal, you had to have a sufficient understanding of Apple's *Inside Macintosh*, a large set of books describing the inner workings of the Macintosh ROMs.

This situation has changed dramatically. Now, almost anyone—not just experienced programmers—can create applications for the Macintosh using HyperCard, which Apple introduced in 1987. HyperCard is a program that mixes elements of a database, a graphics program, and a programming language. Bill Atkinson, the creator of the program, calls it a "software erector set." HyperCard's programming language, Hyper-Talk, represents a real breakthrough in ease of learning and ease of use.

The Strengths of HyperCard

The success of HyperTalk and HyperCard can be attributed to several factors:

- HyperCard is an *integrated* environment, which means that HyperCard includes tools that allow you to manipulate graphics, text, and numbers.

• HyperTalk allows you to create your own programs, in the form of buttons, functions, and other features, that do just what you want them to do. If you have a special need for which there is no available software, you can create your own programs in Hyper-Talk. The major strength of HyperTalk is its English-like syntax that has allowed a large number of people to become conversant in the language very quickly. Existing programs can be examined easily and learned.

• HyperCard features a series of "user levels." Starting with the simplest of these levels, browsing, and then moving to progressively more complicated ones, you can learn HyperCard at your own pace.

• HyperCard is free, included at no extra charge with all Mac-intoshes. You can create HyperCard documents or stacks and dis-tribute them to others, who can use them without purchasing expensive software.

• HyperCard is a new type of program in that it is designed for *publishing* information. Its various features — text fields, fairly fast searching, integrated graphics, sound — make it ideal for organizing information so that it can be delivered to others.

Why SuperCard?

With all the strengths of HyperCard, why is SuperCard necessary? There are several answers to this question.

• HyperCard still lacks a number of features. As we shall see, almost as soon as people started using HyperCard, they began asking for new capabilities that were not included in the original program. SuperCard provides these features without having to wait for Apple Computer to supply them.

• HyperTalk is a tool for programming the HyperCard, not the Macintosh, user interface. The distinction is crucial because there are a number of standard features of the Macintosh user interface (such as menus and multiple windows) that HyperTalk does not support. The fact that SuperTalk (the SuperCard programming language) gives you control over virtually the entire user interface makes it much more useful as a tool for creating projects that more closely mimic standard Macintosh applications.

This control has several implications. First, professional programmers can more easily create full-blown prototypes of applications to test the interface before beginning the hard work of coding the application in C or Pascal. Second, users of your SuperCard projects will probably need to know less about the workings of SuperCard itself to use your applications.

• SuperCard establishes the HyperTalk programming language as a standard. Users who start programming in HyperTalk almost immediately want to have the language available in other programs. Once you get used to HyperCard's Message box as a way of entering complex commands, you will wish you had it in word processors, databases, spreadsheets, and so on. Even painting programs could benefit from a Message box.

Apple has indicated that it plans to establish HyperTalk as a system-wide programming tool. SuperCard, while still strictly in the HyperCard arena, takes the HyperTalk standard one step beyond HyperCard itself.

Changing Your Way of Thinking

When you are moving from HyperCard to SuperCard, or switching between the two environments, you need to do some mental gear-shifting. SuperCard is more than just an enhanced HyperCard; it is in many ways a different *kind* of program, one that you will often use for fundamentally different purposes than HyperCard. Three areas of difference between the two programs stand out: the cycle you go through in developing a project, the features you use in your project, and the manner in which it is delivered to other users.

The Development Cycle

One key area of difference between the two programs is in the structure of the development cycle. Since HyperCard combines the development environment and the using environment, everything is done in one place. Creating a new stack, doing the artwork, importing resources, running the stack, and delivering it to others, are all handled in the same program.

SuperCard's environment, as you will see, is different. Generally, you use the SuperEdit program to create your projects, to lay out much of the design of the project, and to do a great deal of the scripting. You use the Runtime Editor to fine-tune the project, creating new buttons and graphics, modifying programs, and so on. When the project is finished, chances are you will deliver it to your users as a stand-alone application, and they might not even realize you used SuperCard to create it.

Using SuperCard's Features

HyperCard is able to run on all Macintosh computers that have at least 1 MB of RAM. This includes all Macs with at least the capabilities of the Mac Plus; as long as the computer has more than 1 MB of RAM and a hard disk, you can run HyperCard on it. Further, since HyperCard usually uses capabilities that are found on that minimal Mac Plus system, you don't need to worry about implementing features that won't work on minimal machines. If your stack runs on one machine it will, for the most part, run on all machines.

SuperCard, however, is not limited to features that are only available on the basic models of the Macintosh. It can take advantage of features of the Mac II, including color and windows larger than that of the standard Macintosh screen.

This places a burden on the developer of SuperCard projects. When designing a project, you will need to take special care in defining the audience for it, and deciding how to implement its features so that they can work on various models of the Macintosh. Using color, for example, will limit the number of users who can work with your project. When designing cards, you need to consider using larger screens versus smaller screens.

Delivering Projects to Others

When you create a HyperCard stack, you have only one means of delivering that stack to others: as a HyperCard stack. With SuperCard, on the other hand, you can deliver your projects to others in one of two ways: either as a project that is to be used with the Runtime Editor or as a stand-alone Macintosh application. Each method has its unique requirements.

If you are delivering your project to others to run in the SuperCard environment along with the Runtime Editor, you need to make sure that your project acts as a "good citizen" in that environment. It should not insert menus with wild abandon, nor should it make assumptions about what other projects the user might have open at the same time.

If you are delivering your project as a stand-alone application, a different set of rules applies. In this environment, you must make sure to include in your application all the tools your users will need to take advantage of the features of your program. Certain menus (Apple, File, and Edit) should be included as a matter of course. In other respects, however, you have many more choices. It is not as important that your project act as a good citizen. You can safely assume that your project is the only one open at any one time, and therefore you have more control over the environment.

With these requirements in mind, the rest of this chapter discusses features of HyperCard and SuperCard, focusing on how they differ.

The Elements of SuperCard

SuperCard is not a program, but a set of tools that allows you to create your own programs. It features a fast, flexible Editor (SuperEdit) that allows you to build programs — called *projects* — that you can deliver to others. Its built-in programming language, SuperTalk, is a superset of HyperTalk, which means that SuperCard contains all standard Hyper-Talk commands plus extensions that allow it to manipulate elements new to SuperCard from HyperCard.

For SuperCard, virtually every element of HyperCard has been enhanced to include new features.

Projects

SuperCard files, called projects, contain all the other elements of Super-Card. You might think that these projects are equivalent to HyperCard stacks. In one sense they are—they are the largest structure with which the program can deal. However, there is one very important difference. In HyperCard, a stack contains all the cards and backgrounds that are part of that stack, and projects do not. In SuperCard, *windows* contain the backgrounds and cards. In effect, each window is a separate stack.

There are some significant ramifications to this difference. If, for example, you are creating a complex application in HyperCard, you need to decide whether the different facets of your design should be separated into cards of different backgrounds in the same stack, or should be distributed as separate stacks that work together. Activision's Focal Point is an example of a program that uses a fairly large collection of different stacks. Had Focal Point been created with SuperCard, it could conceivably have been distributed as one project, with the different stacks constituting different windows in the project.

Windows

Even though SuperCard's windows are the rough equivalent of Hyper-Card stacks, there are several key differences between the two:

• Windows contain cards. The appearance of cards depends on the size and type of the window that contains the card, and the design of the background that the window is a part of.

• Windows can be of varying size. This is one of the key differences between HyperCard and SuperCard. With HyperCard, you are restricted to a card size of 512 pixels across and 342 down.

• You can have different *types* of windows. Macintosh applications feature different types of windows to present different types of information. *Scrollable windows* allow you to view cards that are larger than the monitor you are using. *Dialog windows* allow you to create dialog boxes to obtain information from your users. *Floating palettes*, such as the tool palettes in HyperCard, allow you to create windows that "float" over the current card.

SuperCard's windows, then, are flexible tools that give you a wide variety of options for viewing the information presented on cards.

Cards and Backgrounds

SuperCard cards are, in many ways, similar to cards in HyperCard. Just as HyperCard stacks are ordered collections of cards, each with an appearance that is based partly on the design of the background it uses, so are cards in SuperCard. The most important difference is that cards in SuperCard can be of different sizes. You can create cards that are as large as 32767 pixels by 32767 pixels. At 72 pixels per inch, this translates into a potential card size of about 30 feet by 30 feet.

Although you'll probably never create a card 30 feet on a side, SuperCard's flexibility in card size can be very useful. For example, one of the standard options that SuperEdit gives you for card size is 8-by-10 inches—close to the size of a standard sheet of paper. You can use this card size to create a variety of cards designed for printed output, such as invoices, reports, letters, and so on.

Just as with HyperCard, the appearance of cards in SuperCard depends on the appearance of the backgrounds they share. And just as is the case in HyperCard, stacks (windows) can include many backgrounds. In SuperCard, you control the size of the card by setting the size of the background. One of the ramifications of this control is that cards in the same window may be of different sizes because their backgrounds have different sizes.

Menus

One of the earliest criticisms of HyperCard was that it did not give you control of the full range of tools that make up the Macintosh user interface, particularly menus. Standard HyperTalk includes no provision for adding or deleting menus, for example. Early in the life of Hyper-Card, external commands were created that allowed you to access your own menus, and many sets of external resources (such as Discovery's HyperSearch), developed their own menus.

SuperCard addresses this weakness by giving you total control over the menu bar that appears when you run SuperCard. This control feature allows you to tailor the tools in your stack precisely to the needs of your stack, giving you the ability to assign COMMAND-key shortcuts to the menu items and to create hierarchical menus. You can insert and remove entire menus from script control and create special "modes" for your projects.

SuperCard defines two special menus—the Apple menu and the Font menu—a handy touch. When you create and insert an Apple menu, that menu automatically displays all the Desk Accessories available from the standard Apple menu. When you create and insert a Font menu, that menu automatically displays the names of all the fonts currently available for your stack. If you are using SuitCase II's option for displaying the names of the fonts in the actual font itself, this option works in the Font menu. These touches are important and speed the process of creating "real" Macintosh applications.

Resources

Resources are standard parts of Macintosh applications that contain many of the tools that those applications use. The resources in a file usually include definitions for such items as dialog boxes, menus, alerts, icons, pictures, and more. Since SuperCard gives you the ability to create menus and dialog boxes, you do not need to use resources to create these objects. On the other hand, a program needs to perform some functions that can only be handled as resources, such as string sounds, external commands and functions, and color lookup tables (more about this later).

SuperCard has added a special "type" of object that allows you to deal with resources in a more direct way than HyperCard. To understand the ramifications of this, let's take a look behind the scenes.

When a Macintosh application needs a resource, it requests one from the Resource Manager, which then locates it on disk; the resource may be in the current System File, or it may be in the application or file itself. The Resource Manager finds the resource and delivers it to the application.

However, the Resource Manager has certain limitations that can cause problems. Because the Resource Manager works best with small files (to allow programs to access relatively small numbers of resources quickly), it is not suitable for large numbers of resources and can in fact manage only 2727 resources. Consider color lookup tables (or *cluts*), which list the 256 colors that are used by a specific picture. In Super-Card, where stacks may contain thousands of pictures with each picture having its own color lookup table, the Resource Manager could break down quickly.

The creators of SuperCard solved this problem in a unique manner. Instead of keeping resources in the resource fork of the file, they created a way of maintaining certain types of resources in the data fork of the project. This allowed them to write their own tools for accessing resources, thus bypassing the Resource Manager and its limitations. Therefore SuperCard can handle color lookup tables, cursors, icons, external commands, external functions, and sounds.

Objects: Anything Can Be a Button

The elements of SuperCard include several types of objects: graphic objects, buttons, and fields. While buttons and fields are part of the standard HyperCard toolbox of object types, graphic objects are new.

Graphic Objects

In HyperCard, each card has two types of graphics on it: the *background graphic*, which is included on every card that shares the background, and the card's *individual graphic*, which is superimposed on the background graphic. SuperCard also has background and card graphics, but they are quite different.

In HyperCard, you have only the size of the card on which to paint. Once you have finished drawing on the card, the drawing becomes "frozen" into the array of dots or pixels that comprises the card. For example, in one corner of a card you might have a small picture of a face and in another corner a small picture of a dog. Even though they are connected by white space, these two pictures are still part of the same *bitmap*, the same array of dots. To move one of the pictures, you must first select it with the selection tool or the lasso, and then move it around on the card.

SuperCard treats graphics in a very different manner. Instead of freezing all graphics into a bitmap that takes up the entire card, it creates separate *objects* that contain the graphics. In the above example, the picture of the face and the picture of the dog are different objects that can be manipulated separately, with the Move command or by clicking on the graphic and dragging the mouse. Each *bitmap object* is defined by a rectangle that contains all points in the object. Within that object, a bitmap is treated just as a bitmap in HyperCard is treated. When you are finished drawing in a bitmap, the bits form an array.

In addition to bitmap graphic objects, SuperCard contains another type of object, called the *draw-type graphic*. Draw-type graphics are of the type created by programs such as MacDraw. The difference is that the forms you create in draw-type objects are stored as mathematical descriptions instead of arrays of dots. For example, consider a line drawn in bitmap graphics compared to a line drawn in draw-type graphics. While drawing in both environments, the tools work the same way. You point to a starting point, hold down the mouse button, drag to form a line, and release the mouse button when finished drawing.

It is what you can do once the line is formed that defines the difference between bitmap and draw graphics. With bitmap graphics, once you have drawn the line, it blends into the background array of dots. To edit it, you must approach each dot individually.

With draw-type graphics, on the other hand, the program remembers that the line is a line and allows you to edit that line. You can grab an end of it to move it, you can stretch or shrink it, or you can give it a different pattern, color, or thickness. The crucial difference is that the program remembers that you are referring to a line and not to an array of dots.

Draw-type objects have strengths and weaknesses. The advantages are that you can easily edit them, and since they are stored as mathematical descriptions, they occupy less disk space and memory. A line that stretches the length of a card takes the same amount of storage space as one that extends only for a centimeter. On the negative side, the tools you have to create draw-type objects are not as "artistic" as those you have for bitmaps. There are, for example, no brush or spray paint tools for draw objects.

Graphic objects can also receive messages, (hence the slogan "anything can be a button"). HyperCard has only three ways of creating pictures that can be clicked on. You can use buttons with icons, but icons have a size limit. You can place transparent buttons over card or background graphics, but then they are fixed into the card bitmap. Or you can create a custom large font and put it into a field, but that takes a lot of work.

In SuperCard, graphic objects have their own scripts, and these scripts allow them to receive the same messages that buttons receive.

Buttons

Buttons also have their own unique characteristics in SuperCard. In addition to their HyperCard properties, including different types of buttons, icons, and so on, SuperCard buttons can have definable shadows, can be disabled (the text in their name becomes greyed out), and are not restricted to a rectangular shape.

Fields

Fields, which are used to contain text in both HyperCard and SuperCard, are still restricted to their rectangular shape, but a few new elements have been added. The primary addition is that text within a field does not necessarily have to be uniform — that is, individual characters within the field can be of a different font, style, or size from the other characters within the field. (You should note, however, that the "overhead" for storing this style of information about individual characters is considerable; projects with a great deal of styled text stored in fields will be considerably larger than projects containing uniform text.)

Color

Perhaps the most dramatic addition to SuperCard is its ability to deal with color. Color, or rather the lack of it, is one weakness that Mac II users first notice about HyperCard. SuperCard, on the other hand, puts at your disposal almost all the color capabilities of the Macintosh II. When creating graphic objects — either of the bitmap or the draw variety — you are free to color those objects any way you like. There are, however, some limitations to the use of color (see Chapter Fourteen for a detailed discussion).

The Macintosh II is theoretically capable of displaying 16 million colors. However, in the most common Macintosh configuration (the one supported by SuperCard) only 256 of those colors may be shown on the screen at any one time. The Macintosh and SuperCard use color lookup tables, which list the 256 colors that are used by a specific picture. As mentioned above, color lookup tables are one of the resources that SuperCard allows you to manage.

Probably the biggest limitation on the use of color is the intended audience for your project. If all of your users will be using Mac IIs with color, or grey-scale capabilities, then you can use color. However, if you are also developing projects to be used by Macintosh Plus or SE owners, you will probably need to forego any use of color. These machines do not display 256-color bitmap images; they appear as "garbage" on the screen.

Animation

SuperCard offers several improvements for handling animation. In HyperCard, your choices on creating animation were limited. You could "flip cards," displaying individual cards quickly to create the illusion of animation. You could cycle through different icons in a button for animation, but that limited you to the size of pictures that could be animated. Or you could create a specific font for animation and quickly switch the characters in a field to give the illusion of animation. However, creating font characters is not easy and may cause a host of problems (most notably, conflicts in font numbering and memory restrictions).

SuperCard gives you the same tools for animation as HyperCard and adds these new techniques:

• *Moving graphic objects* Since all graphics are contained within objects, you can move these objects around the screen with the Move command, and use the visible properties of the objects to hide or show them.

• *PICS animation* PICS is an emerging standard for storing animation files, supported by several programs from different vendors. Essentially, a PICS file contains a series of PICT images that can be displayed quickly. SuperCard allows you to create as well as display these files.

• *Step animation*   This is used when you want your animation to occupy the entire screen. Step animation records a bit image of the entire screen and saves a file that contains a series of these bit images. Step files, however, can take up a great deal of space on disk.

The SuperCard Environment

HyperCard is an *integrated environment*, that is, you use the same program to create new stacks as you do to browse, or use, the stacks created by others. This integration of use and creation has several benefits. First, it allows you to progress easily in the levels of the program. You can, at your own pace, graduate from the Browsing to the Painting to the Scripting modes of the program. Second, it ensures that all users have all the parts of the program they need. And third, scripts in a stack can do anything that a creator of HyperCard stacks can do.

However, this integrated environment also has some disadvantages. The major liability is that HyperCard carries around a lot of "baggage." Even if you are only browsing stacks, you still need to have on disk and, to a certain extent, in memory, all the capabilities of HyperCard even if you are not using them. This means that users of Macintoshes with "only" 1 MB of memory might be limited in the functions they can perform with HyperCard.

SuperCard separates the two environments of creating and running. As we shall see, this has some benefits as well as some drawbacks when it comes to creating projects. Mainly, though, for experienced stackheads, it represents a conceptual change that takes some practice. To see how these two environments work together, let's take a look at the various programs and files that comprise SuperCard.

SuperEdit

SuperEdit is, as its name implies, the editor portion of SuperCard. It is the program you will use most often to actually create your new stacks. While much of the functionality of SuperEdit is included in SuperCard, many elements are not. Here are the major capabilities that SuperEdit allows but SuperCard does not:

1. SuperEdit gives you an overview of your projects by allowing you to look at different elements of each project at the same time. Perhaps this is best explained by looking at the view of cards you have in SuperEdit. When you open a window overview, you are given a list of all the cards that are in that window, in numerical order. You can see the numbers, names, IDs, and background ID numbers of each card. You can go directly to any card simply by scrolling through the list of cards, and double-clicking on the card you want to edit.

Besides showing you only the windows and cards in your project, the program lets you look at all the menus and resources that are in the project.

2. SuperCard is generally nonmodal. In HyperCard, you can have only one script at a time on the screen, and this script is in a *modal* window, meaning that you cannot use such things as pull-down menus to use editing commands. Instead, you must rely on largely undocumented COMMAND-key equivalents. This makes it a nuisance to copy selections of text between different scripts, especially if the two scripts are located on different cards, or in different stacks. Though SuperCard also works this way, SuperEdit allows you to open several script windows at the same time. This makes comparison between scripts, and copying text between them, much easier. Different projects, menus, and cards can also be displayed at the same time.

With SuperEdit, you can copy and paste one card at a time (as you can in HyperCard and SuperCard) or multiple cards; even entire stacks can be copied and pasted between different projects.

3. SuperEdit can import HyperCard stacks. The code that allows SuperEdit to read HyperCard stacks takes up disk space, and there is no need to have it be part of SuperCard (although it would be nice). Since most stacks will need to be edited once they are imported into SuperCard, it only makes sense to have this function be part of SuperEdit.

4. Scripts do not "fire" or execute in SuperEdit, whereas they do in SuperCard. This is a mixed blessing. The feature is not included for several reasons, mainly having to do with memory. The development cycle takes a little longer, as you are fine-tuning scripts (although you can do that in SuperCard).

5. SuperEdit allows you to turn your projects into stand-alone applications. This means that any project you create in SuperEdit can be stored on disk as an application program, and delivered to others without requiring that they have SuperCard. This is a particularly handy feature.

6. SuperEdit includes an Undo feature that is not included in either HyperCard or SuperCard.

7. SuperEdit includes an AutoTrace tool that allows you to translate bitmap graphics, or portions of them, into either buttons or draw-type graphics. This feature is handy for creating unusual draw graphics.

SuperCard

SuperEdit allows you to *create* SuperCard projects, but SuperCard actually allows you to *use* those projects. The best way to describe SuperCard is as a program that knows how to interpret and react to the commands that make up the SuperTalk language. In SuperCard, unlike SuperEdit, scripts are active. This means that menus, cards, buttons, and graphic objects receive messages when you click on them. The Message box is available for typing commands.

An Environment You Can Customize

One of the key features of SuperCard is that it has no built-in menus. In a very real sense, it is a blank slate on which you are free to customize as you wish.

Note that SuperTalk itself includes a great many commands that allow you to edit and create projects while in the language interpreter. Many of these tools work nearly as well as those in SuperEdit, though not necessarily with all the features. Script edit windows, for example, are modal in SuperCard, and nonmodal in SuperEdit.

The Runtime Editor

SuperCard includes no standard menus, windows, cards, or interface. The process of getting started with SuperCard would be tedious if we had to create menus for such simple things as opening other projects, quitting the program, or summoning the Message box.

Fortunately, Silicon Beach Software has provided us with a standard environment. The Runtime Editor includes a wide variety of menus and palettes that you can use to run and edit your projects in Super-Card. You can use the Runtime Editor to create and edit virtually all aspects of a project.

The key item to remember about the Runtime Editor is that it is written in SuperTalk and is therefore completely customizeable. You can change it to work the way you want it to work by adding, changing, or eliminating features.

The SharedFile

The SharedFile is a special project that is analogous to HyperCard's Home stack in important ways but also has differences. Like the Home stack, the scripts and resources in the SharedFile are available to all your other projects. You can insert into SharedFile resources—handlers, functions, external commands and functions, sounds, and icons—that you want to make available to all your other projects.

The SharedFile is the only SuperCard file that actually contains a true resource fork, as HyperCard stacks do. If you need to store resources as true resources, and not as SuperCard's pseudo-resources (which are actually part of the data fork), you can use the SharedFile to do so.

On the other hand, unlike the Home stack, the SharedFile does not serve as a "home base" for your SuperCard activities. There is no equivalent to "go home" in SuperCard (although you could create one).

The Future

You might look at SuperCard not as a "competitor" to HyperCard but as another step in the evolution of the Macintosh system. SuperCard is a step toward a universal programming language that you can use to customize *all* your applications—from word processors to databases to spreadsheets and graphics programs.

Using SuperCard with the Runtime Editor

TWO

Because SuperCard gives you control over the entire interface, including all menus, command keys, windows, and so on, it includes no built-in interface. Instead, SuperCard is simply an interpreter of the extended SuperTalk language.

Instead of building or hardwiring the interface into SuperCard, some of which you might not use when creating your own stacks, Silicon Beach created a complex and powerful project called the Runtime Editor, also known as the SoftEditor.

The Runtime Editor reproduces, in SuperTalk, many of the functions of the HyperCard user interface, and, in addition, gives you many of the capabilities of SuperEdit. You should use it as an example of the kinds of applications you can create. Since it is implemented in Super-Talk, you can add or remove capabilities as you need them. As time goes by, entirely new sets of tools—new menus and palettes—will probably be developed for SuperCard. Additional tools will appear not as buttons, as they do for HyperCard, but as suites of menus and palettes that you can install into the Runtime Editor. Because the Runtime Editor is "soft," the version you are using may be slightly different than the one discussed in this chapter.

This chapter explains how to use the Runtime Editor with various projects, organized by the Editor's menus. (The details of the scripts used by the Runtime Editor are discussed in Appendix B.)

There are three ways to activate SuperCard and the Runtime Editor. The first way is to simply double-click on the file Runtime Editor from the Finder. The Finder will both load SuperCard and open the Runtime Editor with it. You can also double-click on SuperCard itself. After SuperCard is loaded, you are presented with a standard file interface dialog box, asking you to open a project. Find the Runtime Editor and load it.

The third way to start the Runtime Editor is by installing it into one of your projects. This is a handy method for giving your own project access to the Runtime Editor without having to write any scripts. Since this is done from within the Runtime Editor, you'll need to use one of the previous techniques the first time you open your project.

Working in the SuperCard Environment

Before you begin using the Runtime Editor, you should know a few things about SuperCard. First, like HyperCard but unlike SuperEdit, SuperCard is constantly saving changes to your project on disk, reducing the chance of losing data should your machine crash while running the program. On the other hand, it is convenient to be able to experiment with certain things in SuperEdit, knowing that you can safely recover a previous version from disk.

SuperCard's automatic saving feature is slightly different from HyperCard's, which saves changes as they actually occur; SuperCard saves changes (to a card or window, for example) only when that card or window is actually closed. If you experience a system crash, some of your most recent changes might not be saved.

Second, SuperCard features no Undo command. This is not unexpected considering the amount of the Macintosh user interface that SuperCard gives you and the difficulty of programming the Undo facility. HyperCard also lacks an Undo command (it is there, but works infrequently). Keep this in mind when using SuperCard; many of your changes will be permanent.

Script editing is also different in SuperCard than in SuperEdit. In SuperEdit, it is possible to have several script windows open at the same time (see Chapter Three). In SuperCard, script windows are modal: you can only work in one of them at a time, just as in HyperCard.

SuperCard Is "Homeless"

One of the first things you'll notice about SuperCard is that it has no HOME stack. This takes some getting used to, but SuperCard provides two tools that replace Home—the SharedFile and the Runtime Editor.

HyperCard uses Home as a central repository of scripts and resources: since Home is the final stop in the message hierarchy before HyperCard itself, it is the only place that all messages automatically pass through and can be intercepted. The same thing is true of sounds, external commands and functions, and icons. SuperCard's SharedFile serves this same purpose: it is the last stop in the SuperTalk message hierarchy before SuperCard itself, and so can serve as a repository for your standard resources, including scripts.

Home is also used as a "hub" for HyperTalk activity, a central point containing icons that take you directly to different stacks and allow you to open different applications. SuperCard has no such hub although the Runtime Editor works something like one, giving you all the menus and tools you need to navigate through different projects.

SuperCard's Message Box

You'll soon notice the differences between SuperCard's Message box and HyperCard's. The purpose of SuperCard's Message box is the same as HyperCard's: it allows you to send messages to the current card (or to other kinds of objects), to obtain information about the project or about variables, and to test short bits of programming without creating a button or menu.

SuperCard's Message box, however, contains two lines instead of one. This doesn't mean that you can type longer lines into the Message box and see them; rather, it means that many commands and functions return their values to the second line of the Message box. This two-line Message box is discussed under the heading "Message Box (COMMAND-M)" later in this chapter.

An Overview of the Runtime Editor

Because the Runtime Editor is written entirely in SuperTalk, you have the ability to modify it. However, the Runtime Editor does not have the performance of SuperEdit or, in most operations, HyperCard. This is balanced against the fact that you can edit the Runtime Editor itself, adding your own features to it.

The Runtime Editor is comprised of a number of menus. Many of these menus summon either floating palettes or dialog boxes. You should note that floating palettes always float over the top of the current window. When these palettes are on top of a window, however, they do not become the current window; instead they are transparent to many functions.

Menus and palettes in the Runtime Editor might not be as accurately updated as they are in other programs. For example, the Edit menu has a number of commands for obtaining information about the various components of a project. Ideally, the Object Info menu item should be disabled unless an object is selected with the Pointer tool. Unfortunately, this is not possible using SuperTalk. For one thing, no message is sent when the Pointer tool is used (and that is precisely the purpose of the Pointer tool) to click on an object. Since no message is sent, there is no way for a script to determine if an object is selected, and thus no way to dim the menu item. The same is true of many of the palettes that the Runtime Editor uses.

SuperCard's dialog boxes work in much the same manner as dialog boxes in other programs. Although SuperCard dialog boxes are modal— you cannot use other menus or click on other windows while they are active—two functions are hardwired to work around dialog boxes. First, you can always type in the Message box while a dialog is visible. (If the message box is not visible, you can press COMMAND-M to display it.) Second, you can always type COMMAND-Q to quit SuperCard even while a dialog is visible. These functions were built into SuperCard to prevent your computer from being "locked up" while a dialog box is visible; otherwise, you could create a dialog box with no buttons, display it, and shut yourself out of the functions of the program.

You can, by the way, edit the scripts of any of the Runtime Editor's menus by holding down the SHIFT key while you select a menu item. This is a handy feature, allowing you to look "under the hood" of the Runtime Editor. Remember, though, that like HyperCard, projects are always being saved, and when you save a script, you lose the previous version of that script. Keep a separate copy of the Runtime Editor as a backup.

Apple Menu

The Runtime Editor provides you with the standard Apple menu. This menu simply contains an "About SuperCard" item, which displays a dialog box and the name of the program's creator. When the Runtime Editor is started, this window is always presented first. The Apple menu automatically implements the display of all the Desk Accessories available to SuperCard.

File Menu

The File menu, shown in Figure 2-1, provides you with the standard set of tools needed to work with projects.

New Project

As you might expect, this menu item creates a new project. You will be asked to name the project and save it to disk (as noted earlier, Super-Card constantly saves changes to disk).

When your new project is created, a new window—called Untitled—is also created in the file, along with one new card in the window.

Figure 2-1.   The Runtime Editor's File menu

Open Project (COMMAND-O)

This command asks you to locate and click on the name of the project you wish to open. The first window in the project is opened, and the first card in that window is opened.

Note that opening a project does not *automatically* open any of the menus in that project, nor does it automatically open any windows other than the first window in the file. In each case, however, scripts in the project you are opening might do this. This will be something to consider as you develop your projects; you may want to make the first window in the project one that is especially significant to the project.

Close Project (COMMAND-W)

This command closes all the windows associated with the currently open project. You should note that it does not close any menus opened by that project. When creating a project, you should include a closeProject handler, which closes any menus from the project that might be open (see Chapter Eight for a detailed discussion).

New Window

This menu item creates a new window—named Untitled—in the currently active project, and a card to go in that window. The new window will be the size specified in the Preferences dialog in SuperEdit (discussed in Chapter Three).

Set Up Windows

This command allows you to specify which windows in the current project should be open and which should be closed. It presents a dialog box, such as the one shown in Figure 2-2, listing the names or ID numbers of all the windows in the current stack. Currently open windows have a check mark before them. Clicking on a window that is not open places a check mark before its name or ID. Clicking on a window name or ID that has a check mark before it removes the check mark. Changes take effect when you click on the OK button.

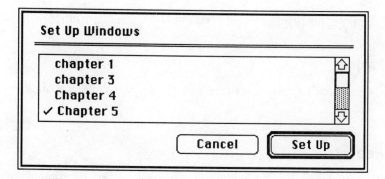

Figure 2-2.   The Set Up Windows dialog box allows you to open and close listed windows

Close Window

Close Window closes the current window, sending the closeCard, close-Background, and closeWindow messages to the current card in that window. If the window is the only open window in the current project, the project itself is closed.

Set Up Menus

This command works in the same manner as the Set Up Windows command. It presents you with a list of all the menus in the current project, allowing you to specify which ones should be open and which should be closed.

Print Card (COMMAND-P)

Print Card prints the current card. If the card is larger than a sheet of paper, the card will be "tiled," that is, printed on several sheets of paper, which you then tape or paste them together.

The Print Card command, like the other print commands, summons dialog boxes that are contained in the project "Print," which is included on the disk called SAMPLES DISK 2, that comes with SuperCard. If SuperCard cannot locate this project, you will be presented with a dialog box asking you to locate it.

Print Window

This command prints all the cards in the current window.

Print Project

This command prints all the cards, in all the windows, of the current project.

Print Report

Since the Print Report menu item is part of the Runtime Editor, and therefore can be used from within any SuperCard project, it will save you a lot of work; you don't need to reinvent the report wheel for your own projects.

When you execute this menu item, you get a dialog box such as the one shown in Figure 2-3. On the left is a reduced view of the report page. On the right is a list box showing all the background fields in the current background of the visible window; clicking on the up or down arrows to the right of this field will show you more of the background fields. If you want to use a different background (in the same window) for your report, click on the Change Backgrounds button, and you will get the dialog box shown in Figure 2-4. This dialog box lists the backgrounds in the current window and allows you to choose a different one. If you want to generate a report based on a different window, you will need to click on the Done button, open the window you want, and choose the Print Report menu item again.

To select a field to print, click on the name of that field and it will be highlighted. Next, click on the Add button below the fields and a number will be placed to the left of the selected field. The numbering indicates the order, from left to right, in which the fields will be printed.

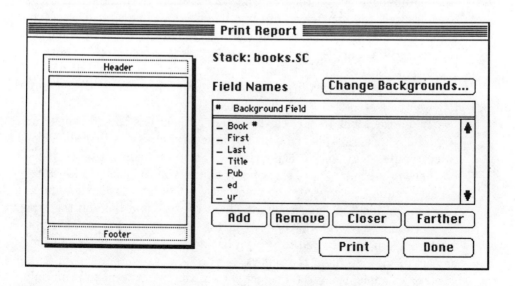

Figure 2-3.   The Print Report window

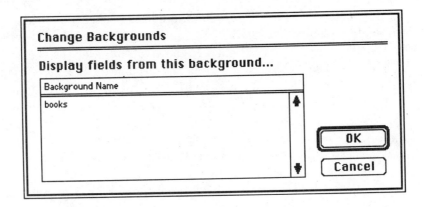

Figure 2-4.   The Change Backgrounds dialog box

As you add new fields, vertical lines will appear on the page representation, indicating how much space is allocated for each field. You can adjust this spacing by clicking on and dragging these lines to the right or left.

The Remove button removes the selected field from the list of those to be printed; the numbering of the other fields will be adjusted accordingly. The Closer button moves the selected field to the left on the report, and the Farther button moves the selected field to the right.

When you are finished defining your report, the Print button will start printing. You will first see a standard Page Setup dialog box, followed by a standard Print dialog box.

When the Print Report card is open, a menu like the one shown in Figure 2-5 appears. This menu performs several functions that allow you to customize your report. The Print Criteria item summons the dialog box shown in Figure 2-6. This window allows you to specify criteria for report printing. You specify the field you want to test by clicking on the name of that field in the scrolling field on the left, and then on the type of operation you want to perform in the Operator field on the right. Note that you do not need to print a background field in order to use it as part of the criteria in the report.

For example, using the Project shown, you might want to print only the books by Benford. To do so, you would first click on the Last field in the scrolling field on the left, and then on the "equals" line in the

Figure 2-5.   The Report menu

scrolling field on the right. Finally, you would click on the Value field, and type **Benford** into this field. When the report is being processed, only those cards that met these criteria would be printed.

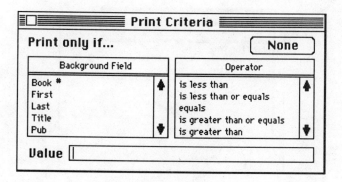

Figure 2-6.   The Print Criteria window

The Field Spacing menu item summons the dialog shown in Figure 2-7. Use this dialog to adjust the height of the fields as they will appear on the report. You can click on the up or down arrows to the right of the fields, or drag the line itself.

The Format Lines menu command summons the window shown in Figure 2-8. Using this window, you can specify the widths and patterns of the various lines that are used in the report. The checkboxes on the left specify which types of lines you are formatting. The column in the middle of the window specifies the width of the line. The array of patterns next to this column specifies the type of pattern to use. And on the right, the top set of checkboxes defines which lines will appear on the report.

The Header and Footer items on the Print Report menu summon the window shown in Figure 2-9. If you use Microsoft Word, this window will be familiar to you; its functions are very close to that of Word. Use the radio buttons at the top of the window to specify whether you are formatting a header or a footer. The row of icons to the right of these radio buttons are used to insert page numbers, the date, the time, and the title of the report, respectively. The text of the header or footer is typed in the first rectangle below these items. Adjust the height of the header or footer using the up and down arrows to the left.

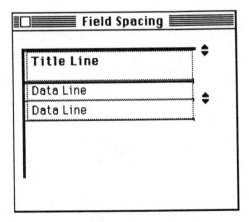

Figure 2-7.   The Field Spacing window

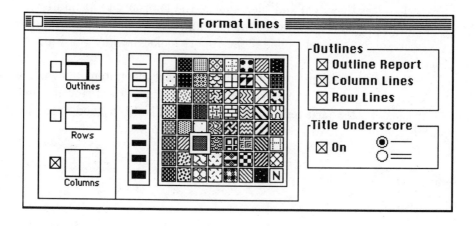

Figure 2-8.   The Format Lines window

The next group of menu items is used to specify the formatting of specific text in the report. These menu items cause other menus to appear (as do similar items used elsewhere in the Runtime Editor) or

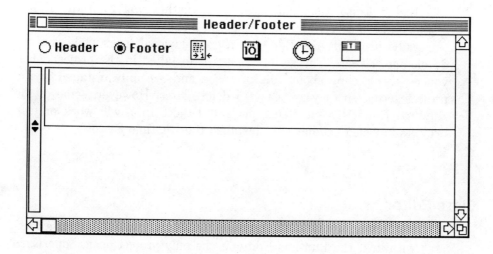

Figure 2-9.   The Header/Footer window

disappear. To set the font, size, style, or alignment of any item in the report, select that item and then choose the appropriate menu item.

Finally, the View Report menu item displays the report on the screen, so you can determine if the report looks the way you want it to look.

Note that the functions of the Print Report menu item, like virtually everything in the Runtime Editor, are constructed entirely in Super-Card, using standard tools of the program. This is a good example of what can be done with SuperCard and SuperTalk.

Print Labels

The Print Labels command is very similar to the Print Report command. It summons a window that allows you to specify which background fields will be used in printing the labels, and includes a menu that allows you to specify which criteria to use in printing. Labels are printed in "three-up"—three labels across the page.

Install Editor

The Install Editor command asks you whether you want the Editor installed in the current stack, giving you a chance to change your mind. Generally, installing the Editor is a good idea, at least while you are developing a stack. The scripts that are installed in the project when you do this occupy about 10K of space and are only installed in the project script, so they are easy to delete later. However, some of the Runtime Editor's menu items, such as Object Info, will work only in projects in which you have not installed the Runtime Editor.

Close Editor

This menu choice closes the Runtime Editor and all the menus associated with it. If the Runtime Editor is the only project open, SuperCard itself will be closed and you will return to the Finder. Do not use this command unless you have a window with a close box or the Message box open; otherwise you might find yourself stuck in SuperCard without a way to quit.

Quit

This command, not surprisingly, quits SuperCard. If you are running under SingleFinder (as opposed to MultiFinder), and launched Super-Card by using the Run command from SuperEdit, you will be returned to SuperEdit, and the current stack and card will be opened.

The command in SuperTalk, by the way, for quitting SuperCard is **Close All Windows**, since SuperCard requires at least one window to be open from a project at all times. You can test this by typing that command into the Message box.

Edit Menu

The Edit menu contains commands that allow you to copy and paste objects and text, as well as to get information about any components of currently open stacks. Remember, an Edit menu is necessary for any application that is running under SingleFinder, and wants to work with Desk Accessories. In MultiFinder, of course, Desk Accessories works with the DA Handler application. The commands on the Edit menu all feature standard COMMAND-key shortcuts.

Cut (COMMAND-X)

This command cuts the selected text or graphic selection and places it on the Clipboard, deleting it, of course, from its current location.

Copy (COMMAND-C)

Copy places the currently selected text or graphic on the Clipboard, and also leaves a copy of it in its current location.

Note that, unlike HyperCard, SuperCard does not allow you to copy a card. You can, however, use the Cut Card command discussed below.

Alternatively, you can use the Select All command to select all the objects on a card, create a new card, and use the Paste command to duplicate the card. Note that this sequence, however, will cause you to lose any text that is in the fields. If you really want to copy cards, use SuperEdit.

Paste (COMMAND-V)

Paste places the contents of the Clipboard onto the current card. If the Clipboard contains a graphic, a new object will be created on the card. If the Clipboard contains text, Paste will not be executed unless the insertion point is in a place that accepts text, that is, the Message Box, a field, or a draw graphic that contains text.

You can find out what type of object the clipboard contains by using the Clipboard function from the Message box. To do so, type **the clipboard** into the message box, and it will display "object" if an entire object is on the Clipboard, or "text" if the Clipboard contains text.

Select All (COMMAND-A)

This command selects all the objects on the current card. It can be handy for deleting all those objects using the Cut command, or for repositioning them using commands on the Palettes or Objects menus.

Info Commands

This series of commands allows you to get information about selected objects. One thing to note about the dialog boxes presented by these commands is that they duplicate virtually all the functions of SuperEdit's Info dialogs, implemented entirely in SuperTalk.

In general, these commands will only work if the Runtime Editor is installed into the current project: they work by sending a special message to the object, that normally has no handler if the Editor is not installed. If you hold down the Command key while choosing one of these menu items, you will, generally, be taken directly to the script of the object you choose. The exception is the Object Info item, which uses the SHIFT key to edit the script of an object. Hold down the SHIFT key while double-clicking on an object, or depress the SHIFT key immediately after you choose the Obect Info menu item (otherwise you will edit the script of the menu item).

New Card (COMMAND-N)

This command creates a new card in the current window using the current background, and makes that new card the current card in the window.

Cut Card

This command deletes the current card. Remember, this command cannot be undone. If you want to restore the card, paste it immediately to avoid losing it altogether.

Bkgnd (COMMAND-B)

The Bkgnd command turns on background editing. When background editing is enabled in SuperCard, you are able to *see* card objects, but you can *select* only background objects. There is no equivalent, in Super-Card, for the options you have for displaying card objects in SuperEdit. Also, in SuperCard, you cannot resize the background. All new objects you create when background editing is enabled are placed on the background layer of the card.

Card (COMMAND-K)

This command turns off background editing and enables card editing. Only card objects, not background objects, are editable when card editing is enabled. All new objects will be placed at the card level.

Go Menu

SuperCard's Go menu implements many of the same commands that are in HyperCard's Go menu and adds some new commands. Since the keyboard shortcuts are the same as in HyperCard they are easy to learn. You will note that SuperCard has no exact counterpart to Home, so it has neither a Go Home command nor a Help command.

Card Navigation Commands

The first four commands in the Go menu are used for navigating among cards. They work the same way as they do in HyperCard. The First and Last Card commands take you to the first and last cards, respectively. The Prev and Next card commands take you to the previous and next cards, respectively. If you use the Prev Card command, at the first card, the command takes you to the last card. If you use the Next Card command at the last card, you go to the first card.

Window Navigation Commands

These commands do for windows what the Card Navigation commands do for cards: they allow you to navigate among the windows.

Message Box (COMMAND-M)

This command is a toggle: if the Message box is hidden, the command displays it; if it is displayed, the command hides it.

As mentioned earlier, SuperCard's Message box contains two lines. The first line constitutes the traditional HyperCard-like Message box. The second line is where values are returned to you when you ask for them without the Put command. For example, open up the Message box, type **Put pi**, and press RETURN. The value "3.141593" is displayed on the first line of the Message box. Now select the text in the Message box and type **pi** without the Put command. Notice that the same value is placed into the second line of the Message box. Most other functions work the same way. When you call them without the Put command, their values are placed into the second line of the Message box.

This comes in handy when you are using the Message box to test your own functions. Since the line you type into the Message box is not immediately replaced by a new line, you can easily edit the first line by selecting text on that line, typing new text, and pressing RETURN.

Find (COMMAND-F)

This command works the same way as the Find command does in HyperCard. When you issue the command, the word "Find" is placed into the Message box followed by two quote marks. The insertion point is placed between the two quote marks, allowing you to type in the text you want to find.

Hide Menu Bar (COMMAND-SPACE)

This command works the same way as the corresponding HyperCard command. If the menu bar is visible, the command hides it. If the menu bar is not visible, the command will reveal it.

Palettes Menu

Most of the commands on the Palettes menu bring up floating palettes that allow you to work with selected objects or to create new objects. This menu is the rough equivalent of HyperCard's Tools menu, as it allows you access to the various tools of SuperCard in addition to various editing palettes. Note that SuperCard's palettes cannot be "torn off" the menu bar as HyperCard's can. Instead, SuperCard palettes are windows.

Also note that, thanks to the Runtime Editor, many of the palettes available on this menu perform functions that are also available in SuperEdit. And thanks to SuperTalk, many functions, such as line smoothing, are available in the Runtime Editor that are not available in SuperEdit.

Most of the facilities available in SuperCard are also available in SuperEdit (for a detailed discussion, see Chapter Four).

Browse Tool (COMMAND-[)

This command simply chooses the Browse tool. In SuperCard, which can have many windows open simultaneously, tools are set for specific windows. This means that when you have two windows open, you may move to one window using the Browse tool, and move to another using the Paint Brush tool. Tool selection generally affects the top window (although you can also write scripts that change the tool for obscured windows).

Changing tools does not usually affect floating palettes. When you move the cursor over a floating palette, it turns into the Browse tool. Generally, this is desirable. Since you often use palettes to choose different tools (button tools, paint tools, and so on) while creating or modifying a window, you don't want to switch manually to the Browse tool just to click on a palette.

The Browse tool works in SuperCard in the same way as it does in HyperCard. Normally it has the appearance of a pointing hand, but when you place it over an unlocked field or the Message box, the pointer shape turns into a text-editing I-beam. When it turns into the I-beam, you can select text, or click to create an insertion point for typing.

Pointer Tool (COMMAND-])

The Pointer tool sets the tool for the top window to the Pointer tool. The Pointer tool is used to select objects and, unlike the various tools in HyperCard, it can select any type of object: button, graphic object, field, and so on. When you click on an object with the Pointer tool, most messages are not sent to that object. (Special messages that *are* sent with the Pointer tool are discussed in Chapter Ten.) Messages are always sent to menu items, though, no matter which tool you are using.

When an object is selected, handles appear at the four corners of the object. If you click on one of the handles and drag, the object is resized. If you click within the rectangle of the object and drag, the object is moved.

You can select multiple objects with the Pointer tool in two ways. The first way is by clicking outside of an object and dragging to form a rectangle that encloses all the objects you want to select. The other is by selecting one object by clicking on it and then holding down the SHIFT key to select other objects.

Generally, to edit an object (aside from text in fields, of course), you will need to use the Pointer to first select the object before you can use any of the palettes or menu items to modify that object.

Paint Tools

The Paint tools command opens the Tools palette of the Runtime Editor and selects the Paint. (If you examine the Runtime Editor with Super-Edit, you will find that the various suites of tools on that palette are merely different cards in the window.) The Tools palette with the Paint tools selected is shown in Figure 2-10.

This palette has two sections. The column of buttons on the left chooses the *type* of tools displayed. The array of buttons on the right chooses the *actual* paint tools. For more discussion on using the painting tools, see Chapter Four.

When painting in SuperCard, the usual first step is to create a graphic object—sometimes called a "bit bucket"—to contain the painting. If you choose one of the painting tools, and click on a part of the card that does not already contain graphics, the cursor will change to a circle with "crosshairs." Use this cursor to create a rectangle, which will contain the graphic object. After you have created the rectangle, you will be able to paint in it. If, on the other hand, you click on an existing bitmap object, you can paint immediately.

Figure 2-10.   The Runtime Editor's Paint tools

Figure 2-11.   The Draw tools

Draw Tools

Choosing the Draw Tools command from the Palettes menu, or clicking on the Draw tools icon in the floating tools palette, displays the Draw tools, as shown in Figure 2-11.

Button Tools

The Button tools are shown in Figure 2-12. To create a new button in SuperCard, simply choose the tool that corresponds to the type of button you want to create, and draw the button—you do not need to hold down the COMMAND key, as you do in HyperCard. For details about the different kinds of buttons, see Chapter Four. The scripting of buttons is discussed in Chapter Ten.

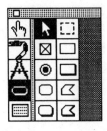

Figure 2-12.   The Runtime Editor's Button tools

Field Tools

The Field tools, shown in Figure 2-13, are discussed in Chapter Five, and scripting of fields is discussed in Chapter Eleven.

Brushes

The Brush palette, shown in Figure 2-14, shows the standard Super-Card brushes, and the current brush is highlighted. Note that there is no method of editing a brush in SuperCard. To create and use brushes of different shapes, you must use SuperEdit.

Lines

The Line palette, shown in Figure 2-15, is used to set the line width of selected draw objects, or undrawn lines in bitmap objects. The palette uses SuperCard to give you a feature that is not available in SuperEdit. In SuperEdit, you are limited to the eight widths of brushes shown at the left of this palette. However, with this palette you can set the height and width of the brush separately, each up to 43 pixels on a side.

Patterns

The Pattern palette, shown in Figure 2-16, contains two sections. On the

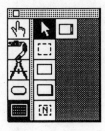

Figure 2-13.   The Field tools

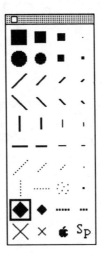

Figure 2-14. The Brushes palette

right of the palette are SuperCard's 64 patterns. On the left, the top rectangle shows the fill pattern. The bottom rectangle indicates the line pattern. To reset the pattern for a draw object, simply select that

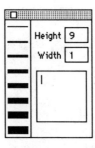

Figure 2-15. The Line Width palette from the Runtime Editor

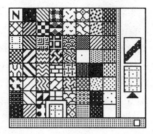

Figure 2-16.   The Patterns palette

object with the Pointer tool and then click on the pattern you want to use. If the arrow is pointing to the top rectangle, the fill pattern will be set. If the arrow is pointing to the bottom rectangle, the line pattern will be set.

Note that SuperCard, unlike HyperCard and SuperEdit, has no method of creating new patterns.

Colors

The Color palette displays all 256 colors available in the current color lookup table, if your Macintosh is capable of displaying color. If your Macintosh is not capable of displaying color, the Color menu item will not be displayed. See Chapter Fourteen for a discussion of color.

Objects Menu

As with the items on the Palettes menu, the items on the Objects menu act on specific objects. In order for these commands to have an effect, you will in general first need to select an object with the Pointer tool.

Send To Back (COMMAND-=)

This command places the selected object(s) behind other objects and changes its numbering. For example, if you have two graphic objects on the screen, the one that is in front will have the higher number, in this case 2. If you use the Send To Back command with that object selected, its number will change to 1 and the other object will become object 2.

This command and the next replace HyperCard's Bring Forward and Send Back commands—instead of adjusting the object numbering one number at a time, they adjust them in big jumps.

Bring To Front (COMMAND--)

This command does the opposite of the Send To Back command. It brings the selected object to the front, and gives it the number that equals the number of objects. The numbers of all the other objects are set one less than they were before.

Relocate and Resize

The dialog box summoned by this menu item performs much the same function as the Nudge and Displace palettes (discussed later in the chapter). It displays the size and location of the selected object and allows you to type in new numbers for those properties.

Rotate Polygon

This command places a handle at the top point of the selected Draw or Button polygon, allowing you to use that point as an axis of rotation. It will not do anything if you have selected an object (field, paint graphic, oval, and so on) that cannot be rotated.

Reshape Polygon

If you have selected a Draw or Button polygon, this command places handles at the points of the polygon, and allows you to click and drag with those points to reshape the polygon. If you select this command with an object that cannot be reshaped, nothing happens.

Flip Polygon Vertical

This command flips the polygon vertically. It works with bitmap objects, draw objects, and polygon buttons but does nothing on rectangular objects, of course.

Flip Polygon Horizontal

This command flips polygons horizontally.

Font

Choosing this menu item inserts a new menu in the menu bar, Fonts, which lists all the fonts currently available to SuperCard. If the Fonts menu is already visible, it removes that menu.

The Fonts menu affects selected text in a field, selected text in a draw object, or all new text created with the Draw or Paint text tools.

Style

This menu item inserts a standard Style menu on the menu bar or removes that menu if it is already there. It contains a standard set of text style commands: plain, bold, italic, underline, outline, shadow, condensed, and expanded. This command affects selected text in a field or draw object, or new text created with the Draw or Paint text tools. To remove all styles, use the Plain command on this menu.

Size

The Size menu item inserts a Size menu on the menu bar or removes it if it is already there. As with the other Text commands, this command affects selected text in a field or draw graphic, or new text created with the Paint or Draw text tools.

Note that in most applications, certain sizes of text listed in Size menus or dialogs are outlined to indicate the actual sizes of the text available. SuperCard has no means of finding this information (though an external function could be written to do this) so it is not displayed.

Palette Projects

Aside from the functions built into the Runtime Editor, a number of palettes are also included in the folder Palette Projects on the disk called SAMPLES DISK 2 included with SuperCard. You can access these palettes in two ways. The first is to use the Open Project command on the Runtime Editor's File menu. This lets you choose a palette from a standard Open File dialog box. You can also open the project UTILITIES, which places a menu of that name on the menu bar. This menu lists all the palettes in the Palette Projects folder. You can then open any of these palettes with a simple menu selection.

Align Objects Palette

This palette, shown in Figure 2-17, is quite different from the one

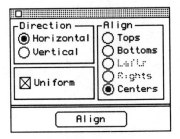

Figure 2-17.   The Align Objects palette

SuperEdit uses. It does not allow you to set vertical and horizontal alignment at the same time. Instead, you set these alignments in separate steps.

Note the checkbox labelled "Uniform." If this box is checked, the selected objects will be evenly spaced on a line. If you are performing horizontal alignment, the leftmost object will become the beginning of the line and the rightmost will become the end of the line. Objects between the two will be distributed uniformly across the line.

Displace Palette

This palette, shown in Figure 2-18, allows you to move selected objects in either a vertical, horizontal, or diagonal direction. You can specify the distance to move the selected objects by typing numbers into the appropriate fields or by using the mouse to indicate the direction and distance in the square below the fields.

Go Palette

The Go palette includes four buttons that perform the same functions as the Go Card and Go Window commands on the Go menu.

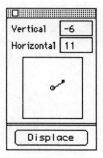

Figure 2-18.   The Displace palette

Inks Palette

The Inks palette (shown in Figure 2-19) allows you to set the ink effects for the selected object. Since buttons and fields do not have ink effects, the command does not apply to those types of objects. Ink effects are discussed in detail in Chapter Fourteen.

Nudge Palette

The Nudge palette, shown in Figure 2-20, allows you to precisely size objects or windows. If the Object radio button at the top of the palette is highlighted, selected objects will be stretched. If the Window radio button is highlighted, the top window will be stretched.

The Edge radio buttons determine which edge of the object will be stretched, and the Nudge field determines how far it will be stretched.

At the bottom of the palette are four arrows. Clicking on one of the arrows stretches the object or window in that direction. Note that you need to coordinate between the Edge radio buttons and the arrows. If you have highlighted the Right radio button, you can only click on the Left or Right arrows to stretch or shrink the object.

Radio Button Links Palette

Use this palette, shown in Figure 2-21, to link a group of radio buttons.

Figure 2-19.   The Inks palette

Figure 2-20.   The Nudge palette

Radio buttons are handled in groups: when one is highlighted, the others in the group should not be. This palette simply places a small script into each of the radio buttons that handles this function. Use the Pointer tool to select a set of radio buttons, then click on the Link radio Buttons button. Again, SuperCard displays the ability to handle fairly complex problems in a standardized manner by allowing you to create floating palettes.

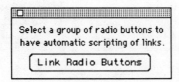

Figure 2-21.   The Link Radio Buttons palette

Scale Objects Palette

The Scale Objects palette, shown in Figure 2-22, stretches or shrinks selected objects (including buttons, fields, and graphic objects) according to the radio button settings on the palette.

Smooth Palette

This palette uses SuperTalk to create a smooth line out of a jagged line created by the Draw Curve or Draw Polygon tools. It does not, of course, work on Paint objects. The Divisions Per Segment field allows you to type in the number of new points that will be created between any two existing points: the higher the number you type in this field, the smoother the line will become and the longer the action will take to perform.

Utilities

This project allows easy access to the palettes in the Palette Projects folder but contains no palettes of its own. It consists of one window and one menu. The window is hidden so that it does not actually appear on your screen when you open the project; a new menu—Utilities—is

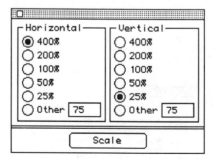

Figure 2-22.   The Scale Objects palette

inserted when you open this project. This menu simply lists the names of the projects contained in the Palette Projects folder, allowing easy access to those palettes.

Window Style Palette

The Window Style palette, shown in Figure 2-23, sets the style of the top window. When you first open this palette with the menu command, the current style of the top window will automatically be highlighted.

The SharedFile: A Resource Repository

The SharedFile works in SuperCard just as Home works in HyperCard: as a repository for resources, including icons, sounds, external commands and functions, and your own handlers and functions. The Shared-File is the last stop in the Message hierarchy before the message reaches SuperCard itself. Therefore, all messages that are not handled before reaching the SharedFile can be handled there.

The SharedFile, like the Home stack in HyperCard, has many uses. Many people place handlers that they use often in the Home stack in

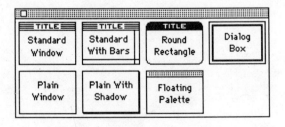

Figure 2-23.   The Window Style palette

order to make them available to all their stacks. This method does not readily apply to SuperCard. Much of what you want to add to the program can be added by way of menus and palettes in the Runtime Editor.

The SharedFile is also unique in SuperCard in that it is the only project that actually has a resource fork open. As mentioned in Chapter One, SuperCard stores the resources that projects use as part of the data fork of a project. However, some external commands and functions will not work properly without resources in the resource fork, and some other programs, such as Farallon's SoundEdit, cannot place resources into SuperCard's resource structure. Therefore, you will use the Shared-File as a repository for many of the resources you use in SuperCard. Resources are discussed in detail in Chapter Nine.

Creating Projects with SuperEdit

You will use SuperEdit to do a lot of the "dirty work" of creating your SuperCard projects. Much of this work can also be handled within SuperCard itself, with the added ability to test scripts as you are writing them. But the SuperEdit environment is much faster than the SuperCard environment, and you have the use of some tools and capabilities that you do not have in SuperCard.

SuperEdit is a multifaceted program. It includes a wide variety of tools that you use to create all the various objects that make up a project. It includes tools for performing such tasks as importing Hyper-Card stacks, resources, and graphics. It also includes a sophisticated text editor for creating scripts, is able to work with multiple projects at the same time, and most important, it includes a sophisticated graphics program. This chapter covers the basics of the SuperEdit program and shows you how to work with windows, menus, and resources. The Card editor, where you actually create cards, is discussed in Chapter Four.

Two key ideas you need to keep in mind when using SuperEdit:

1. Unlike SuperCard, SuperEdit does not automatically save your changes; you must save them yourself. Use the Save and Save As commands on the File menu.

2. SuperTalk scripts do not "fire," which means you cannot test your scripts as you write them. For that you must use SuperCard.

Starting SuperEdit

You start SuperEdit from the Finder, either by double-clicking on its icon, or by selecting it and then choosing the Finder's Open command. When SuperCard starts, you are presented with a standard file dialog box allowing you to choose which project you want to edit or to create a new project.

Because SuperCard projects will normally open SuperCard and not SuperEdit when you double-click on them, you cannot simply double-click on the project's icon and open SuperEdit. Instead, if you want to open SuperEdit and have it automatically open a specific project, you can select the SuperEdit icon, SHIFT-click the project icon, and, with both icons highlighted, choose the Finder's Open command. Of course, this only works if both SuperEdit and the project are in the same folder.

SuperEdit Basics

Although SuperEdit is a powerful program, it is not a complex program to learn and use. This is because a number of techniques and tools are common to all its components, and because many of the tools operate in a consistent manner.

Common Menus and Tools

Three menus — File, Edit, and Windows — are always visible and active, regardless of the component with which you are working. Here's a rundown of what each of these menus does:

• *The File menu* The commands on the File menu are virtually always available. These commands are generally used for working with projects, and allow you to do such things as create new projects, open existing ones, and print the current window.

• *The Edit menu* The Edit menu contains six commands that are standard to virtually all Macintosh programs: Undo, Cut, Copy, Paste, Clear, and Select All. They function in the standard manner. However, you should note that when you copy any selected object with this command, all the objects contained within the object are also copied. Thus, when you copy a window, all the backgrounds and cards, and all the objects on all those cards, are copied as well. This can be a very handy tool, as you will see later in this chapter.

• *The Windows menu* The Windows menu always lists all the open windows you have in SuperEdit. You use this menu to move quickly between open windows. Choosing one of the window names brings that window to the front.

Aside from the standard items, the Edit menu also includes commands for working with the currently selected object or objects. This second tier of menu items allows you to create a new object (window, card, menu item, and so on), open the object for further editing, edit the script of the object, or open an Info window about the object. These four standard operations have standard COMMAND-key combinations associated with them:

Operation	COMMAND-Key
New	N
Open	O
Edit Script	E
Get Info	I

These COMMAND-key combinations become second nature after a while, and you will find yourself using them often. Double-clicking on an object is also a handy shortcut for opening that object. Note that some objects cannot be opened; it makes no sense, for example, to open a graphic object. In this case, double-clicking on the object will give you an Info dialog about that object.

Below these commands on the Edit menu is a second group of commands, performing the same set of functions on a different set of objects. These functions work the same as the ones above but do not have keyboard shortcuts. Generally, the top level of edit commands will work on the currently selected object, while the bottom set will be more generic and will work on the *type* of object, or on the object containing the current object. Therefore, when you are editing a window, the shortcut commands will refer to the selected window, while the second level will work on the project.

Overview Windows

Most of the windows you work with in SuperEdit, aside from the Card windows and dialogs, are called *Overview windows*. These windows contain a list of all the objects contained within the current object. For example, the overview of a window lists all the cards, in numerical order, contained in that window. You will be working with these Overview windows a lot in SuperEdit, and will become more familiar with them when you start working with projects.

Preferences

Under the Apple menu is an item called "Preferences." Choosing this item brings up the dialog shown in Figure 3-1. This dialog allows you to specify certain characteristics of the way SuperEdit works.

The first of the three checkboxes at the top of the dialog allows you to specify whether or not a new window and card is automatically created when you create a new project. Generally, you will want to do so, since SuperCard cannot actually open projects with no windows or cards. If, on the other hand, you are creating projects that consist only of menus, you can leave this box unchecked.

The next two checkboxes specify whether or not scripts are to be automatically inserted into new projects and projects converted from HyperCard stacks. The script that is automatically inserted provides support for the Runtime Editor; if you are creating projects that will be running in this environment, it is a good idea to include these scripts.

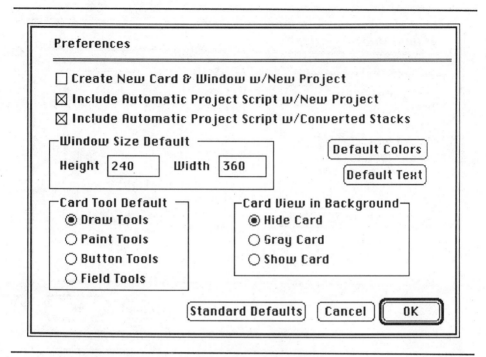

Figure 3-1.   SuperEdit's Preferences dialog box

The Window Size Default fields are self-explanatory: they specify the height and width of new windows that you create. The Default Colors button summons a list dialog of all the color lookup tables (cluts) available, and allows you to specify which color lookup table will be automatically used for new cards.

The Default Text button summons the dialog box shown in Figure 3-2. Using this dialog, you can specify which fonts and sizes are used as the defaults (that is, the fonts of new text), for card objects and for scripts. The default for card fonts affects all text that is created on a card, whether it is using the Draw or Paint or Field tools.

The two sets of radio buttons determine which set of tools are visible when you open a card, and the default value for how card objects are displayed when you are editing cards. Chapter Four discusses card editing in more detail.

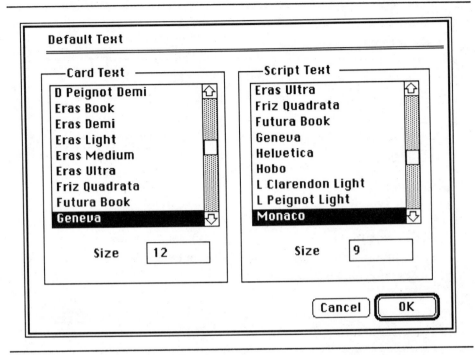

Figure 3-2.   The Default Text dialog box, summoned from the Preferences dialog box

Projects

Projects, you will remember, are SuperCard documents, containing all the elements that comprise a SuperCard application: menus, windows, and resources.

Creating a New Project

To create a new project, you can either choose "New" from the File menu, or click on the New button in SuperEdit's Open File dialog box. Depending on the settings of your Preferences, when you create a new project, SuperEdit might do two things automatically.

First, it creates a new window for that project and one new card in that window. SuperEdit does this because all projects must have at least one window and one card; otherwise, SuperCard cannot open those projects. Second, SuperEdit automatically opens the new window and the new card. The new card will automatically have the size you specified in the Preferences dialog. The assumption is that the first thing you will want to do with a new project is edit the first card in that project.

Because your new project is *not yet named*, it has not been saved on disk. To give your project a name, use the Save or Save As commands on the File menu.

After creating the new project, you will see a window much like the one shown in Figure 3-3. This Overview window is the "hub" of the project. The window's title bar shows the name of the project, in this case "Untitled-1," since it is the first new project created since Super-Edit was opened. Subsequent new projects would also have the name "Untitled," followed by a number.

The top panel of the overview tells you the size and free size of the project, and the date it was last modified (in this case, the date the project was created).

You can find out more about the project by choosing the Project Info command under the Edit menu. Issuing this command displays the

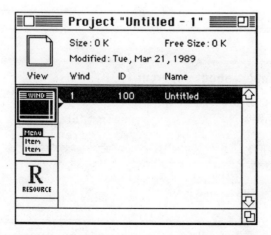

Figure 3-3.   The Project Overview window for a new project

dialog box shown in Figure 3-4. This dialog is roughly similar to the Stack Info dialog box in HyperCard. Unlike HyperCard, this dialog box does not tell you how many cards the project contains, but it does tell you how many windows, menus, and resources it contains. It also tells you how much space it takes up on disk and how much of that space is free space. You can also use this dialog box to set the password for a project.

Other Ways to Create Projects

Aside from the ways mentioned in the previous section, there are two other ways to create a new project.

Convert a HyperCard Stack

Converting a HyperCard stack also creates a new project. To do so, choose the Convert Stack command on the File menu. You are presented with a standard File dialog box that shows only HyperCard stacks. When you have selected a stack to convert, you are then asked to name the new stack, and SuperCard proposes a new name that is the same name as the old stack, with the characters *.sc* appended to it.

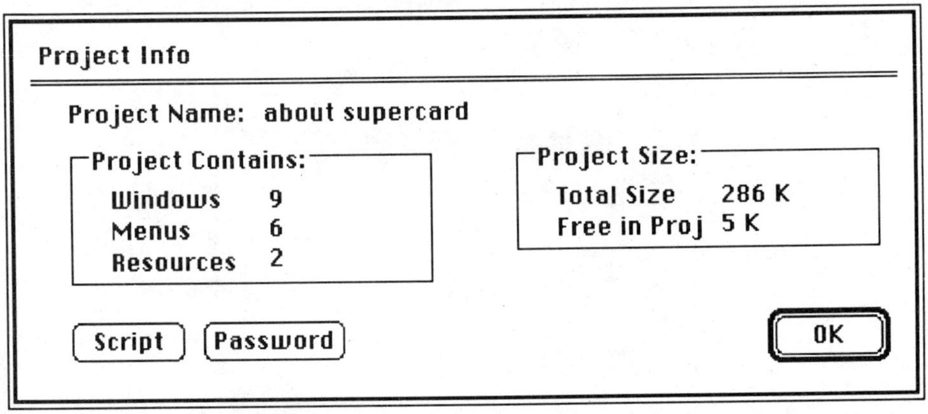

```
 Project Info
 ─────────────────────────────────────────────
   Project Name:  about supercard
  ┌Project Contains:─────┐      ┌Project Size:──────┐
   Windows     9           Total Size    286 K
   Menus       6           Free in Proj  5 K
   Resources   2
  └──────────────────────┘

  ( Script )  (Password)                    ( OK )
```

Figure 3-4.   The Project Info dialog box

While stack conversion is taking place, you will see an alert similar to the one shown in Figure 3-5. Depending on the size of the stack being converted, the process can take some time. Not only is SuperEdit reading the stack and saving it into a new format, it is performing some translations on the scripts in the stack.

Import Resources

Another way to create a new project is with the Import Resources command—a handy, unique command that allows you to bring into SuperCard resources from other programs. This includes all the resources that SuperEdit knows how to deal with: windows, cursors, icons, color lookup tables, sounds, and external commands and functions.

You might use this function if you are creating a project that trains others to use a specific application. Most programs define their windows and menus using standard resources, and this would allow you to create a project that has virtually the identical appearance as the original application. Of course, you would have to simulate the functionality of the software on your own.

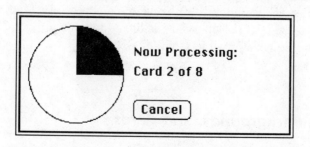

Figure 3-5.   This alert shows you how SuperEdit is progressing in converting a HyperCard stack

Other Project Commands

Several other commands on the File menu provide special services specific to working with projects.

Compacting Projects

As with HyperCard, when you create a project and work with it, a certain amount of free, or wasted space is generated in the project. To eliminate this free space, use the Compact command on the File menu.

The Run Command

If you are not running MultiFinder, this command quits SuperEdit and starts SuperCard with the current project opened. This command makes it fairly easy to switch between the editing mode of SuperEdit and the running mode of SuperCard.

If you are running MultiFinder, you can switch between the two applications, provided you have enough memory to load both programs at once. Otherwise, SuperEdit will quit, and your Macintosh will beep.

Building Applications

You can also use SuperEdit to transform your SuperCard project from a document into an application that can be executed directly without requiring SuperCard. This process has sometimes been called "compiling," but that is not an accurate term. Unlike a compiler, SuperEdit does not translate your SuperTalk commands into a language that can be more quickly understood by your computer. Instead, the language interpreter that is in SuperCard is linked to your project. This process is discussed in more detail in Chapter Sixteen.

Windows, Backgrounds, and Cards

Windows, key elements of SuperCard projects, are roughly analogous to HyperCard's stacks: all the cards in your projects are contained in windows, though any project can have multiple windows. To view the list of windows in your project, select the window icon at the top of the list of icons on the left side of the Project window, as shown in Figure 3-3.

With the window icon selected, a scrolling list of all the windows in your project will be displayed, including the number of the window, its ID number (generated automatically by SuperEdit, and cannot be edited by you), and the name of the window.

Creating New Windows

There are two ways to create a new window: by using the New Window command under the Edit menu, or by double-clicking on either the window icon or on the top panel of the project window.

The new window will be named "Untitled" and will be placed in the scrolling list at the point indicated by the small right pointing arrow at the left edge of the scrolling list of windows. To move this arrow, click on the left edge of the list at the point where you want the arrow to appear; normally it will be at the end of the list. Note that you can use this arrow to change the order of numbering for windows: select a window, use the Cut command, move the pointer, and paste the window at the new location. When you cut or copy a window, all its associated backgrounds and cards are copied with it. Note also that this same technique works for any items that appear in these scrolling lists.

Once you have created the new window, you can name and define it with the Window Info command on the Edit menu. This command brings up the dialog box shown in Figure 3-6. Aside from the standard information (name, number, ID, number of cards, and backgrounds), this dialog also allows you to control the appearance of the window, including its type and size.

Remember that no matter which object you have selected, in any of SuperEdit's displays you can summon an Info dialog box about that object by pressing COMMAND-I.

Window Types

This dialog allows you to choose one of seven standard types for your window. Select the type you want by clicking on its icon. To the right of these icons are checkboxes showing various window properties. As you

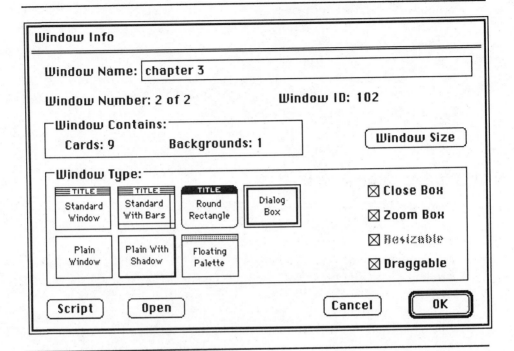

Figure 3-6.   The Window Info dialog box

select different types of windows, some of these checkboxes become greyed out, depending on whether or not they are applicable to that type of window. Zoom boxes, for example, are not appropriate for windows other than the standard windows with scroll and size bars. The uses of the various types of windows are discussed in more detail in Chapter Seven.

Sizing the Window

To set the size of the window, click on the Window Size button on the right of the Window Info dialog. This button summons the dialog box shown in Figure 3-7. This dialog box has three sections.

The section at the top of the dialog box allows you to specify the size of the monitor. Click on the pop-up menu next to "Monitor Size" to see a list of common Macintosh monitors, or type the width and height

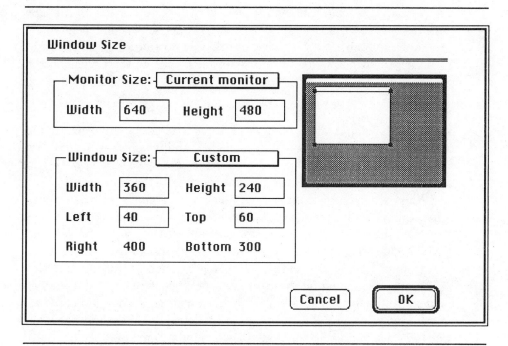

Figure 3-7.   The Window Size dialog box

of the monitor in the appropriate fields, and select "Custom Monitor" from the pop-up. You use this to assist SuperCard in determining the relation of the monitor to the window in the small display to the right of this information. Don't worry that if you select a certain value here, your project will not execute correctly on a machine with a different monitor. Instead, you can use it to determine how your window will appear on various-sized monitors.

The next section of the dialog sets the size of the window. Again, a pop-up menu features some standard sizes. You can choose one of these sizes or type in a custom size.

Another way to set the size and location of a window is by dragging and sizing the representation of the window on the right section of the dialog. To resize the window, grab it by any of the four "size handles" (the small black squares that appear on the window's corners). To reposition it anywhere on the screen, click anywhere within the window representation, and drag the window to its new location.

Note that setting the window size *does not set the size of the card contained within the window.* These two properties are independent.

To accept the new size, click on the OK button at the lower right. To return the window to its original settings, click on the Cancel button.

Backgrounds

Much of the appearance of a card is controlled by its background. Remember that all objects—buttons, fields, and graphics—that are contained on a background appear on all the cards associated with that background. Backgrounds also control the size of the card.

When a new card is created in a cardless window (as when Super-Edit automatically creates a new window when you create a new project), a new background is automatically created; you cannot have a card without a background. Aside from this, you can also create a new background (and a new card on the background) by using the New Background command on the Edit menu. Figure 3-8 shows an Overview window containing a number of cards. A new background (and card) has been added after card 3 by clicking on the left edge of the Overview just under card 3, and using the New Background command.

Card	ID	Bkgd	Name
1	101	100	Untitled
2	103	102	Untitled
3	104	102	Untitled
4	121	120	Untitled
5	105	102	Untitled
6	106	102	Untitled
7	107	102	Untitled
8	108	102	Untitled

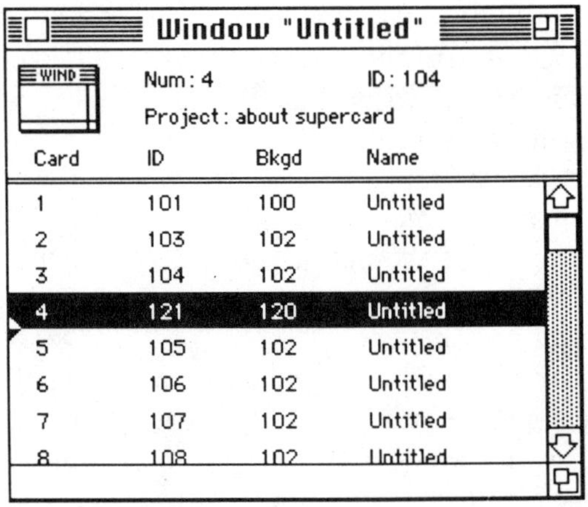

Figure 3-8.   A Window Overview window

There are two ways to size the new background. The first way is to use the Background Info dialog box. To get to this dialog box, select a card, and use the Background Info command (you *cannot* type COMMAND-I, as that will get you Card Info). The Background Info dialog is shown in Figure 3-9.

This dialog lets you set a background name, as well as the cantDe-lete property (if the checkbox is checked, SuperCard, not SuperEdit, will prevent you from deleting the last card using this background, but only when SuperCard is running, not SuperEdit), and the size. You can set the size by entering numbers for the height and width in the appropriate fields. You can also use the pop-up menu above these fields to choose from some standard background sizes.

The second method of sizing the background will be discussed in Chapter Four.

If you want to edit a background, and not a specific card, you can choose the Open Bkgnd item on the File menu; the Card editor will be launched, and you will be in Edit Background mode.

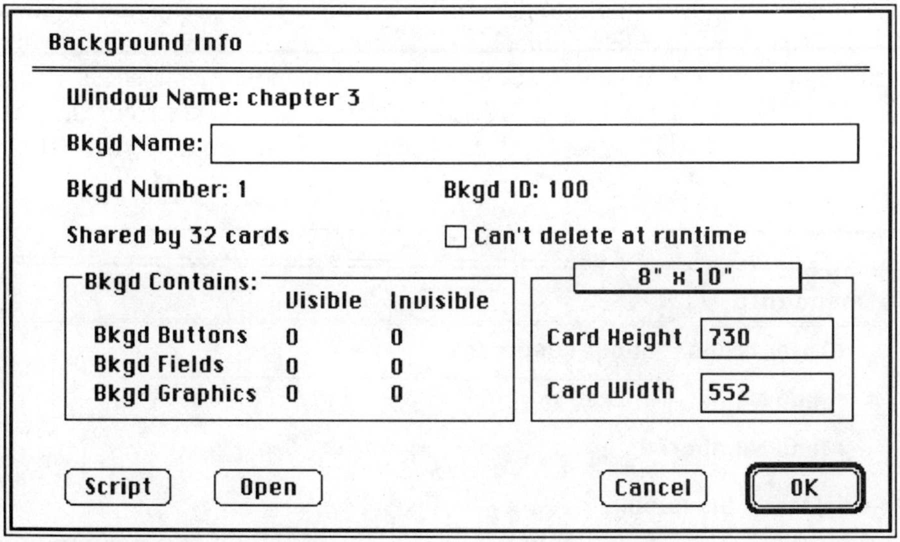

Background Info

Window Name: chapter 3

Bkgd Name:

Bkgd Number: 1   Bkgd ID: 100

Shared by 32 cards   ☐ Can't delete at runtime

Bkgd Contains:
	Visible	Invisible
Bkgd Buttons	0	0
Bkgd Fields	0	0
Bkgd Graphics	0	0

8" x 10"

Card Height 730

Card Width 552

Script   Open   Cancel   OK

Figure 3-9.   The Background Info dialog box

Menus

Menus are an essential part of any Macintosh application, and since SuperCard allows you to create standard applications, menus can be a key part of your SuperCard projects as well.

Menus often need special planning. If you are creating a project that is designed to be run exclusively with the SoftEditor, you don't need to spend much time thinking about special menus; almost everything you need to do while strictly in the SuperCard environment can be handled by the SoftEditor.

If, on the other hand, you are creating a project that you plan to distribute as a stand-alone application, you should give a great deal of thought to your menus, particularly because your application will likely run in a number of quite different environments; some of your users will be running MultiFinder, for example, while some will not. You should include three menus as a matter of course: the Apple menu, the File menu, and the Edit menu (if your users want to access Desk Accessories and not run MultiFinder). Scripting of menus and items is discussed in Chapter Eight.

Creating a menu is quite simple: in the Project Overview window, select the menu icon, and double-click on the panel above the empty list. A new "Untitled" menu will be created. To name a menu, select it, and open the Menu Info dialog box (by selecting Menu Info from the Edit menu, or pressing COMMAND-I). This dialog box is shown in Figure 3-10.

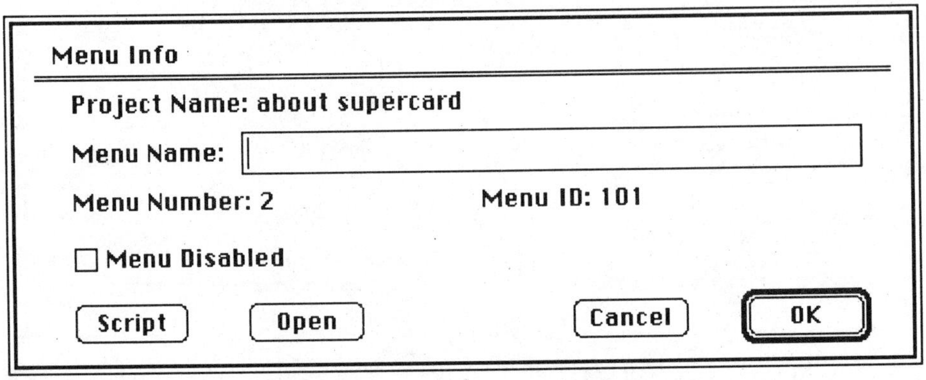

Menu Info

Project Name: about supercard

Menu Name: [   ]

Menu Number: 2   Menu ID: 101

☐ Menu Disabled

(Script)   (Open)   (Cancel)   (OK)

Figure 3-10.   The Menu Info dialog box

The only property of a menu that you can set is the disabled property, which you set by clicking on the Menu Disabled checkbox on the left of this dialog box. If a menu is disabled, its name will be greyed out, and none of its items will be selectable (though it will drop down when you press the mouse button on it).

When you open a menu to display its Overview window, the new menu is displayed on SuperEdit's menu bar. If you click on this menu name, the menu will be activated and you will see the items associated with this menu. Since SuperEdit does not "work"—that is, scripts don't execute—your menu won't do anything, but you do have a chance to test its appearance and function. A menu is basically a name on a menu bar. Its *items* actually do the work.

Menu Items

Creating an item for a menu is the same as creating a new card: with the Overview window open for a menu, double-click on the top panel of that window, and a new, untitled menu item will be created.

Once the new item is created, open the Item Info dialog box, as shown in Figure 3-11. This dialog allows you to name the new menu ("Untitled" might be satisfactory for a card or window name, but it is useless as a menu name) and assign a COMMAND key to it. If you assign a COMMAND key to that menu, the COMMAND-key symbol and that keyboard key will automatically be displayed to the right of the item name.

Menu items have a number of attributes, which you can control with the Item Info dialog box. The checkboxes in the left column of the dialog box allow you to set these attributes. Controlling these properties from SuperTalk is discussed in Chapter Eight.

- *Disable Item* If this box is checked, the menu item will be greyed out. When you pass the mouse over the item, it will not highlight.

- *Simple Dividing Line* If this box is checked, the menu item will be a dividing line that separates groups of menu items. If the mouse is released on a dividing line, nothing happens.

- *Mark Item With Check* If this is checked, a check mark will appear to the left of the menu item.

• *Text Styles*   The column of attributes to the right of the dialog box controls the appearance of the text in the menu item.

Special Menus

SuperCard includes predefined support for two key menu types. This predefined support facilitates the creation of these sometimes complex menus.

Apple Menu

The Apple menu is commonly the first menu on the menu bar and displays a list of Desk Accessories. Instead of requiring you to write the programming necessary for the desk accessories to be displayed in

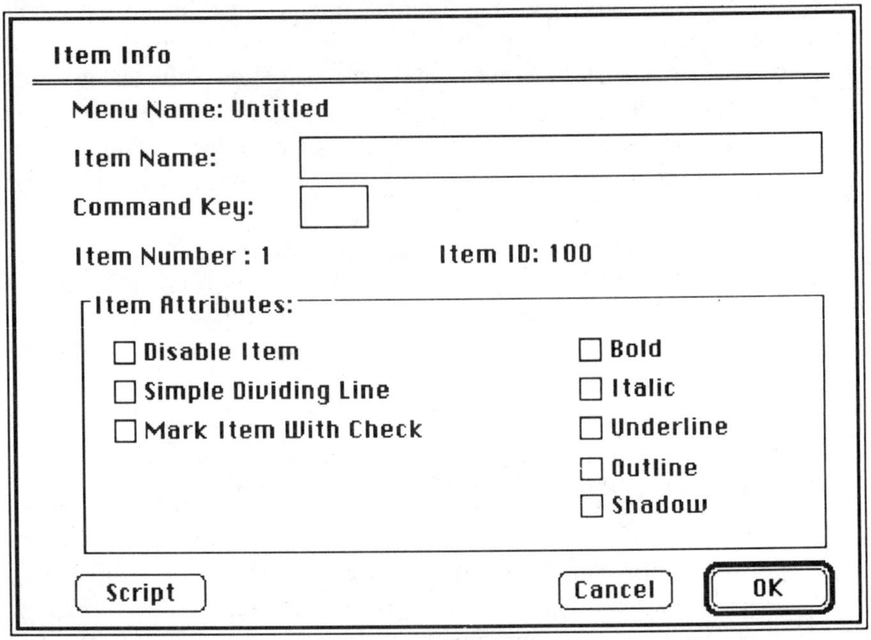

Item Info

Menu Name: **Untitled**

Item Name:

Command Key:

Item Number : 1   Item ID: 100

┌ Item Attributes: ─────────────────

☐ Disable Item   ☐ Bold

☐ Simple Dividing Line   ☐ Italic

☐ Mark Item With Check   ☐ Underline

                            ☐ Outline

                            ☐ Shadow

[Script]   [Cancel]   [OK]

Figure 3-11.   The Menu Item Info dialog box

this menu and summoned when the menu items are selected, SuperCard takes care of this function for you. To make a standard Apple menu, simply create a new menu, and name it "Apple." It will automatically display the names of currently available Desk Accessories (including those loaded with utilities such as SuitCase and Font/DA Juggler).

Generally the first item under the Apple menu, before the Desk Accessories, is one that summons an information screen about the application. The Finder's "About the Finder" menu item is an example. If you create a menu item to display an "About box," be sure to include a dividing line below it, to separate that item from the list of Desk Accessories.

Font Menu

Font menu support, like Apple menu support, is standard in SuperCard. If you create a menu called "Fonts," this menu will automatically list all the fonts available to the application. This includes, like the Apple menu, all fonts loaded with utilities.

Resources

Resources are essential components of Macintosh programming, whether you are using HyperCard, SuperCard, or a traditional programming language to create your application.

Resources, in standard Macintosh applications, are tools that the program uses to create the Macintosh user interface. They are separate from the actual code (program instructions) that comprise the program and are instead used by that code. In most Macintosh applications, objects such as windows, menus, icons, dialogs, and alerts, and so on are defined by resources. Using resources, programmers can alter these elements of the user interface (to provide foreign language support, for example, or change the appearance of dialogs) without recompiling the entire application.

In HyperCard or SuperCard, resources are often used to provide tools that are not directly supported by the language. External commands and functions (XCMDs and XFCNs) are examples of these resources. They are essentially new commands for the language — commands that were created using a traditional, compiled programming language.

Creating New Resources

SuperCard allows you to create and manage directly three types of resources: icons, cursors, and color lookup tables. To create a new resource, double-click the Resource icon in the Project display. The dialog shown in Figure 3-12 will appear, asking which kind of resource you want to create. A new icon will be created and will appear in the list of resources.

Note that the Resource Info dialog box that appears for resource items (shown in Figure 3-13) differs from other Info dialogs in one key factor. Resources have ID numbers, but no other numbers, and further, those ID numbers are initially assigned by SuperEdit, but can be edited by you. That means you can assign your own numbers to resources.

Once you have created a resource you double-click on that resource to work on it. Techniques for working with the three types of resources, not surprisingly, depend on which kind of resource you are editing.

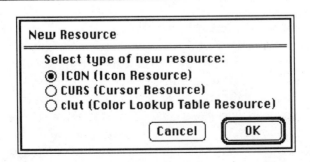

Figure 3-12.   The New Resource dialog box

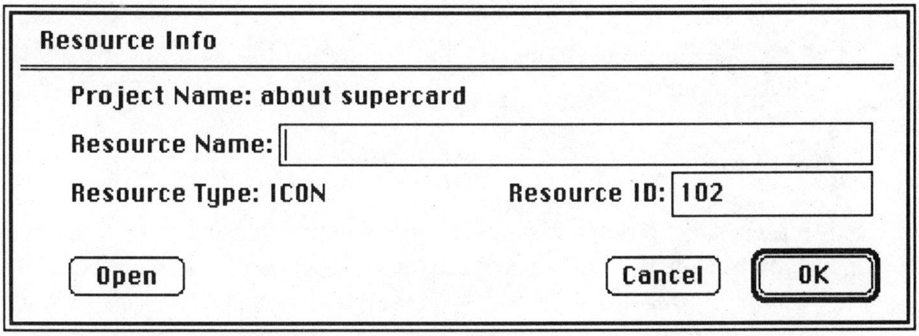

```
┌─────────────────────────────────────────────────────────┐
│ Resource Info                                           │
│ ───────────────────────────────────────────────────────│
│   Project Name: about supercard                         │
│   Resource Name: │                                    │ │
│                  └────────────────────────────────────┘ │
│   Resource Type: ICON          Resource ID: │102      │ │
│                                              └─────────┘ │
│   ┌──────────┐              ┌──────────┐  ┌──────────┐  │
│   │  Open    │              │  Cancel  │  │    OK    │  │
│   └──────────┘              └──────────┘  └──────────┘  │
└─────────────────────────────────────────────────────────┘
```

Figure 3-13.   The Resource Info dialog box for an icon

Icons

The Edit Icon dialog box, shown in Figure 3-14, has three parts. On the right is a large box showing a "fat bits" or zoomed version of the icon. Icons are 32 pixels high by 32 pixels wide. To place a pixel at a particular location, click on that location; to erase a pixel, click on that pixel.

To the left of the zoomed view of the icon is an actual-size view of the icon, showing you how it will appear when it is displayed.

Below the actual-size view of the icon are four buttons:

• Revert allows you to abandon any changes you have made to an existing edit, so you can experiment with the appearance of an icon, without changing the original.

• Cancel is similar to Revert, in that it discards any changes you have made to the icon. However, it also closes the Edit Icon dialog box. Using Cancel is the equivalent of using Revert and then OK.

• Paste places the graphic on the clipboard, assuming it is no larger than 32 × 32 pixels, into the icon shape. This gives you several techniques for working with icons. You can use all the graphic tools in SuperEdit's Bitmap editor, for example, to create icons, copy them, and then paste them into this dialog. You can also capture icons used by other programs by taking a snapshot of the screen, importing that screen shot into a card, then copying the icon.

• OK saves the changes you have made to the icon and closes the Edit Icon dialog box.

Cursors

Editing cursors is quite a bit different from editing icons because they move around on the screen and are generally more complicated. Since the cursor represents the tool you are using, it is one of the most important elements of your user interface: the tool can determine how you approach the problem at hand, and how you perceive your software.

The cursor has three components, represented by the three panels in the Edit Cursor dialog box, shown in Figure 3-15. The *cursor image* is the image of the cursor as it will appear *when it is shown against a*

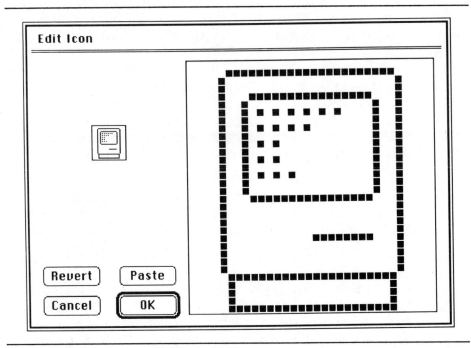

Figure 3-14.   The Edit Icon dialog box

white background. You will typically draw the cursor in the cursor image panel. The black pixels you create in this panel show the cursor as it will normally appear.

The *cursor mask* determines the appearance of the cursor when it is placed against a black or grey background. The white areas in the mask will be transparent when the cursor is over pixels that are black or grey. Note that in Figure 3-15, the entire hand and finger in the cursor mask panel is blackened. This makes the bulk of the cursor visible when it is over a black area.

The *cursor hot spot*, shown in the rightmost panel, is the precise, "sensitive" point on the cursor that indicates exactly which pixel on the screen you are pointing at. If you examine several different cursors, you will note that the location of hot spots within the cursors varies considerably. The hot spot of the standard Macintosh arrow cursor, for example, is at the upper-left corner of the pixel region. The hot spot of a cross-shaped cursor is at the junction of the two lines that form the cross.

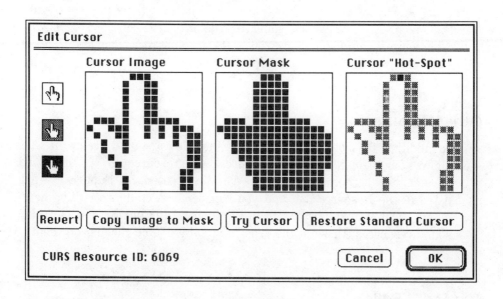

Figure 3-15.   The Edit Cursor dialog box

Note that the display in the hot-spot panel is automatically updated in grey as you draw the cursor in the cursor image panel. Only one pixel in this panel is active at any one time. To relocate the hot spot, simply click on the new location of the hot spot.

To the left of the three panels are three small boxes showing the actual size of the cursor, as it appears against white, grey, and black backgrounds. Keeping an eye on these three boxes will help you draw your cursor. Note that lines only one pixel wide tend to disappear when shown against dark backgrounds. If you want to create a "cross" cursor, the cursor image should be a single line, but the lines in the cursor mask should be wider to make it stand out better against dark backgrounds.

By clicking on the Copy Image to Mask button below the panels, you can automatically duplicate the cursor image in the mask panel, eliminating the need to redraw the cursor to create the mask. All you need to do is darken the white spots on the original cursor.

Cluts

Color lookup tables, or "cluts," are necessitated by the fact that, while the Macintosh can display some 16 million colors on the screen with 8-bit color, it can display only 256 of these colors at a time. See Chapter Fourteen, which discusses all aspects of color.

Other Resources

In addition to the resources SuperEdit allows you to create, it also allows you to manage other resources. All resources in a SuperCard document—whether or not they can be created by SuperEdit—are listed in the Resource list, and you can perform standard editing commands (Cut, Copy, Paste, Clear) on them. Additionally, you can play sound resources (those of the type "snd ") by double-clicking on them.

The Script Editor

If you have edited scripts in HyperCard, you have probably been frustrated, at least occasionally, by the HyperTalk script editor. Since it is a modal dialog box, it has some serious limitations, including lack of menu support (you must use largely undocumented COMMAND-key combinations to perform many actions), no Undo command, and the inability to open two scripts at one time to facilitate copying and pasting. The Script editor in SuperEdit solves all these problems.

Getting Into Scripts

There are two ways to open the script of any object when in SuperEdit. The first and more complex way is choosing the Info command for that object under the Edit menu and then clicking on the Script button in the resulting dialog. The second, easier way is choosing the Script command near the Info command for any object on the Edit menu. The Script Edit window is shown in Figure 3-16.

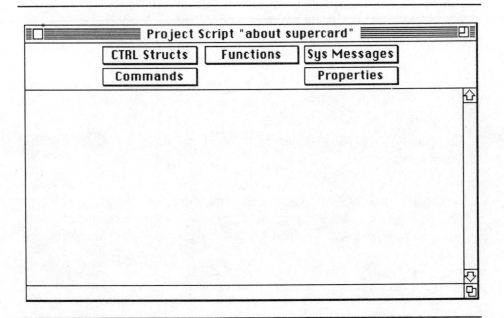

Figure 3-16.   The Script Edit window

Pop-up Menus

At the top of the Script Edit window are five pop-up menus, containing all the commands, functions, messages, and other components of Super-Talk. You can use these pop-up menus to help you enter these components correctly into a script. Note that in some cases, more than just a word or two will be placed for you; these items are denoted by the ellipses after their name. The If structure, for example, is followed by three dots, and if you choose this item, this text

```
if then
xxx
else
xxx
end if
```

will be placed at the insertion point. The string of x's indicates where your commands are to be placed.

Script Menu

When you open a Script window, you will notice a new menu on the menu bar, called "Script." This menu contains commands to assist you in script editing. The menu is shown in Figure 3-17.

Set Text Font

This command summons a dialog that shows in a scrolling list the names of all the fonts available to SuperEdit, and allows you to choose the font and size of the current script.

Set Tab Size

This command allows you to set the *tab size,* or the number of spaces that lines are indented, for the current script. The standard in Hyper-Card is two spaces, but you might prefer larger indentation, which can sometimes be easier to read. SuperCard's default indentation is four spaces.

Comment/Uncomment

The Comment command places comment markers (two dashes: --) in front of the currently selected line. The commands are greyed out if

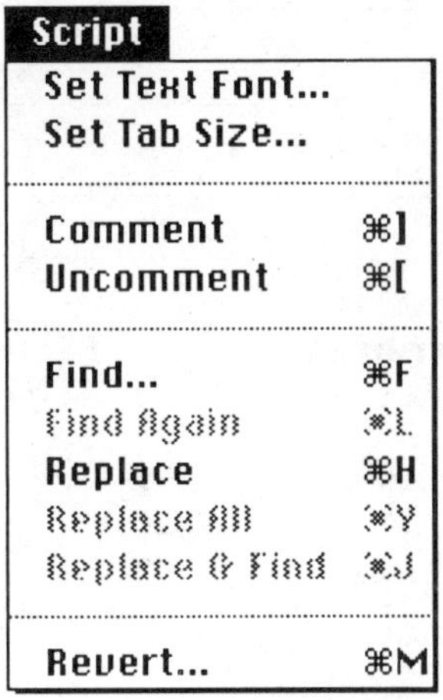

Figure 3-17.   The Script menu appears when a Script Edit window is active

entire lines are not selected. If you want to comment a block of lines, a second pair of dashes are added at the beginning of the line. This is done so that when you later use the Uncomment command, you will not lose original comments.

Find Commands

The Script menu has five commands for searching for and replacing text. If you choose the Find command, you will get the dialog shown in Figure 3-18, in which you can enter the text you want to find. If you are performing a simple Find, after the first occurrence of the text is found, using the Find Again command (COMMAND-L) will find its next occurrence.

The Replace command brings up the dialog box shown in Figure 3-19. This dialog box contains fields for the text you wish to find and for the text with which to replace it. If the checkbox labeled "Stop at end of script" is checked, it will do so; if this box is not checked, when the end of the script is reached, the operation will start over again at the beginning of the script.

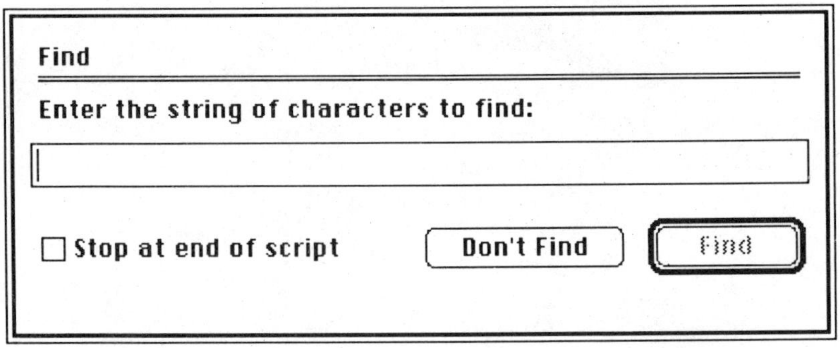

Figure 3-18.   The Find dialog for searching through scripts

Revert

The Revert command on the Script menu provides an "Undo" that reverses all the changes you have made to a script since you opened the script. It is analogous to the "Cancel" button in the HyperCard or SuperCard Script editor.

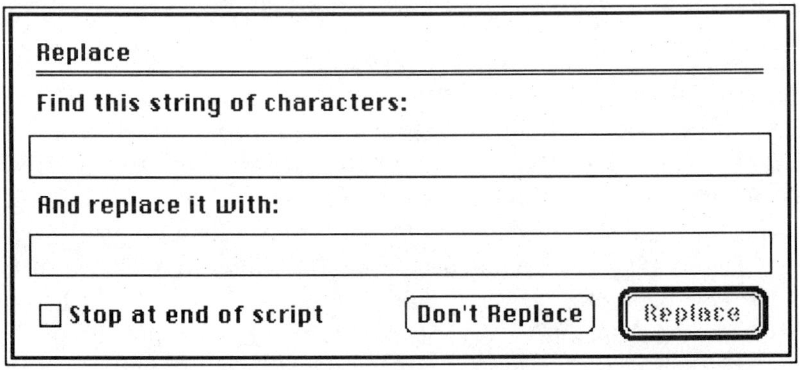

Figure 3-19.   The Replace dialog for searching and replacing text in scripts

Nonmodal

The Script editor in SuperEdit is nonmodal, which means that while the window is open, you are not limited to working only within that window. Instead, you can choose any appropriate command from the SuperEdit menus, including the standard Cut, Copy, Paste, and Clear commands. The Undo command also works, allowing you to reverse your last actions. As long as you choose the Undo command immediately after performing some action (whether deleting or adding text), that action will be reversed.

One of the best features of the nonmodal Script editor is the fact that it allows you to view, simultaneously, scripts from other objects — even if they are in other projects. This can be very handy when working on complex projects. If you are using numerous global variables, for example, it is sometimes difficult to remember the exact names of those global variables when they are used in many scripts. By opening several Edit windows, you can easily copy the declarations of those globals from script to script.

Selecting Objects

SuperEdit gives you several tools for finding objects. Some of them work in the Card editor, and will be discussed in the next chapter. However, when Overview windows are active, the View menu, which includes commands allowing you to cycle among the three major types of objects in SuperCard, includes a Select command that you can use to select objects meeting certain criteria. The dialog box summoned by this command is shown in Figure 3-20.

Note: If an overview of a window is visible, the View command disappears and is replaced by an Options menu. This menu contains a Select command that serves the same purpose, with minor variations, as the more general Select command discussed here.

This dialog box is one of the most innovative and handiest in SuperCard, particularly when editing scripts. Its basic operation is simple: click on the radio button to indicate how you want to find text, type

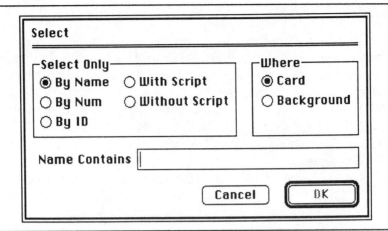

Figure 3-20. This Select dialog box allows you to search for specific objects

the text you want to find, and click the OK button. All the objects in the current Overview window that contain the text will be highlighted. You can then do such things as cut, copy, or clear the objects, open them, or edit their scripts.

Perhaps the most useful of the radio buttons is the one labeled "With Script." When you use this option, all objects that contain the specified text *within their scripts* will be highlighted. This is useful if you are trying to find, for example, all scripts that contain a specified global variable, or are searching for all the scripts that call a specific function or handler. When the objects are highlighted, you can then use the Edit Script command to open all the scripts at once.

If you select the "Without Script" radio button, all objects that *do not contain scripts* will be selected.

When a Card window is opened, the Select command works differently, and that will be discussed in Chapter Four, which covers the Card editor.

Working With Cards in SuperEdit

Graphics, text and buttons — virtually all the things that comprise the project — are contained in cards. Only windows (which contain cards), menus (which control cards), and resources are not part of the card structure. Fittingly, SuperEdit's flexible Card editor is at the core of the program, and you will probably use it a great deal.

When working with SuperEdit, always remember that changes you make are not automatically saved, as they are in SuperCard and Hyper-Card. Therefore, you should perform two tasks fairly frequently: use the Save command on the File menu to save your changes, and use the Save As command on the File menu to save different versions of your projects, which will allow you to revert to previous versions should you make some drastic changes.

Managing Cards

You will use SuperEdit's Window Overview to manage the order of cards in your stack. Because HyperCard has no analog to this window, it has no easy way to change the order of cards in your stack without sorting or extensive copying and pasting, which can be quite a nuisance. However, SuperEdit has no Sort command to sort cards automatically — for that you need to use SuperCard.

Backgrounds and Cards

The Window Overview shown in Figure 4-1 is an example of a fairly standard window, containing ten cards and four backgrounds. You should note two things about this Window Overview. First, cards and backgrounds are not shown in order of their creation. The card with ID 112 comes before the card with ID 103 (card IDs are assigned in

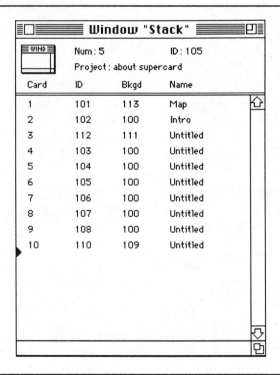

Figure 4-1.   A Window Overview shows you all the cards in a window in a scrolling list

SuperCard, as in HyperCard, in order of their creation). Backgrounds are also not necessarily shown in order of their creation. Second, some of the cards are titled, and some are not.

Using this window, you can create a new background (and a new card to go with it) by using the New Background command on the Edit menu. Remember that the new card will be inserted at the point denoted by the insertion triangle at the left edge of the window. Normally this insertion triangle will first appear at the end of the list, but you can position it elsewhere by pointing to the desired location at the left edge of the window and clicking.

Copying and Pasting Cards

To copy or cut cards, simply select the card or cards you want to copy, and then select the appropriate command from the Edit menu.

To select a contiguous group of cards, click on one of the cards at either end of the group, then hold down the SHIFT key and click at the other end of the group. In the window shown in Figure 4-1, for example, if you want to select cards 5 through 7, first click on card 5, hold down the SHIFT key, and click on card 7. Or you could do it the other way around.

To select a discontiguous group of cards, use the COMMAND key when you select the second and following cards. In the same example, if you want to select cards 3 and 5, but not 4, first click on card 3, hold down the COMMAND key, and click on card 5. Card 4 is not selected.

Once you have selected a group of cards, you can copy, cut, or clear the cards. Clearing the cards, you will remember, deletes them, so you are prompted with a dialog box, which asks if you really want to remove them. However, you are not so prompted when you cut a selection of cards. This is problematic because the Undo command is not enabled after this cut, so if your selection is discontiguous, you cannot immediately paste the cards into the different areas from which they came.

When you paste a card or group of cards, they will be inserted at the point of the insertion triangle. If the card (or cards) is being pasted into a window that contains other cards with the same background, the background ID will remain the same. If the card is being pasted into a new window, or into another window that does not contain the same background, a new background will be created.

Note that card-numbering is dynamic: when you cut or clear cards, all cards after the card you cut or clear are renumbered to make the numbering contiguous. Card IDs, though, are not dynamic. Pasting a card back into the window from where it came will preserve the card's ID. However, pasting a card into a different window will give that card a new ID. If it were otherwise, two cards in a window could have the same ID numbers.

Also note that pasting location is governed strictly by the location of the insertion triangle; you cannot paste over cards that you have selected by clicking on them.

Replacing Backgrounds

One of the best features of the Window Overview is the ability it gives you to select certain cards and to replace their current backgrounds with other backgrounds. This facility will be a welcome addition to experienced HyperCard users.

To replace the background, select the cards whose background you want to replace, and note the ID number of the desired background. Then choose the Replace Bkgnd command from the Options menu that is visible when you are using the Window Overview. The dialog box shown in Figure 4-2 will appear.

This dialog box simply lists the ID numbers of all backgrounds in the current window. Find the desired background for the selected cards, click on the ID of that background, and then click on OK.

Note: You cannot undo the Replace Bkgnd command. If you use this command to replace the background of the only card that uses that background, that background design will be lost.

Selecting Cards Automatically

Like the Select command discussed in Chapter 3, the Select command located on the Options menu allows you to select cards meeting certain criteria. Using this command summons the dialog shown in Figure 4-3.

This dialog allows you to search for cards or backgrounds with certain names, numbers, or ID numbers. There are a number of uses for this facility. Suppose, for example, that in ordering your project you have somehow separated the cards sharing a certain background, so

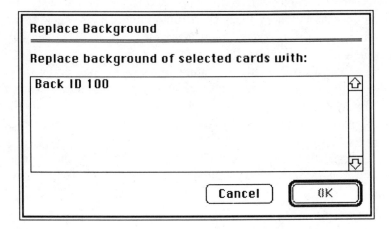

Figure 4-2.   The Replace Background dialog box allows you to replace backgrounds on selected cards with different backgrounds

that they are not contiguous in the project. To make them contiguous, choose the Find command, and then click on the Background button on the right side of the dialog box. Click on either the "By Name," "By Number," or "By ID" radio buttons, and enter what you are looking for in the field. Click on the OK button, and all the cards meeting the search

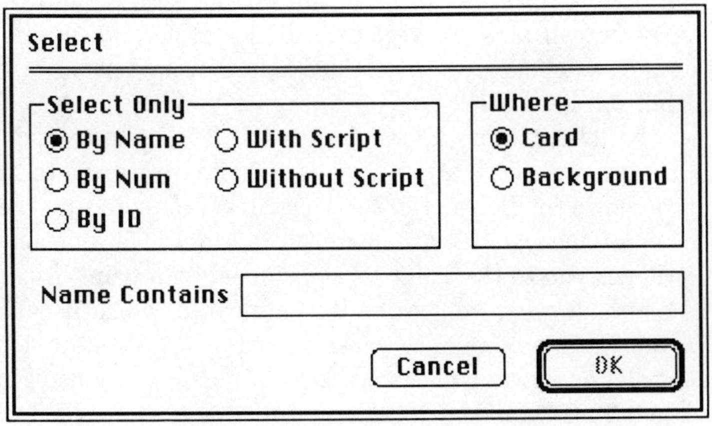

Figure 4-3.   The Select dialog box searches for cards

criteria will be selected. With those cards selected, use the Cut command to remove them from their current locations, click to move the insertion triangle to the point where you want to place the cards, and use the Paste command.

You can also use this command to perform such actions as replace the background of all the cards containing a certain background with a new background. Use the Select command to locate and select all those cards, and then the Replace Bkgnd command to replace those backgrounds.

Card-sorting is a chore in HyperCard, but using the Window Overview in SuperEdit to change the order of cards in a window is very easy.

The Card Editor

The Card editor, shown in Figure 4-4, is in a resizeable window, with the standard close, zoom, and size boxes, all of which allow you to reshape the window to the needs of your screen and the card you are editing. Within the window is an outline of the card, in its actual size.

The area outside the card is similar to the Pasteboard in Page-Maker. You can place objects on this area if you want to use them later. They will not be displayed when the project is run in SuperCard, nor will you be able to scroll to see them (scrolling is limited to the card size). Objects can also overlap: part of the object can be on the card, part on the pasteboard. In SuperCard only that part of the object on the card itself will be visible.

On the left side of the window is the Tool palette—actually four Tool palettes, and there are two ways to switch from one to another. In the card shown in Figure 4-4, the Draw tools (denoted by the compass at the top of the palette) are currently selected. Clicking on this compass switches you to the Paint tools, signified by a paint brush. Clicking on the brush switches you to the Button palette, which in turn switches you to the Field palette. You can also change to a different palette by choosing the one you want from the View menu, or by using one of the associated COMMAND keys.

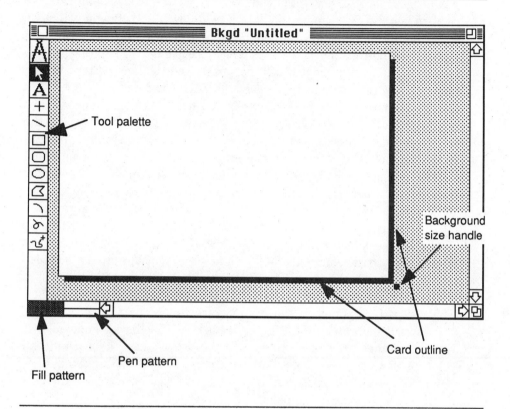

Figure 4-4.   The components of the Card editor window

Patterns and Colors

Draw objects have two components that govern their screen appearance: the Fill pattern and the Pen pattern. The Fill pattern governs the appearance of enclosed areas of draw objects. The Pen pattern governs the appearance of the lines that define the object.

You control the appearance of the Fill pattern with the small rectangle at the lower-left corner of the Card editor (see Figure 4-4). This rectangle displays the current Fill pattern, or the Fill pattern of the selected draw object.

If you are using a black-and-white monitor (or a color monitor set to two colors), when you hold down the mouse button on the left rectangle, a palette will pop up showing the patterns currently available, as in Figure 4-5. To select a new pattern, move the mouse pointer to the pattern you desire, keeping the button held down. A rectangle will move with the mouse pointer, outlining the different patterns. When you release the button, the pattern to which the pointer is pointing will be selected. The pop-up palette will disappear, and the new pattern will be shown in the rectangle at the lower-left of the Card editor.

If you have a color monitor, when you hold the mouse button down on this rectangle, you will see three palettes. The first palette, at the left, represents the foreground color. The second shows the pattern itself, and the third shows the background color. On two-color monitors the foreground color is the one that is generally shown as black, and the background color is the one generally shown as white. These color patterns show all 256 colors available in the current color lookup table.

The rectangle next to the Fill pattern represents the Pen pattern. It works in the same manner as the Fill Pattern rectangle, except it contains an extra column at the far right—the Pen Width palette, which sets the width of the lines. The Pen Pattern rectangle will show you a display of the current settings of the Pen pattern, including line width. The Pen pattern pop-up is shown in Figure 4-6.

In its default state, the Fill pattern is grey. The background color is black, and the foreground color is white. To change the background color, point to the rectangle, depress the mouse button, and while it is still held down, drag through the palettes until you have chosen the new background color from the palette to the right.

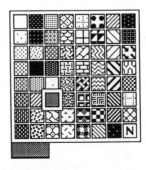

Figure 4-5.   The Fill Patterns palette pops up when you click on its rectangle

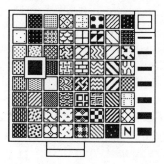

Figure 4-6.   The Pen Pattern menu controls the width and pattern for lines

You can change the Fill and Pen patterns for buttons, draw objects, and fields *after you have drawn them.* For paint objects, these settings only affect new paintings; you cannot edit the pattern of a paint oval after it has been drawn, for example.

Generally, objects you create in SuperEdit are opaque; they completely obscure other objects that are underneath them. However, using the Object Info dialog box for bitmap and draw objects, you can change the Ink Effects for that object. Ink Effects control how objects on top of one another are affected by the presence of other objects. SuperCard's Ink Effects are discussed in detail in Chapter Fourteen.

Background and Card Layers

All cards in SuperCard or HyperCard have two layers: the background layer and the card layer. All changes made to the background layer affect all the cards that share that background; changes to the card layer affect that card only. You can choose the layer by selecting the appropriate command from the View menu—COMMAND-B for background and COMMAND-K for card. You can also use the Open Bkgnd command with a card selected in the Window Overview to open the selected card and go directly to background editing.

When working on one layer, you have some flexibility about how the items on the other layer are displayed. For example, when you are in the card layer, you can have the background objects hidden, displayed as grey, or shown in full color. You can use the Preferences command (discussed in Chapter Three), under the Apple menu, to set the default method SuperEdit will use to display card objects when you are editing the background.

Unlike HyperCard, SuperEdit lets you select only objects that are part of the layer you are currently editing. This restriction is a mixed bag: it is not as flexible as HyperCard's approach but prevents you from thinking you are on one layer when you are really on the other, as sometimes happens with HyperCard. This is especially true of graphics.

Note that you can size backgrounds when you are working on the background layer. When you are editing the background layer, a small box, or handle, appears at the bottom-right corner of the window (see Figure 4-4). You can click on this handle and drag it to resize the background (and therefore all the cards associated with that background). This technique is useful when creating small cards, particularly palettes and dialog boxes, but it is not so useful when working on larger cards because it gives you no feedback about the actual dimensions of the new background. If you need precision, use the Background Info dialog box.

Cards and Colors

Each card in a window can have a separate color lookup table (clut) associated with it. To choose a clut use the Select Colors command on the Options menu, and you will see the dialog box shown in Figure 4-7. The four cluts shown in the figure are standard cluts that are part of the Macintosh system software. If your project has any other cluts, they will be shown in the scrolling list.

The Color Matching radio buttons govern how existing colors on the card will be matched to the colors in the new clut you choose. Colors and color matching are discussed in detail in Chapter Fourteen.

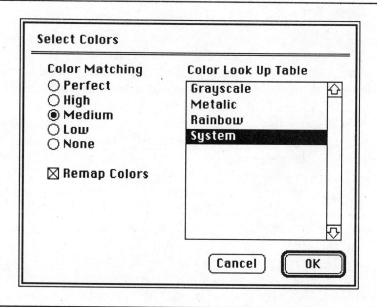

Figure 4-7.   The Select Colors dialog box

If the Remap Colors checkbox is checked when you choose the new clut, existing colors will be matched to the new colors; in addition, you will later be unable to reset the colors of any bitmap objects on the card to their original values. The Undo command does protect you against this, but you must choose it immediately after selecting new colors.

About Tools

You create the objects that will appear on the card with tools, which are located on four separate palettes.

In discussing these tools, we will use the names for the tools as they appear in the SuperTalk language. All the tools (with the exception of the AutoTrace tool) can be used under script control in a project or manually in SuperCard as well as in SuperEdit.

The Pointer Tool

Two of the tools are common to several of the palettes—the Pointer tool and the AutoTrace tool. The Pointer tool is located at the top of all four palettes, directly below the icon indicating which palette is active. The Pointer tool has the same appearance as the standard Macintosh pointer—the one active in the Finder, for example.

The Pointer tool is used to select all objects, no matter which tool palette is currently active. It is also used to move (drag) and resize any object. It is the default tool: when you open the Card editor or switch palettes, this tool is automatically selected.

You can select multiple objects either by SHIFT-clicking on the objects you want to select, or by clicking on an area of the card that does not contain any objects, and dragging the mouse to draw a rectangle around the objects you want to select (this is the same technique you use to select multiple icons in the Finder). If you wish to deselect one particular object when you have already selected a group of them, you can hold down the SHIFT key and click on that object.

In SuperEdit, the Pointer tool replaces the separate Field and Button tools in HyperCard. In HyperCard, you must choose a specific Button tool to select or resize a button, and you must do the same with the Field tool. In SuperEdit, the Pointer tool is used for selecting and working with *all* objects. You will find the pointer very convenient; it is easier to use one tool than to switch to different tools to perform similar tasks. (In SuperCard, you still have the Field and Button tools, which work as they do in HyperCard. You also have a Graphic tool, which selects graphics only, along with the Pointer tool.)

The AutoTrace Tool

The AutoTrace tool is available in SuperEdit, but not in SuperCard itself. In SuperEdit, this tool is available on the Draw and Button palettes. It is used to trace the rough outlines of regions of bitmap graphics and transform them into buttons or fields. It is handy for importing bitmap graphics (such as maps and the like) and transforming them, piece-by-piece, into draw graphics, or for making irregular areas on bitmap graphics act as buttons.

The AutoTrace tool operates in three modes, depending on which keys you use with it. You normally use it without any key at all. Select the tool, click where you want the draw object to be outlined, and then encircle the area of the bitmap you wish to trace. Release the mouse button when you have enclosed the area. This mode of the AutoTrace tool operates in much the same way that the standard Lasso tool in HyperCard works; most other applications that allow you to work with bitmaps, such as paint programs work in the same way. However, while the lasso will select pixels that are not connected to one another, the AutoTrace tool will only transform pixels that are actually connected into draw graphics.

The second method for using the AutoTrace tool is with the OPTION key. If you hold down the OPTION key while clicking and dragging with the AutoTrace tool, you will draw a rectangle. This makes it easy to select large areas to transform and doesn't require that you encircle the area. Control of the area selected is not as precise as with the lasso mode, so it is not useful in all cases.

Finally, you can use the COMMAND key with the AutoTrace tool. Using this key eliminates the need to encircle an area. When you COMMAND-click on a point with the AutoTrace tool, the tool uses this point as the inside of the area you want to select; it "looks outward" to the next white or black pixels, and it creates a region based on what it finds. If you click on a white pixel surrounded by black pixels, the white area will be traced to a draw object or button; if you click on a black pixel, all contiguous black pixels will be traced. This mode works the same as the Paint Bucket tool: any area that would be filled with the Bucket will be traced by this tool.

At the same time, SuperEdit lets you do a "reverse AutoTrace" — that is, convert any other type of object into a bitmap. This capability is discussed in the "Paint Tools and Bitmap Objects" section later in this chapter.

Draw Tools and Objects

The ten draw tools are used to create draw objects. Draw objects are considerably different from paint objects. Paint objects create *bitmaps*, which are arrays of dots on the screen; *draw objects* are mathematical descriptions that store the shapes that you draw on the screen. Draw objects have several benefits:

• They can be edited. You can edit bitmaps too, but only by erasing pixels and replacing them with new pixels. You can resize, rotate, and reshape draw objects, and the essential characteristics of the shape are maintained.

• They are smaller in terms of the space they occupy in memory and on disk. Instead of having to store the location of each of a series of bits, the program only has to store the location and size of the object. This feature is especially beneficial to users who have color monitors.

• Draw objects are faster to display on the screen. Since they take up little room on disk and in memory, they consequently load onto the screen much faster than do bitmap objects.

The Draw Tools palette is shown in Figure 4-8. If you have used a draw-type program before, such as MacDraw, Canvas, or the draw layer of SuperPaint, you will be familiar with these tools.

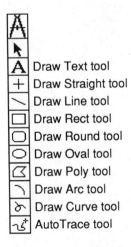

Figure 4-8.   The Draw Tools palette

Draw Text Tool

The Draw Text tool creates a draw object that contains text. This tool is useful for such functions as labeling fields on the screen. Draw text can be edited and styled, either in SuperEdit or SuperCard.

To use this tool, select it, and draw a rectangle. After you draw the rectangle, click in the rectangle and type your text. The rectangle will only be large enough to contain one line of text; however, when you type the text and press RETURN, or type enough text so that it needs to wrap, the text area will automatically enlarge to hold it. If the rectangle you create is too large for the text you type, you can shrink the rectangle with the pointer tool. If you draw a rectangle, then choose another tool without first typing any text, no text object is created.

You can set the style of any text in a draw object by selecting that text and using the Text Styles command under the Object menu. Note that this means that draw text objects can have varying styles: changes made with the Text Styles dialog affect only selected text in the object.

SuperCard gives you only one method of changing the color or pattern of text in draw objects. You create a second draw object and place it directly on top of the text. Next, choose the colors you want for the text, using the Fill pattern. To make the underlying text object adopt the characteristics of the object on top of it, double-click on the overlaying object and click on the Inks button. Then, if you want to change the color of the text, choose the addPin effect.

Draw Straight Tool

The Draw Straight tool is used to draw vertical or horizontal straight lines. If you move to the right or left, it will draw a horizontal line; if you move up or down, it will draw a vertical line. While drawing, if you move the mouse more than 45 degrees from either pure vertical or horizontal, the line will shift its orientation.

Draw Line Tool

The Draw Line tool draws straight lines at any orientation. If, after the line is drawn, you click on one of its ends while holding down the SHIFT key, the line will "snap" to either a pure vertical or horizontal orientation, and you will then be unable to move it off that orientation.

Draw Rect and Draw Round Tools

These two tools are used to draw rectangles. The first draws rectangles with 90-degree corners, while the second draws rectangles with rounded corners. If, while you are drawing a rectangle, you hold down the SHIFT key, the rectangle will be drawn as a square. You can also transform an existing rectangle into a square by resizing it with the SHIFT key held down.

Draw Oval Tool

The Draw Oval tool is used to create ovals. It works in the same way as the Rectangle tool—that is, using the SHIFT key constrains the oval to a circle.

Draw Poly Tool

The Draw Poly tool enables you to draw polygons. To use it, click at the point where you want to start the polygon, release the mouse button, and move the mouse to the location of the second point. You will notice a "rubber band" line following your mouse. When you have reached the second point, click the mouse button again, and repeat the process. When you click the mouse button on the same point at which you began the polygon, the object will be finished, and you will be switched to the Pointer tool. If you double-click the mouse at any point, the polygon will be finished with a line that extends directly to your starting point.

Once you have created a polygon with this tool and selected it with the pointer, two commands on the Objects menu—Rotate Polygon and Reshape Polygon—become enabled.

When you select Rotate Polygon, one handle will be created, at the top of the selected polygon. Click on this handle, and drag to the left or the right. The polygon will rotate. Since it might be hard to rotate the polygon back to its precise location later, you should immediately evaluate whether you like its position or not. You can use the Undo command to reset it to its original state.

The Reshape Polygon command creates handles at all the corners of the polygon. By clicking on one of the handles and dragging, you can reposition it, reshaping the polygon.

Note that both these commands also affect polygons drawn by the Draw Curve tool, discussed shortly.

Draw Arc Tool

This tool draws arcs. Click with the tool at the beginning point of the arc, and drag the mouse to form an arc. When you have finished dragging, the arc will be filled with the current Fill pattern and color (if any). If you hold down the SHIFT key while you draw the arc, the created arc will be from a perfect circle, that is, the distance from any point on the arc to the center of an imaginary circle formed by extending the arc will be the same.

After drawing an arc, you can then use the Reshape Arc command on the Objects menu. Handles will be created at either end of the arc, and dragging one of the handles will change the length of the arc.

Draw Curve Tool

The Draw Curve tool operates much the same as the Draw Poly tool, except that you do not need to click the mouse button at each juncture of the object. Instead, it allows you to draw freehand objects. To use it, simply click where you want to begin the object, and drag the mouse with the button held down.

Like objects created with the Draw Poly tool, those drawn with the Curve tool can be reshaped and rotated using the appropriate commands on the Objects menu.

Paint Tools and Bitmap Objects

SuperEdit's Paint tools, shown in Figure 4-9, are used to create bitmap graphic objects. If you are familiar with other painting programs, such

▢	Paint Select tool
℘	Paint Lasso tool
✏	Paint Pencil tool
▱	Paint Eraser tool
A	Paint Text tool
🖌	Paint Brush tool
🖋	Paint Spray tool
🪣	Paint Bucket tool
＼	Paint Line tool
▢	Paint Rect tool
◯	Paint Round tool
◯	Paint Oval tool
◿	Paint Poly tool

Figure 4-9.   The Paint Tools palette

as MacPaint, HyperCard, or the paint layer of SuperPaint, these tools will be familiar to you.

The Bit Bucket

The Paint tools in SuperEdit (and SuperCard) differ from those in other programs in that before you can use them, you must create a *bit bucket*—a rectangular bitmap object—to contain the bitmaps. The rectangle you create will define the limits of the object, and you can constrain the rectangle to a square by holding down the SHIFT key as you drag. Once you have created the object rectangle, you can paint anywhere in that rectangle with the current tool. If you choose another tool and click on an area that is within a current bitmap object, you will draw on that object.

Once created, both the graphic object and the bitmap it contains can be resized. To resize the object, click on it with the Pointer tool and drag one of the handles that appears at its corners. Note that if you make the object itself smaller—that is, if you make the rectangle smaller than the bitmap it contains—that part of the drawing that becomes obscured by the rectangle is lost. You can get it back with the Undo command, but not by later resizing the object rectangle.

If you hold down the SHIFT key while stretching the object rectangle, resizing the object will be constrained in either the horizontal or vertical direction, depending on the direction in which you first move.

To resize the object, and resize bitmaps that are contained in that object, hold down the OPTION and COMMAND keys as you reshape the object. Bitmaps within the object will be stretched or shrunk to fit within the new object rectangle. Again, you can use the SHIFT key to constrain the new proportions of the object to a square.

As mentioned earlier in this chapter, you can copy anything on the card into a bitmap. To do so, hold down the OPTION key while you are dragging with the mouse to form a bit bucket with any of the Paint tools. The design of all card objects under the rectangle you draw, including other bitmap objects, draw objects, fields, and buttons, will be copied into the new bit bucket. This technique is useful if you have several bitmap objects on the card and want to create one new object out of them.

Bitmaps and Colors

Another difference between bitmaps and draw objects is in the area of color. Bitmaps cannot be edited after they are drawn, and this is especially true of colors. If you paint an object in a specific color and pattern, you cannot change its color or pattern without redrawing it. Before you start drawing, then, consider the patterns and colors, and choose the ones you want.

Using the Object Info dialog box with a bitmap object selected allows you to change a bitmap from a color object to a black and white object, and vice versa. When you change a color object into a black and white object, SuperEdit generates a *dither*—a set of black-and-white patterns that approximate the shades in the original—for that object. (Note that the Undo command, which you must use before you do anything else, is the only way to reverse this action. You may change the object back to color again later, but the colors in the original have been lost.)

Paint Select Tool

The Paint Select tool is used to select portions of bitmaps for cutting, copying, or clearing. To select an area of a bitmap, simply draw a rectangle around the area with this tool. When an area has been selected, the Flip and Rotate commands in the Objects menu, and the Nudge and Scale commands in the Arrange menu, become available.

When using this tool, of course, you need not first draw a bitmap object. Instead, when you click inside any existing bitmap object, that object becomes active. Double-clicking on this tool with a bitmap object selected selects the entire bitmap object. You can also use the Select All command on the File menu to select the entire active paint object.

If you hold down the COMMAND and OPTION keys while dragging with the Paint Select tool, the rectangle you create will shrink to the smallest rectangle that can hold all the bits you have selected (similar to the Shrink command in HyperCard). If you hold down the OPTION key as you drag to form a rectangle with this tool, when you release the mouse button you will be switched to the Lasso tool (discussed below), and only the actual bits you outlined — not the white space — will be selected.

Paint Lasso Tool

The Lasso tool works just as it does in HyperCard. To select an area of a bitmap, draw a line around that area with this tool, and that area will be selected. Remember that only nonwhite pixels are selected with this tool. As with the Select tool, the Flip and Rotate commands in the Objects menu, and the Nudge and Scale commands in the Arrange menu work with these selections.

Paint Pencil Tool

Due to SuperCard's support of color, the Paint Pencil tool works differently in this environment than it does in HyperCard.

When you are using color, the Paint Pencil tool draws in the currently selected color. Clicking with the pencil on a white pixel changes that pixel to the selected color, as does clicking on a pixel that is of a different color than the current color. Clicking on a pixel of the current color erases that pixel.

If you COMMAND-click with the Paint Pencil tool at a specific location, you are taken into the Zoom Bits editor, permitting you to edit one pixel at a time. You can also enter the Zoom Bits mode by double-clicking on the Pencil tool in the Tool palette, or by choosing Zoom Bits from the Objects menu.

Paint Eraser Tool

The Paint Eraser tool erases all the bits in a 16-pixel-by-16-pixel area around which you click. If you are in the Zoom Bits mode, it instead erases an area 4 bits by 4 bits.

The Paint Eraser tool is constrained to horizontal or vertical movement with the SHIFT key. Double-clicking with the Eraser erases the current bitmap object.

Paint Text Tool

The Paint Text tool allows you to place paint text in a bitmap object. You can set the style of the text either before you type the text, or after you have typed text but *before* you click the mouse someplace else.

Paint Text ignores colors and patterns; the text itself is always black against a white background. A white rectangle is created within the bitmap to define the text.

If you double-click on the Paint Text tool on the Tool palette, SuperEdit opens the Text Styles dialog box, allowing you to specify the font, size, and style of text to be typed. You can change the style of text already typed by choosing Text Styles from the Objects menu (or by pressing COMMAND-T), as long as you have not clicked anywhere else on the card since you typed your text.

Paint Brush Tool

You will use the Paint Brush tool to create most of your paintings. It paints in the current pattern, using the current foreground and background colors. To use it, simply hold down the mouse button and drag; if you click outside of a bitmap object, you will need to create one first.

The default size of the paint brush is a square 16 pixels on each side. By double-clicking on the paint brush, or by choosing the Brush

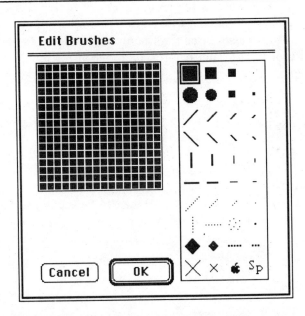

Figure 4-10. The Edit Brushes dialog box

Shapes command from the Objects menu, you can edit the shape of the brush in the dialog box shown in Figure 4-10. In this dialog box, the large area on the left is where you edit the brush; click on a black pixel to make it white, or on a white one to make it black. On the right is a box showing all the brush shapes. The current shape is surrounded by a box; to edit a different shape, click on it.

When painting with the brush, the SHIFT key constrains the brush movement to horizontal or vertical directions. The COMMAND key causes the brush to only affect areas that are currently filled with black pixels; white and colored pixel areas are left alone.

Paint Spray Tool

The Spray tool operates in much the same way as the spray tool in HyperCard—drag it with the mouse button held down, and it sprays a pattern of dots in the current pattern and colors.

Double-clicking on the Spray tool summons the Edit Patterns dialog box (shown in Figure 4-11) that allows you to edit the patterns used by

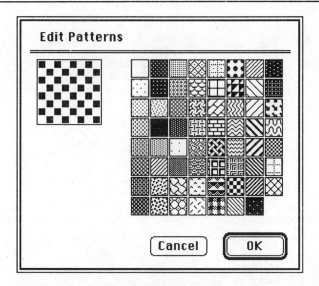

Figure 4-11.   The Edit Patterns dialog box

the Paint tools. On the left of the dialog box is the editing area; the available patterns are shown to the right.

The Spray tool works with different keys in the same manner as the Brush tool: the SHIFT key constrains it to horizontal or vertical movement, and the COMMAND key causes it to change the color of black pixels only.

Paint Bucket Tool

Use the Bucket tool to fill white pixels in a bitmap with the current pattern and color. If the hot spot on the bucket is on a white pixel when you click on it, then only contiguous white areas—those connected to one another with white pixels—are painted. If you click on a nonwhite pixel, only contiguous pixels *of the same color* will be filled.

Double-clicking on the Bucket tool also brings up the Edit Patterns dialog box.

Paint Line Tool

The Paint Line tool works in roughly the same manner as the Draw Line tool, except, of course, that you cannot edit the line once it is drawn. The line is drawn using the current pattern, color, and line-width settings. Using the SHIFT key constrains the line to either a horizontal or vertical alignment.

Paint Rect and Paint Round Tools

The Paint Rect and Paint Round tools are used to draw rectangles. With the Paint Rect tool, the corners of the rectangles are at 90 degrees; with the Paint Round tool, the corners are rounded. The SHIFT key constrains these shapes to squares. You can set the line width of the border, along with its pattern and color, by using the Pen pattern rectangle at the lower-left portion of the window.

Paint Oval Tool

The Paint Oval tool is used to draw ovals. Use the SHIFT key to constrain the oval to a circle. Use the Pen pattern rectangle at the bottom-left portion of the window to set the pattern and width of the border.

Paint Poly Tool

This tool is used to create bitmap polygons. Click at the initial point of the polygon, drag the mouse, and a rubber band line will follow the pointer until you click again. Repeat the process for each side of the polygon. When you are finished, either double-click the mouse (and the polygon will be finished with a line from that point to the initial point), or close the polygon by clicking at the original point. The polygon will be filled using the current patterns and colors, and the line will have the current line settings.

While you are drawing with this tool, you can hold down the SHIFT key to constrain any side of the polygon to a horizontal or vertical line.

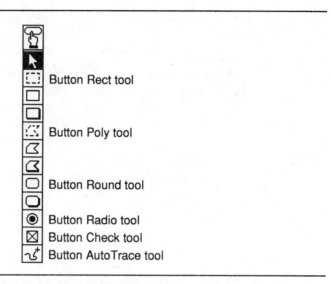

Figure 4-12.   The Button Tools palette

Zoom Bits

Zoom Bits are used on bitmaps (*not* draw objects) to allow you to edit individual pixels. There are two ways to enter Zoom Bits: COMMAND-click with the Pencil tool at the location you want to edit, or choose Zoom Bits from the Objects menu with a bitmap object selected. The latter method is less precise as to the location you want to edit.

Zoom Bits work the same way as Fat Bits in HyperCard, with a couple of differences. When you enter the Zoom Bits mode, all you can see of the card is the current bitmap object. You cannot scroll to see different parts of the card; it is as if the bitmap has expanded to fill the entire card.

To leave Zoom Bits, you can again select Zoom Bits from the Objects menu, COMMAND-click with the Pencil tool, or switch to a different tool palette.

Button Tools

Use the Button tools to create buttons. Buttons are the "prime movers" in HyperCard, but they are not quite as important in SuperCard. In

SuperCard much of your user interface will use menus instead of buttons. Nevertheless, buttons are quite powerful. The Button Tools palette is shown in Figure 4-12.

Even after you have created a button, you can change the style of buttons using the Button Info dialog shown in Figure 4-13. To get this dialog, either double-click on a button, or press COMMAND-I with a button selected. As you can see from this dialog, you can use the Button Style rectangle on the lower-right to change the style of the button. You can also set other button properties (whether its name is shown, the Auto-Hilite of the button, and so on) using the rectangle on the left. These properties are discussed in detail in Chapter Ten.

A new feature in SuperCard is the ability to set the depth of the shadow visible for a button or field. You do this with the dialog shown in Figure 4-14. This dialog is summoned by clicking on the Shadows button on the Button Info dialog box.

The Shadow dialog box has two ways to set the depth of the shadow. You can type a number into the Shadow Offset field, indicating

Button Info

Card name: Untitled

Button Name: [   ]

Button Number: 1   Button ID: 100

[Shadows...]

Button Properties:
☐ Show Name   ☐ Disable Button
☐ Auto Hilite ☐ Default
☒ Visible

Button Style:
◉ Round Rect
○ Rectangle
○ Polygon
○ Check Box
○ Radio Button

[Script]   [Icons...]   [Cancel]   [OK]

Figure 4-13.   The Button Info dialog box

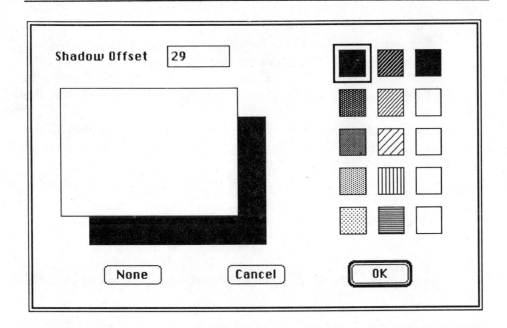

Figure 4-14.   The Shadow dialog box

how far from the button the shadow is cast. You can also set the depth
of the shadow by pointing to the inside of the white rectangle (which
represents the button) and dragging the mouse. The dialog box constantly updates the display of the shadow. To the right of the dialog box
are 15 patterns, allowing you to specify the pattern of the shadow that is
cast.

Button Rect Tools

Three tools allow you to create rectangular buttons. To use any of these
tools, simply draw a rectangle with the mouse. The SHIFT key constrains
the shape of the button to a square. The first Button Rect tool creates a
transparent button, which will be visible to you in SuperEdit as a grey
rectangle but will be hidden in SuperCard. Transparent buttons cannot,
of course, have shadows.

In HyperCard, transparent buttons are generally used to create
buttons on top of graphics, giving the appearance that clicking on a
portion of a graphic does something. Since graphics in SuperCard are

objects in and of themselves, you will have little need for this kind of button, unless you want to add AutoHiliting to a graphic.

The second tool draws a rectangular button with a white fill pattern and a black pen pattern. You can change these settings by selecting the button, and using the fill and pen rectangles at the bottom-left corner of the screen. You can set the shadow of a rectangular button with the Shadow dialog box.

The third Rectangle tool draws a button in the same manner as the previous version of the tool but automatically gives a shadow with an offset of 1 to the bottom.

Button Poly Tools

Three tools allow you to create polygonal buttons. To create these buttons, use the same techniques as for the Draw Poly tools. These buttons behave in the same manner as the three Button Rectangle tools.

Button Round Tool

The two Button Round tools create standard Macintosh buttons with rounded corners. There are only two, since it does not make sense to create a transparent button that has rounded corners. The only difference between the two tools is that the second automatically adds a standard shadow, with an offset of 1, to the button.

When you are using either of these tools, you can hold down the OPTION key while you click on the card. A new button with a default height and width will be created, and centered at the point you click.

Button Radio Tool

The Button Radio tool draws a radio button. While it is possible to set the shadow for a radio button, it will not be displayed.

Button Check Tool

The Button Check tool creates a checkbox.

AutoTrace Tool

The AutoTrace tool on the Button palette operates in exactly the same manner as the AutoTrace tool on the Draw palette. That is, it transforms an area of a bitmap graphic into a polygonal button.

Field Tools

Fields are used to hold text on cards. Fields are created with the Field Tools palette, shown in Figure 4-15.

The Field tools are variations on the Rectangle tools used on SuperEdit's other menus. To use them, click at one corner of the rectangle you want to define, then drag to form the field. Fields, unlike buttons and draw objects, can only be rectangular.

You can set many characteristics of fields with the Field Info dialog box shown in Figure 4-16. As you can see from this dialog box, fields, like buttons, can have shadows. The process of setting the shadow for a field is the same as it is for a button.

Also in the Field Info dialog box is a button that takes you to a Text Styles dialog box. This dialog allows you to specify the font, size, and

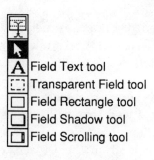

Figure 4-15.   The Field Tools palette

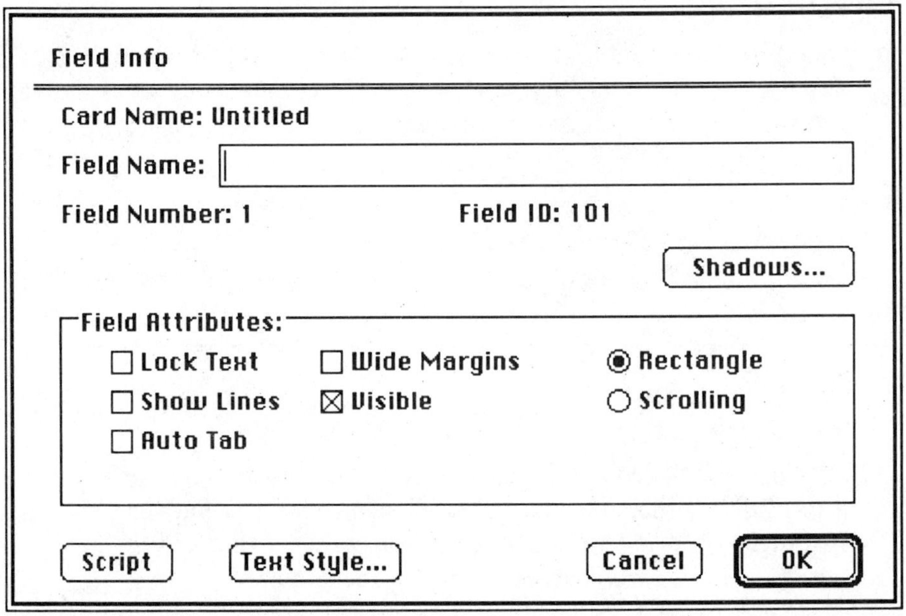

Figure 4-16.   The Field Info dialog box

style of all the text in the field. This default style can be changed.
Other properties of a field are discussed in Chapter Eleven.

Field Text Tool

Once you have finished drawing any field with a Field tool, you are switched to the Field Text tool, which allows you to enter text into the field. You can also switch to this tool manually, to enter or edit text in a field.

One key difference between HyperCard and SuperCard is the latter's ability to include styled text within a field, as illustrated by the Field Text tool. Enter text in a field, select some of it, and then choose the Text Styles command from the Objects menu. When you format selected text with this dialog, only the selected text will be formatted. You should not use this feature capriciously, however. Formatted text can take up quite a bit more room on disk than unformatted text.

Various Field Tools

As mentioned, the Field tools work like Rectangle tools, and, except for the Transparent tool, you can use the Field Info dialog box to change the style of a field from one to another. You cannot change a transparent field into one that is not transparent, nor can you change one that is not transparent into one that is, using SuperEdit.

When fields are drawn, the border of the field is automatically black and the fill pattern is automatically white. You can change these settings by selecting a field, and choosing different patterns and colors from the rectangles at the lower-left of the Card editor window. However, when choosing colors, be careful to use schemes that result in clear, readable text.

Scrolling fields are identical to the other fields in that they present a standard scroll bar at the right side of the field. One nice feature provided by SuperCard but not by HyperCard is that the elevator box is not visible when text does not reach below the lower limits of the field.

Working With Objects

Aside from simply creating objects, you can do some other work with them in SuperCard.

Selecting Objects Automatically

Within the Card Editor, you can use the Select command on the View menu to help you locate specific objects. This command summons the dialog box shown in Figure 4-17. As you can see, this dialog box allows you to search for objects by name, number, ID, or search the scripts of objects. Use the checkboxes on the left of the dialog to restrict your search to specific types of objects. When SuperEdit finds the specified objects, they are automatically selected.

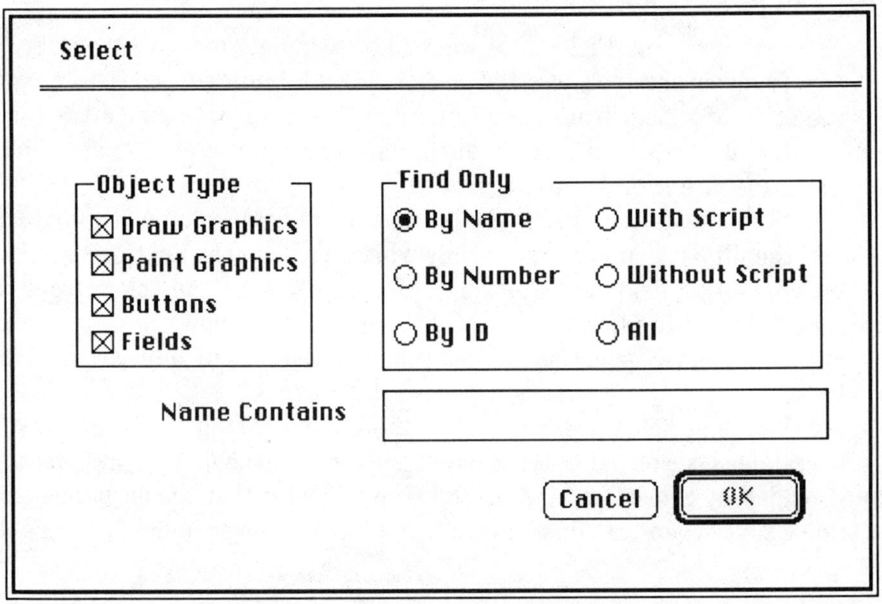

Select

Object Type
- ☒ Draw Graphics
- ☒ Paint Graphics
- ☒ Buttons
- ☒ Fields

Find Only
- ⦿ By Name   ◯ With Script
- ◯ By Number   ◯ Without Script
- ◯ By ID   ◯ All

Name Contains [   ]

[Cancel] [OK]

Figure 4-17.   The Select Objects dialog box

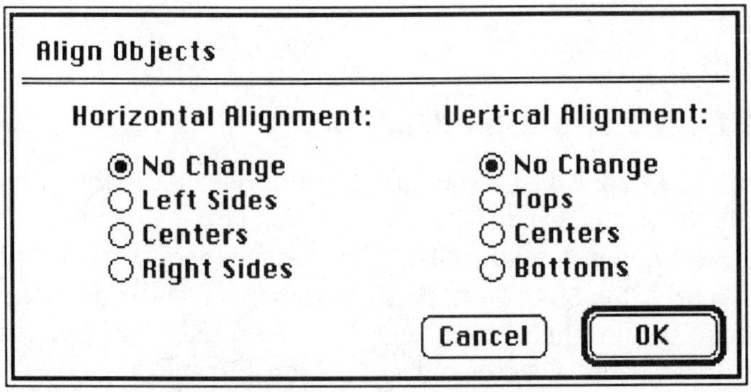

Align Objects

Horizontal Alignment:
- ⦿ No Change
- ◯ Left Sides
- ◯ Centers
- ◯ Right Sides

Vertical Alignment:
- ⦿ No Change
- ◯ Tops
- ◯ Centers
- ◯ Bottoms

[Cancel] [OK]

Figure 4-18.   The Align Objects dialog box

Aligning

With several objects of any type selected, you can use the Align Objects command on the Arrange menu. This command will come as a welcome addition for experienced HyperCard users: aligning objects in Hyper-Card is very difficult. The Align Objects dialog box, shown in Figure 4-18, is self-explanatory. The radio buttons in the left column determine horizontal alignment; those in the right column determine vertical alignment. To give two objects the same center point, for example, you would select the two objects, choose the Align Objects command, and then click on the Centers buttons in both columns.

Grouping

Grouping allows you to take several graphics objects — whether they are bitmaps, draw objects, or objects of both types — and group them. When two or more objects are selected, the Group command on the Arrange menu performs this operation. Choosing Ungroup from the Arrange menu returns the objects to their original, individual, status.

Grouping, in effect, creates one new object where there were several before. When graphic objects are grouped, they lose their individual identities, and you lose the ability to edit them. Draw objects cannot be resized, and bitmaps cannot be painted in, unless you are resizing, rotating, or flipping the entire group, nor do any of the original objects receive messages in SuperCard. You can give this entire group its own script, with the Object Info dialog box that appears when you double-click on it.

The Dangers of Grouping

Grouping, or rather ungrouping, can be dangerous. As mentioned above, groups can have their own script and identity. When you ungroup some objects, the object formed by the group is, in effect, deleted. Therefore, before you ungroup, make sure you are not losing some important scripts.

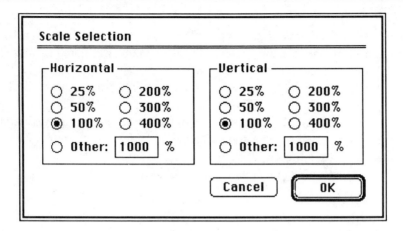

Figure 4-19.   The Scale Selection dialog box

Scaling Graphics

When a graphic object or a portion of a bitmap object is selected, the Scale Selection command on the Arrange menu is enabled. This command produces the dialog box shown in Figure 4-19. As you can see from the dialog box, you have independent control over horizontal and vertical scaling. You can use one of the default values or enter your own new values in the fields.

Locking

You can lock or unlock an object by selecting the object and choosing the appropriate command from the Arrange menu. Locking an object is a good way to save yourself from accidentally altering or deleting it.When an object is locked and you select it, the size handles normally displayed on the object are greyed out, which signals that you cannot modify the object.

Nudging

Nudging allows you to move a selected graphic or group of graphics in any of four directions, one pixel at a time. The Nudging tool in Super-Card (not included in HyperCard) comes in very handy when you are putting the final design touches on a card.

Importing Graphics

There are several ways to import graphics into SuperEdit from other programs. One common way, of course, is the standard Macintosh Clipboard, which is supported by SuperEdit. Some programs come in very handy for moving graphics from application to application, such as Open It!, the desk accessory from TenPoint0 that allows you to open graphic files, select portions of them, and place them on the Clipboard for pasting into SuperEdit.

Importing graphics from HyperCard is handled automatically when you convert a stack using the Convert Stack command. SuperEdit itself imports graphics in PICT, TIFF, or MacPaint file formats, using the Import Graphics command under the File menu. This command is only available when you are editing a card. After the program has read the file, it will present you with a dialog box indicating that the graphic has been placed on the Clipboard. You can then paste it onto your card.

When you paste any color image onto a card, SuperEdit will notify you that the image has a color lookup table associated with it and ask whether you want to add that clut to the resource list. If you click on "Yes" in the dialog box, you will be given a Resource Info dialog, into which you can type the name of the new clut. If you answer "No", the image will be pasted, and the colors will be matched to the existing clut. SuperEdit does not check through the existing cluts to see if a clut matches the one you are importing.

FIVE

A Scripting Refresher

SuperTalk
Objects
Referring to Objects
Dealing with Messages
Script Components

The purpose of this chapter is to present a quick refresher course in the basic concepts of scripting in HyperCard and SuperCard. If you are familiar with HyperTalk, HyperCard's scripting language, much of this chapter will be old hat to you. However, even if you are familiar with HyperTalk, you should at least skim through this chapter, as it does present some ideas you will need to consider when learning to script in SuperTalk.

If you are unfamiliar with HyperTalk, this chapter should help you understand some of the concepts. However, this chapter does *not* cover all the elements of the scripting language. You should, instead, refer to one of the many sources of information about HyperTalk such as *Hyper-Card: The Complete Reference,* by Stephen Michel, [Berkeley, Ca: Osborne/McGraw-Hill, 1989].

SuperTalk

SuperTalk is SuperCard's scripting language. It allows you to instruct SuperCard objects to perform certain actions in response to messages sent by you and by SuperCard.

You program in SuperTalk by opening the script of an object and inserting a *handler* that tells the object what to do when the message is received.

Objects

SuperCard is an *object-oriented* environment. When creating SuperCard documents or projects, you are assembling a collection of objects. Some of the objects you create will be active in that they respond to messages and perform actions. Other objects will be passive in that they are used for containing text or displaying a graphic. The distinction is up to you and the needs of your design.

Following is a discussion of the various types of objects that Super-Card contains.

Graphics

In HyperCard, there are no graphics objects. Instead, you have two "layers" of bitmap graphics: the background layer and the card layer. In SuperCard, there are two types of graphic objects: bitmap objects and draw-oriented graphics. Bitmap objects are always rectangular and contain arrays of dots (bits), which can be any color. Draw graphics can have complex shapes (not necessarily rectangular), and each dot in the graphic is *not* necessarily addressable. Instead, you use special draw tools to construct the objects.

Graphic objects, of either kind, can receive messages. This means you can put scripts into these objects and send them messages by clicking the mouse button on them, or in other ways.

Graphics are different from other SuperCard objects in one key way: fields and buttons, even if they do not contain scripts, always receive messages. If you click on a button, the mouseUp message is always sent to that button. However, if you click on a graphic and that graphic has nothing in its script, it does not receive the message.

Fields

Fields contain text—usually text that you wish to present to the user but also text that the user of your projects enters. The kind of field you choose depends on the kind of text you are presenting.

Fields, like buttons, can receive and handle messages. In different circumstances, however, different messages are sent to fields. Since you usually want to edit text when you click in a field, certain mouse messages are not always sent to a field. Instead, most messages are only sent to a field when that field is *locked.*

Buttons

A *button* is a special type of object. When you click the mouse button on a button, it performs an action responding to (or handling) a series of messages that are sent to it.

One interesting feature of SuperCard is the increased flexibility you have in creating objects that are explicitly designed to receive messages. In HyperCard, virtually your only choice is the button, and buttons are limited to a rectangular shape. In SuperCard, however, anything can be a button, including graphic objects. Since draw objects are not limited to a rectangular shape, this gives you more flexibility in designing your cards. Buttons can do only a few things that graphic objects cannot. Specifically, buttons have a highlight property that can automatically darken the button when the pointer is on the button and the mouse button is depressed. SuperCard buttons also have a shadow property that provides a great deal of flexibility in button design. Buttons can also be disabled.

Cards

The card is the basic unit of information in SuperCard. Cards contain fields, buttons, and graphic objects. Only one card is visible within a window at any one time, but several cards can be visible at one time if you display different windows.

Backgrounds

A *background* is a set of design elements—buttons, fields, graphic objects—that are shared by a number of cards. If a card is associated with a particular background, all the elements of that background will appear on the card.

Note that you may, however, use card-specific elements that obscure background elements. In this way you can differentiate one card from others in a common background.

Backgrounds also determine the size of the card.

Windows

The windows of SuperCard are analogous to stacks of cards in Hyper-Card. SuperCard projects can have one or many windows. When running SuperCard, you can have one or an almost unlimited number of windows visible on the screen.

Menus

Menus, new to SuperCard, respond to messages sent to them when you select a menu item. A *menu* is composed of two parts: the menu itself and the items it contains. The menu name is what appears on the menu bar; the items appear when you point to a menu and depress the mouse button.

Projects

A *project*, the largest element of SuperCard, is the document created when you use the Save As menu command. A project is a collection of all the elements that comprise a SuperCard application: resources, menus, windows, backgrounds, and cards.

Referring to Objects

You may need to refer to objects for several reasons:

- To send messages to that object.

- To determine what object received the message your script is handling.

- To set properties, which define many characteristics of an object.

- To make the object visible on screen if it is a card, background, or stack.

To refer to an object, you need to include several general descriptors, as well as one specific descriptor. General descriptors define the *kind* of object to which you are referring: button, field, card, background, or stack. If the object resides on a card or background (that is, a button or a field), you must also include in the descriptor the designation *background* or *card* to indicate whether the object is part of the background design or is specific to the individual card. (If the object is a button and is on a card, you need not use the *card* descriptor; if it is a field and is on the background, you need not use the *background* descriptor.)

Buttons, fields, cards, and backgrounds have three types of specific descriptors—object names, object numbers, and object ID numbers. Projects have one specific descriptor, which is the complete pathname of the project.

Object Names

Names are optional for all SuperCard objects, except for projects. (Since projects are documents on Macintosh disks, they must have names; projects do not have any of the other specific descriptors discussed here.) Even though names are optional, they are very useful for describing many SuperCard objects: a name is easier to remember than a number.

You assign a name to a SuperCard object by typing it into the dialog box that appears when you use the Object Info menu. Names can include any characters, including spaces and numbers. Names can be as long as 31 characters, though you should keep them shorter.

When referring to an object by name, you should put the name of the object in quotes. A statement such as **Go to card "menu"** is preferable to **Go to card menu**. Though the latter usage often works, Super-Card might interpret the word *menu* as a variable or stack name, instead of the name of a card. Following that logic, you should see why it is not wise to include quotes as part of the object's name. Numbers are also problematic, since SuperCard might interpret **Go card "1941"** as an instruction to go to card *number* 1941 instead of the card *named* 1941.

Object Numbers

In SuperCard, virtually all objects except projects are numbered. These numbers often, although not always, refer to the order in which they were created. They do, however, always refer to the order in which the object exists within its container. Card 7 is the seventh card in the stack, for example, and background button 5 is the fifth button on the background.

Note that the number of an object can be changed. If you sort the cards in a window project, for example, the first card might become the last depending on the order in which you sorted the stack. You can change the numbers of buttons and fields with the "Send Further" and "Bring Closer" items on the Objects menu.

There are three ways to express the number of an object:

1. With an integer following the general descriptor. **Card 47, Background 2**, and **Background field 3** are examples.

2. With a numeric constant. SuperCard defines ten numeric constants (one, two, . . . ten), which you can use to refer to objects. **Card ten** and **Background Field seven** are examples. Of course, these only work for the first ten objects in a container.

3. With an ordinal. SuperCard defines ten ordinal constants, which are similar to the numeric constants mentioned above. These are

first, second, third, and so on through the tenth. The ordinals are used *before* the general descriptors, which only makes sense grammatically. **First card** and **second background button** are examples.

In addition to the ten ordinal numbers, which are useful only for the first ten objects, SuperCard defines three other special ordinals: **middle**, **any**, and **last**. You can use these special ordinals in this manner:

```
Go to middle card of this window

Go to any card

Go to last card
```

"Middle" refers to the object that is in the middle of the list of objects. For example, if the window contains 10 or 11 cards, the statement above will take you to card number 6.

"Any" causes SuperCard to pick an object at random. At present, the uses of this special ordinal are obscure.

The special ordinal "last" refers, of course, to the last object in a container. Last is an easy way of going to the last card in a window.

Object ID Numbers

When a new object is created, SuperCard generates a new ID number for that object. The ID number, unlike the object number, remains constant for each object; it is not affected by sorting. ID numbers are always created sequentially with new, larger numbers being assigned automatically to new objects.

Referring to objects by ID number is generally faster than referring to objects in other ways. This is especially true when going to different cards in windows with many cards. However, ID numbers are not nearly as easy to use, since they are more difficult to remember than names and not as intuitive as ordinal numbers.

To use an ID number in a descriptor, you insert the word **ID** after the general descriptor and before the actual ID number. **Go to card ID 1770** and **Edit the script of card graphic ID 3770** are examples of statements that use ID numbers.

Dealing with Messages

SuperTalk scripting is "message driven." This means that all SuperCard activities are responses to messages that are either generated automatically by the software or triggered by your actions. These messages can be sent in several ways. For example, they may be initiated by the mouse—by clicking on a button or a field or by choosing a menu item. They may also be initiated by the keyboard—by typing something into the aptly named Message box. Messages may also be generated automatically. When you go to a card, for example, the message "openCard" is sent to that card, just as the message "openWindow" is sent to a window when you open that window.

The Hierarchy of Message Passing

Which messages are sent to which objects and when? Most messages are sent to specific objects on cards, but some messages are sent directly to cards. Consider two examples.

When you point to a button with the mouse, a series of messages are sent to that button. As the mouse enters the rectangle of the button, the message "mouseEnter" is sent to the button. For as long as the pointer is in the area of the button, the message "mouseWithin" is sent to the button. When you click the mouse button within a button, the message "mouseDown" is sent to the button; when you release the mouse, the message "mouseUp" is sent.

When you go to a new card, the message "openCard" is sent to the new card. If the script of this card has no handler for this message, the message is then passed up the hierarchy to the script of the background of which the card is a part. If the background script has no handler, it is passed to the script of the project. If no handler is there, the message is sent to the script of your SharedFile, and if no handler is there, on to SuperCard itself. Because SuperCard does not handle the openCard message, nothing happens.

Figure 5-1 illustrates this hierarchy of messages. Note that in the case of the current project, the SharedFile, and SuperCard itself, the message can also be handled by external commands (XCMDs) or functions (XFCNs).

In addition to taking advantage of SuperCard's standard message passing, you can explicitly send messages to SuperCard objects with the Send command.

SuperCard's message hierarchy may be suprising if you are used to working with HyperCard because in SuperCard you can have multiple projects open simultaneously. This is especially noticeable in the case of menus.

In SuperCard, a menu from one project may be on the menu bar when the current card on the screen is part of a different project altogether. If you choose a menu item from one of these menus, you might expect that the hierarchy of message passing for that menu item might include the project of which the menu is a part. Instead, messages generated by that menu—or by any other handler—are sent directly to *the card that is open* (see Figure 5-1), regardless of what project contains the object sending the message.

Stand-alone applications that are created with SuperEdit have a different hierarchy of message passing (see Chapter Sixteen).

Defining Your Own Messages

You can also create handlers for messages that are *not* sent automatically by events in SuperCard, and then, in effect, send them yourself. Doing this constitutes much of the process of programming.

Here's an example. Suppose you need to draw a circle on a card using SuperCard's draw tools, and to repeat, under script control, the same circle several times. As a first attempt, you might include these three lines in your script whenever you need to draw the circle:

```
choose draw oval tool

drag from 50,50 to 100,100

choose browse tool
```

(Although these lines should be self-explanatory, consult Chapter Ten for a discussion of choosing tools and Chapter Twelve for a discussion of drawing if you have any questions.) This solution works well if you need to draw the circle only a couple of times, but if you need to draw this circle often, these three lines could add quite a bit of bulk to the script and mean a lot of extra typing.

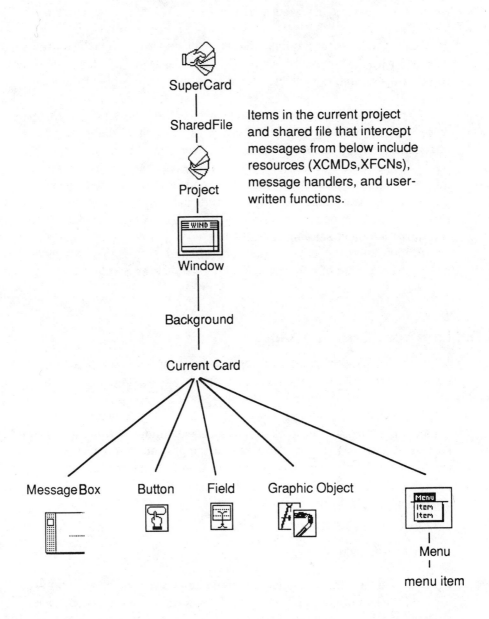

Items in the current project and shared file that intercept messages from below include resources (XCMDs,XFCNs), message handlers, and user-written functions.

Figure 5-1.   SuperCard's message hierarchy

A better solution is to create a separate handler that performs this function, and call the handler "drawCircle." Here's how it would read:

```
on drawCircle
    choose draw oval tool
    drag from 50,50 to 100,100
    choose browse tool
end drawCircle
```

With this handler whenever you need to draw this circle, you need only include one line in your script:

```
drawCircle
```

When this line is encountered in a script, the message "drawCircle" is sent up the message hierarchy in the same way that the standard system messages are sent. If the drawCircle handler is found in this hierarchy, its commands are executed. When the handler has finished executing, the original script (the one that included the "drawCircle" line) will continue executing.

Script Components

As you have seen, scripts are contained in objects and tell those objects how to react to messages. All SuperCard objects (except resources such as icons and cluts) can contain scripts, which in turn, have different components, handlers, and functions.

Handlers and Functions

A handler is the script unit that tells the object what to do when a specific message is received. For example, the most common handler to be placed in the script of a button is the "mouseUp" handler, which tells the button how to respond to the mouse being clicked on it. (Actually, it tells the button how to respond to the release of the mouse button while the mouse pointer is on the button.)

The form of this handler is:

```
on mouseUp
  series of commands
end mouseUp
```

The first line of a handler always begins with the word "on" followed by the message to which the handler is supposed to respond. This line tells SuperCard that the lines following the handler name are a series of commands to be executed in sequence.

The last line of a handler is the *end* statement, which includes the word "end" and the name of the handler. This line tells SuperCard that the sequence of commands to be executed in response to the message are finished and that this handler is ended.

Control Structures

Normally, statements within a handler or a function are executed in a step-by-step sequence. Sometimes, however, you need to change the order of the statements or execute a series of statements repeatedly. SuperTalk has several "control structures" that allow you to do this.

The most basic form of the control structure is the "on...end" structure discussed in the previous section. The two basic types of control structures used within handlers are the "repeat" and "If" control structures. "Repeat" structures tell SuperCard to repeat a sequence of commands a specified number of times, or to repeat a sequence when some condition is true. "If" structures tell SuperCard to perform one command or a sequence of commands in one condition and perhaps another command in a different condition.

Commands

In order to tell HyperCard or SuperCard to perform an action, you use a *command*, which is an instruction for the program. "Go" is a command, and is followed by an "expression" that tells the program where to go. You might, for example, type **Go first card**, where "Go" is the command and "first card" is the expression that tells SuperCard to go to the first card of the current stack. Here are some other forms of the Go command:

```
go stack "help"
go background "environment"
go second card of bg "test"
```

A handler is in essence a sequence of commands that tells the program to perform certain functions when the message that triggers the handler is passed.

Operators

An operator derives new values from other values, as when two values are added together. For example, in the statement

```
put 3 + 5
```

the "+" is the operator and returns the value "8." Many of SuperTalk's mathematical capabilities lie in its operators, but you can also use operators to join two strings of text together.

Typically, operators need to work with a command. In the above example, if you enter "3 + 5" into the Message box, the value "8" will be displayed; the "put" is implicit in the line. However, if you include that line within a handler, SuperTalk will not know what to do with it. You must include "put" in the script.

Functions

A *function* is a portion of a statement that generates a value. Similar to an operator, a function generally needs to be accompanied by a command for SuperTalk to know what to do with it.

Functions *return* values; they can almost be considered "retrievers" for values. An example is the "sqrt" function, which returns the square root of a number. When you type and enter this statement in the Message box:

```
put sqrt(4)
```

SuperCard puts "2" into the message box. The "put" command instructs the sqrt function to take 4 as its source value, and return the result.

Functions can also operate on text. You can define your own functions, just as you can define your own handlers. To do so, you use this form of the basic control structure:

```
function functionName inputs
   return value
end functionName
```

Properties

All SuperCard objects, and SuperCard itself as it is executing, have *properties* that determine the behavior of an object. If, for example, the AutoHilite property of a button is true, the button will automatically blacken (highlight) as you depress the mouse button while the pointer is on that button and return to normal when you release the button.

In a script, you can set the status of any of SuperCard's properties. You can also read the status of any property.

Values

Programs and programming languages work with data. *Data* is the "raw material" that you put into the program. In a word processor, the text you enter is the data. In a spreadsheet, the data is generally numbers. In SuperCard, you can work with numbers, dates, or text. Usually, you store the data you are working with in fields so that it is saved from session to session. But there are other sources of data—variables, chunks of text, and so on. These are generally called *containers* because they contain data.

Fields

Fields are where you store text (including numbers) that you want to preserve on disk from one session to the next. Fields are capable of holding approximately 30000 characters.

You store text in fields (in SuperCard, as in HyperCard, all data, whether it is numeric, date, or text data, is stored as text) to make it readily visible to the user and to save it, so that if you quit SuperCard, the data is accessible the next time you start SuperCard.

Variables

A *variable* is a container that scripts use to store text on which they are working. Variables are names that stand for their contents. A variable name can be of any length, it must begin with an alphabetic character, and it can contain any alphanumeric character including the underscore character and digits. Variable names cannot include spaces.

You use the Put command to assign a value to a variable. Once the variable has something in it, you can perform a number of operations on that variable.

The following are two statements that illustrate how you work with variables:

```
put "steve" into myName--myName is the variable name
put character 1 of myName--puts "s" into the message box
put 1 into theNumber--theNumber is the variable name
add 2 to theNumber--theNumber now contains 3
divide theNumber by 2--theNumber now contains 1.5
```

When used in this way, variables are "local" only to the handler in which they are used. This means that those variables have meaning and are active only during execution of the handler. If you want to make variables available to all handlers, you must first "declare" them to be global variables. You do this by using the following statement

```
global variableName
```

in the handler, *before* the variable is actually used. A global variable can then be accessed by any other scripts that are executed.

Constants

A *constant* is a container that always holds the same value, allowing you to work with certain values without having to explicitly put something into them. HyperCard and SuperCard each have several constants built into them.

Some of the built-in constants such as "one", "two", and "three", contain numbers. You can use these constants instead of using the actual numbers, as in the line

```
go card three
```

Another constant contains the value of pi or 3.141593. You can use "pi" anytime you need this value without having to type the actual number from memory. For example, a short function that returns the diameter of a circle is:

```
function diameter radius
   return pi * radius ^2
end diameter
```

Literals

A *literal* is text that represents itself. A literal is always "quoted," that is, it is surrounded by double quotation marks. When SuperCard encounters text that is enclosed in quotes, it does not attempt to interpret that text (as a command, function, or variable name), but instead uses that text as itself.

Numbers

Numbers, of course, are values. Numbers are very straightforward, as in the following.

```
put 3 into temp--assigns the value 3 to the variable temp
add 3 to temp--temp now contains six
divide temp by 2--temp now contains three again
go card 2
```

Chunk Expressions

Sometimes you do not need to work with all the data that is contained in a field or variable. SuperCard's *chunk expressions* allow you to refer to certain portions, or chunks, of text. (In SuperCard, as in HyperCard, all data is stored as text and can be referred to as text.) Text in SuperTalk can be referred to in several ways.

A *character* is a single letter of the alphabet, number, or other symbol (space, return, and so on). You can refer to any character or range of characters in a container. Some uses of containers are:

```
put "SuperCard" into temp--the variable temp contains
"SuperCard"
put character 1 of temp--puts "S"
put character 1 to 5 of temp--puts "Super"
put character 6 to 10 of temp--puts "Card"
```

A *word* is a group of characters that is separated from other characters by spaces or returns. Only spaces and returns separate words; punctuation is considered part of the word. Here are some examples:

```
put "Mr. Jones" into temp
put word 1 of temp--puts "Mr." (note the period)
put word 2 of temp--puts "Jones"
```

Items are composed of any characters, including punctuation, spaces, and lines, that are separated by commas.

```
put "a,b,c,d" into temp
put item 1 of temp--puts "a"
put item 2 of temp--puts "b"
put item 2 to 4 of temp--puts "b,c,d"
```

A *line* is any group of characters, including puncutation, that is separated by a return character. The line structure is similar to the paragraph structure used by most word processors. Lines are displayed in the same way in SuperCard fields—a line wraps around in the field, and you can "force" a wrap by putting a return character into the field. This means that the number of "lines" visible in a field may or may not reflect the number of lines that SuperTalk considers to be in that field— some of those visible lines might be caused by the wrapping of text to fit in the field.

Externals

Externals are additions to the language written in more sophisticated, powerful languages, such as C or Pascal. They are different from handlers written in SuperTalk in that they are stored in a form that allows the Macintosh to execute their statements directly, rather than in the interpreted form in which scripts are executed. Externals have two forms: external commands (XCMDs) and external functions (XFCNs).

A key difference between HyperCard and SuperCard is the way in which externals are installed into the program. In HyperCard, externals are stored in the resource fork of either the stack that contains them or the Home stack. Since SuperCard has no Home stack, you can install resources into the SharedFile. And since the resource fork of a file is not opened, in SuperCard you must convert and install the resources into the data fork of the file, using SuperEdit. Resources are discussed in more detail in Chapters Nine and Sixteen.

Projects

**S
I
X**

Managing the SuperCard project is more complicated than managing the HyperCard stack for several reasons. First, projects are inherently more complicated than stacks. Even though it has the capability of dealing with different backgrounds, the HyperCard stack is relatively homogeneous: all cards are the same size, there is only "one stack per stack," and the only types of objects you need to deal with are buttons and fields. In SuperCard, however, a single project can contain a multitude of windows (each of which is roughly equivalent to the HyperCard stack), and each window can contain multiple backgrounds and cards. Further, you may have several projects—each with its own multiple windows and menus—open at one time.

You will also need to decide *how* your project is going to be running. Is it designed to work in the SuperCard/Runtime Editor environment or as a stand-alone application? The answer will determine some of the features you will need to include in it.

Working in the Runtime Editor Environment

Working in the Runtime Editor environment is, in many ways, similar to writing a HyperCard stack that is to interact with other stacks. In

HyperCard, you may easily switch from stack to stack, and only one stack can be open at a time. In the Runtime Editor, you also may easily switch from project to project—and have many projects open at a time, with multiple windows and menus open from those projects.

Depending on the purpose of your stack, you will generally need to decide early in the design process what mode your stack will run in. If you are creating a stand-alone project, you must make sure to include in that project everything it will need to execute, such as palettes, menus, and the like. If your project is going to be running alongside other projects using the Runtime Editor, you must take steps to assure that your project is existing as a good citizen with those other projects.

Opening Projects

There are several ways to open a project with SuperCard. One common method is to use the Open Project command from within SuperCard. You can use this command by typing it into the message box, as with the statement **Open project "runtime editor"**. This command is also used when you use the Open Project command on the Runtime Editor's File menu.

A project can also be opened by double-clicking on its icon in the Finder. If SuperCard is not open, the Finder will then open SuperCard and that project.

The third way to open a project is with the Go command, which implicitly opens a project. SuperCard's Go command is similar to Hyper-Card's Go command, except that you can specify more than just the stack or card number to go to; in fact, if you do specify a card to go to, you must specify the window that contains that card.

Finally, a project can be opened when it has been built as a stand-alone application with SuperEdit.

Each of these means of opening projects creates special demands on the project creator. Depending on the nature of your project (the windows and menus it contains), you will need to plan accordingly. But no matter which mechanism is used to open a project, three actions occur in the following order.

1. The first card of the first window in the project is opened and displayed on the screen.

2. The message openProject (discussed later in this chapter) is sent to that card. It proceeds up the hierarchy, going first to the card, then to the background, then to the window, and then to the project itself, until it encounters a handler.

3. Other messages are sent to the first card in the first window to signal opening the window, background, and card.

Because the first window is always opened first, you cannot display another window or card with the Open Project command. This is similar to HyperCard, in which the first card of a stack is always displayed when you use the Open Stack command.

Note: *No* menus or other windows are opened automatically—you must use an openProject handler to automatically open other windows or to insert menus.

Project Messages

As with HyperCard, a set of SuperCard messages is sent notifying your scripts of specific events at the project level. For the most part, you will use these messages to set up which windows and menus are to be open, to establish global variables, and other functions—just as you do with HyperCard.

The startup Message

This message is sent when SuperCard is first opened. You should use this handler *only* for dealing with those tasks that are required for initially setting up SuperCard, since the message is not sent to a project when it is opened after SuperCard has been launched.

You can see how this is the case in the startUp handler that is part of the Runtime Editor. This handler is placed in the project script of every project into which you have installed the Runtime Editor. This

Startup Script is used to install the editor itself, that is, to open the various Runtime Editor menus. Since these menus only need to be installed at startup and not when a project is opened, this is the perfect time to install those menus.

The openProject Message

This message is sent when the project is opened. Since the first card of the first window in the project is automatically opened when a project is opened, the message is, in effect, sent to this first card.

OpenProject handlers are ideal for setting up the manner in which projects are to be run. Specifically, you should use them to insert any menus that are specific to projects (see Chapter Eight), and to open any windows except the first window of the project.

When you examine the structure of the Runtime Editor, you will see that the first window in this project is called "About Runtime Editor," which is first opened and displayed when the project is opened. Including an "about" or "startup" message in the first window is a good practice; your users can read it while the rest of the project is loading. This is an especially nice feature if your openProject handler has a lot of tasks, such as installing menus, opening other windows, setting up global information, and so on.

The closeProject Message

This message is sent when a project is closed. The closeProject message is sent at two different times:

1. The last open window from a project is closed, and then the project itself is closed. On this occasion, the message is sent to the current card in that window. This is what the Close Project command in the Runtime Editor does—it closes all the windows (and menus) in the current project, one by one. The Quit command in the Runtime Editor does the same thing, with the Close All Windows command.

2. As in HyperCard, a project might be closed when the Go command is used to go to a different stack. However, in HyperCard, you can only have one stack open at a time, so the current stack is *always* closed when you go to a different stack. In SuperCard, the current project is closed *only* when the current window is the *only* open window in a stack when the Go command is used.

In Chapter Eight, you will see how the closeProject message to remove any project-specific menus you might have used while the project was open.

The newProject Message

This message is sent to a project when it is created. Since new projects do not have any scripts in them, the message is never acted upon. The message can only be handled by scripts in the SharedFile.

The Compact Command

The Compact command performs the same action as the Compact Stack menu command in HyperCard: it removes all the free space from a project, thus making it a little smaller on disk. As a project is being compacted, you see the watch cursor icon. Compacting large projects can take quite a while.

Generally, it is a good idea to compact a project automatically when the free space in that project has reached a certain level. Script 6-1 shows a handler that checks the free space in a project and, if that space exceeds 20 percent of the total size of the project, asks you if you want to compact the project.

You can call this handler from a closeProject handler that you place in the SharedFile. Such a handler might read

```
on closeProject
  checkProject
end closeProject
```

Global Properties

These global properties are not properties of projects per se, but they do determine some characteristics of the environment under which your project is running.

The IdleTicks Property

the idleTicks
set the idleTicks to integer

As with HyperCard, the Idle message is constantly sent to the current card when no other scripts are running. In HyperCard the Idle message is sent continuously. In SuperCard, however, you can set this property to control how often the message is sent. This is useful if you have an Idle handler in your card or project script that takes some time to execute. While the idle message is being sent and the handler is executing, such things as typing into fields or the Message box can be sluggish, disrupting the feel of the program.

```
on checkProject
  set numberformat to "0"
  put the freesize of this project into theSize
  if theSize > the size of this project / 5 then
    answer theSize/1024 & "K wasted.  Compact?" ¬
    with "No" or "Yes"
    if it is "Yes" then
      Compact
    end if
  end if
end checkProject
```

Script 6-1.   Call this handler from a closeProject handler to automatically compact excess free space from a project

The value returned by this property, or the value to which you set it, is measured in ticks, which are 1/60 of a second. To cause the Idle message to be sent only every 1/4 of a second, set the idleTicks to 15.

The heapSpace Property

get the heapSpace

This global property contains the amount of free or unused memory currently available to SuperCard. This function or property has many uses. The most common use is to determine whether SuperCard, in the configuration in which it is running, has enough memory to perform a specific task, such as displaying a bitmap picture on a screen. Through testing this function, you can determine how much RAM will be required for a specific picture to be displayed. To do so, type **put the heapSpace into memCount** into the message box, and press RETURN. Then go to the card that displays the picture whose size you want to determine. When this card is displayed, type **subtract the heapSpace from memCount** into the message box, and strike the RETURN key. Next type **put mem-Count**, and the message box will display the amount of memory the card requires.

Once you have determined the amount of memory a specific picture requires, you can put a handler, such as the one in Script 6-2, into the button that displays that picture.

```
on mouseUp
  if the heapSpace < 8000 then
    answer "Not enough memory to go to that card!" ¬
    with "Oops"
  else
    -- insert commands here to go to the card
  end if
end mouseUp
```

Script 6-2.   This handler can check the script of a button that goes to a large card to see if enough RAM is available to display that card

The Clipboard

> **the clipboard**
> **clipboard( )**

This function returns either **card, object, text, or empty** depending on the contents of the Clipboard. For more details about manipulating the Clipboard, see Chapter Ten.

The SharedFile Function

> **the sharedFile**
> **sharedFile( )**

This function returns the pathname of the current SharedFile, allowing you to discover which folder the SharedFile is in located on the disk. You cannot use this function to change the SharedFile: the location of this project is recorded in the file SuperCard Preferences. When you first start SuperEdit or SuperCard, if the program cannot find the SharedFile, you will be asked to locate it, using standard Macintosh file- and folder-navigation techniques.

If your project is running as a stand-alone application, the Shared-File is not used, and this function returns "None."

Project Properties

Projects, like stacks, have four properties that you can use to determine certain facets of the project.

The Name Property

> **the {short ¦ long}**
> **name of this project**

This property, not surprisingly, contains the name of the project. Unlike HyperCard's corresponding property, the Name property in SuperCard is *read-only*; that is, you can determine the name of the project, but you cannot *set* the name of the project by changing this property.

Using the *long* or *short* descriptors changes not only the amount of information that is returned, but also the manner in which it is returned. When you use the *long* descriptor, the phrase returned includes the word "project," followed by the full pathname (including the name of the disk and folders containing the project) in quotes. When you use the *short* descriptor, the phrase returned does not include the word "project," but returns only the name of the project without surrounding quotes. Using no descriptor works just as does the long descriptor, except the full pathname of the project is not returned—just the project's name.

The Size Property

the size of projectDescriptor

ProjectDescriptor is the word "project" followed by the pathname of the project (including, if necessary, the names of the disk and folders containing the project). You can type **the size of this project** to find the size of the current project. The size is simply the number of bytes that the project takes up on disk. This property is, of course, read-only; you cannot use the Set command to change this value.

The FreeSize Property

the freeSize of projectDescriptor

Like HyperCard, SuperCard generates a certain amount of wasted space as changes are made to the project, including adding and deleting windows, cards, text, and graphics. Sorting a stack also generates free space. The freeSize property simply tells you how much free space is in the project. You can remove this free space from a project by using the Compact command, discussed earlier in this chapter.

The Script Property

edit script of projectDescriptor
set script of projectDescriptor to newScript

As with HyperCard, scripts of SuperCard projects (and all other objects) are properties. Unlike the other properties discussed in this section, however, you can set the script of a property to a new value. In the set statement above, *newScript* would be any container that held the new script of the project.

Altering scripts in this manner is not the preferred way to change scripts; most of your script changes are handled with the Script editor. You can use this property, though, to change a script under program control.

The Version

the version [of this project]

This property contains the version number of SuperCard. In its first release, SuperCard returns "SuperCard 1.0" when you use this command. You can also use the long form of the function to determine the version of SuperCard that created a particular project.

Installing the Runtime Editor

When you use SuperCard with the Runtime Editor and create a new project, the Editor will automatically ask you if you want to install the Runtime Editor scripts into that project. Generally, you should do so. The Runtime Editor scripts are fairly small, adding less than 1000 characters to the script of the project, and they facilitate working with your project in the Runtime Editor environment; many of the Runtime Editor functions will not work correctly if your project does not have these handlers installed. This is particularly true of the Object Info command on the Runtime Editor's Edit menu. This menu command sends the message "doubleClick" to the selected object, and that message is handled in the Runtime Editor script that is placed into your project; if the script is not there, this menu item will not work.

If you later convert your project from one that runs in the Runtime Editor environment to one that runs as a stand-alone application, you will need to remove the Runtime Editor scripts from your project since you cannot assume that other users have SuperCard.

Modifying the Scripts of the Runtime Editor

The scripts of the Runtime Editor are discussed in detail in Appendix B, but a few words about them are appropriate here.

There are several ways, and several locations, in which you can modify the handlers inserted into your project when you install the Runtime Editor. First, after the Runtime Editor handlers have been installed into your project, you can directly modify them there. Changes made to one project, of course, have no effect on other projects.

You can also modify the standard scripts that are installed in each project when you install the Runtime Editor. You can use either Super-Card or SuperEdit to do this, though it is somewhat easier in SuperEdit. In the Runtime Editor project is a window called Boot Script. This window has one card to it, but the card is not important. Instead the Runtime Editor handlers are part of the script of this window itself. To modify these scripts from SuperEdit, simply open the Runtime Editor project, locate the Boot Script window in the Window Overview, and use the Window Script command on the Edit menu to open that script.

To edit this script from within SuperCard, type this line into the Message box: **edit script of window "boot script" of project "runtime Editor"**. (This line just fits into the Message box.) SuperCard will open the script of that window.

Generally, you should avoid modifying the existing handlers in the Runtime Editor for several reasons. First, you should make sure that you completely understand these lines—changing them might have adverse effects on the performance of the Editor. Second, later versions of the Runtime Editor might modify some of these handlers, causing your changes to be lost.

It *is* a good idea to add handlers. Handlers that you add to the Boot Script will be automatically placed in all projects into which you install the Runtime Editor.

Determining Which Projects Are Open

Sometimes it is useful for a script to know which projects are currently open. As you will see in later chapters, SuperTalk provides functions that allow you to determine which menus and windows are currently open, but it has no built-in function for determining which projects are opened.

Script 6-3 is a function that returns a list of all the projects currently open. The list is in the form of lines, and one project is listed on each line.

This function is relatively simple. It first puts *empty* into the *theProjs* variable, to declare this variable the temporary holding area for the names of the current projects. It next uses *the number of current windows* (discussed in Chapter Seven) and the related currentWindow function to cycle through each of the windows. The SetWindow command (discussed in Chapter Seven) is used to make the various open windows the current window, so that *this project* will refer to the project containing each of the windows in turn. (This technique is used often in the Runtime Editor scripts.) If the short name of that project is not already in the variable *theProj*, that name is added to the list.

```
function currentProjects
  -- returns a list of all the projects currently open,
  -- one project to a line
  put empty into theProjs
  put the long name of this window into thisWindow
  repeat with x = 1 to the number of current windows
    setWindow currentwindow(x)
    if the short name of this project is not in theProjs then
      put the short name of this project ¬
      into line (the number of lines in theProjs + 1)¬
      of theProjs
    end if
  end repeat
  setWindow thisWindow
  return theProjs
end currentProjects
```

Script 6-3. This function returns a list of all the currently open projects

The Go and Open Commands

These two commands behave somewhat differently in SuperCard than in HyperCard. The differences are subtle and take a little getting used to.

The Go Command

go [card ¦ window ¦ project]

In HyperCard, you use the Go command to go to a specific card, background, or stack. The card you go to becomes the current card on the screen in the HyperCard window.

The Go command in SuperCard works similarly. Whatever card, background, or window you go to becomes the current card, replacing the card *in the current window*.

The Open Command

Open [project ¦ window]

The Open command is used in HyperCard to open a program other than HyperCard itself. If you use this command while running SingleFinder, HyperCard quits, the other program runs, and when you quit that program you return to HyperCard. When running under MultiFinder, the Open command opens the specified application in a different Multi-Finder "partition," assuming you have the free memory.

In SuperCard, however, the Open command does *not* open other programs; for that, you should use the Launch command, discussed later in this chapter. Instead, use the Open command to open the first window of a different *project*.

The Open command, therefore, has different results than Super-Card's Go command. As mentioned earlier, the Go command causes the specified window or card to become the current window or card, replacing the one that was current when the command was issued. The Open command *opens a second window* and makes that the current, visible one on the screen, but the original window is still there.

The best way to see this is with a Project window open on the screen. If you type a Go command into the Message box, causing a new window or project to be opened, you can see the existing window transform itself to take on the characteristics (size, style, and so on) of the new window. If you use the Open command, you will see a new window appear.

If the new window or project opened with this command is already open, but is not active (that is, if it is behind other windows on the screen), it becomes the currently active window.

Note: Variations on the Open command as used in HyperCard, such as Open File, work in the same manner in SuperCard as in HyperCard. Additional variations on the Open File command for opening animation files are discussed in Chapter Fifteen.

Launch

launch applicationDescriptor [with documentDescriptor]

In HyperCard, the Open command is used to Open other programs on disk and to specify which documents, if any, to open with those programs. The Open command in SuperCard is used to open different cards, windows, or projects. Therefore, the Launch command has been added, which serves the same function as HyperCard's Open command.

Launch takes one argument: the pathname of the application you wish to launch. You can also optionally include the pathname of a document you wish to open with that application. For example, if you have a program called "Draw," in a folder called "Apps" on your hard disk named "Hard Disk," you would use this command to launch that application:

launch "hard disk:apps:draw"

If you want to open a document called FloorPlan with that Draw application, you would use a statement such as this:

launch "hard disk:apps:draw" with "hard disk:apps:floorplan"

Note that in this case the document and the application are in the same folder; you still need to supply the complete pathname for the document.

If you issue this command while running in the standard or Single-Finder, SuperCard will quit, and you will be shifted into the other application. When you quit that application, you will be returned to SuperCard.

If you issue this command while running under MultiFinder, the Macintosh will attempt to open the application, and SuperCard will still be running in a different MultiFinder "partition" or memory segment. If there is not enough memory to do so, you will be notified of that fact and returned to SuperCard. There is no way for you to test, under script control, whether you have enough memory to run the other application or not.

Just as with HyperCard, you can use the Print command to open another application and then print a document with that application.

Windows, Backgrounds and Cards

Windows
Backgrounds
Cards

The SuperCard window is a rough analog of the HyperCard stack. Within each window is a stack of cards. The appearance of those cards is determined in part by the appearance of the background with which they are associated. A singular difference between HyperCard and SuperCard is the ability of the latter to include multiple windows—in effect, multiple stacks—within the same project. This chapter examines the methods SuperTalk gives you for manipulating SuperCard's windows, backgrounds, and cards.

Windows

Along with icons and pull-down menus, windows are one of the most recognizable aspects of the Macintosh user interface. In Macintosh word processing programs, painting programs, and more, windows are a key element of the Macintosh environment.

Macintosh windows allow you to look into a larger world than is visible on the screen; in a word processor, a window allows you to display, and scroll through, a larger document than can fit on the screen. In HyperCard, there is a one-to-one relationship between the window and the card it displays: they are always the same size. The SuperCard window is separate from the card it views. The window can be small and the card large, or vice versa.

The appearance and size of windows is important. The scrollable window signals the user that there is more to the card than meets the eye. You can find the other portions of the card by using the Size box to make the window larger, or you can use the scroll bars and elevator boxes to bring different parts of the card into view.

Windows also signal different functions based on their appearance. Scrolling windows serve different purposes than do dialog boxes or floating palettes.

As mentioned, a SuperCard window is analogous to a HyperCard stack. All the cards in your project are part of windows, and you can only use one window at a time to look at a "stack" of cards.

Creating Windows

You can create windows in either SuperEdit (see Chapter Four) or SuperCard. This chapter focuses on working with windows from within the SuperCard environment.

To create a window using SuperCard, simply type **New Window** into the Message box and a new window will be created in the current project. You can also use the New Window command in the File menu of the Runtime Editor. The new window will be added to the list of windows in the current project—you cannot change the numbering of windows within SuperCard, or insert new windows before others.

When a new window is created in SuperCard, the window will have the default size specified in the preferences, as set in SuperEdit. The window will automatically be a Standard window without scroll bars. Once the new window is created, the newWindow message is sent to the card in that window and up the hierarchy, followed by the newBackground and newCard messages.

Window Commands

SuperTalk has several commands that allow you to manipulate windows. In SuperCard, the word "window" can be abbreviated "wd".

The Open Window Command

Open window windowDescriptor

This command opens the specified window and displays the first card of that window on the screen. If the window you are opening is part of another project, you need to specify that project in the *windowDescriptor*. The openWindow, openBackground, and openCard messages are sent to that card. If the window is part of a different project, the message openProject is sent first.

You can use this command to open specified windows in projects currently not open. For example, if you want to open the project "test" on your hard disk and go directly to window 2 without opening window 1 at all, you can use a command such as this:

open window 2 of project "test"

The Go Command

You can also use the Go command to open any window and optionally specify a card within that window to go to. The Go command works differently than the Open Window command in that when you use the Open command, the new window is opened separately from the active window. When you use the Go command, the new window is opened *in place of* the active window, which will be closed.

See Chapter Six for a discussion of how the Go, Open, and Launch commands work in SuperCard.

The Close Window Command

Close Window windowDescriptor

This command closes the specified window, sending the closeCard, closeBackground, and closeWindow messages to the current card in the specified window. The full descriptor of the window must be used if the window is not the current window. If the window is the only currently opened window of its project, that project is also closed and the closeProject message is sent.

A variation on this command, Close All Windows, closes all the currently open windows and causes SuperCard to quit.

The Delete Window Command

Delete Window windowDescriptor

This command deletes the specified window from its project.

The New Window Command

New Window

With this command, a new window is created in the current project, along with a background and card. The new window will be a Standard (nonscrolling) window named "UNTITLED."

The new window will be located at the top-left corner of the screen, 40 pixels from the left edge of the screen and 60 pixels from the top. The size of the new window will be the size determined by the SuperTalk Preferences file on your disk. You can change the standard size of the new window with the Preferences command on the Apple menu in SuperEdit.

Once the window has been created, the messages newWindow, newBackground, newCard, followed by openWindow, openBackground, and openCard, will be sent to the new card created in the new window through the project hierarchy.

Later in this chapter under "The newWindow Message," a handler is presented that asks you to name for new window when it is created.

The setWindow Command

setWindow windowDescriptor

This command, used under script control only, makes the specified window the active window. It does *not* bring that window to the top of the stack of windows, nor does it make the specified window the top window.

Use setWindow when you are writing scripts—especially for menus and palette buttons—that you want to work with a variety of windows. Once you use setWindow, requests for information, such as

the name of this project
the name of this window
the number of cards in this window

all refer to the window you have set as the current window.

Scrolling with the Grabber Command

Grabber

The Grabber is a special tool that can only be used within a handler; you cannot use the Choose Tool command to select the grabber. Here is a short function that illustrates its use:

```
on mouseDown
   grabber
end mouseDown
```

With this handler in the card or window script, holding the mouse button down on a card causes the pointer to turn into a small hand (grabber). If you continue to hold the mouse button down and move the mouse around the window, the window scrolls to display different portions of the card. When you release the mouse button, the mouse pointer will revert to the Browse tool. If you have used MacPaint, the function of the grabber will be familiar to you.

Window Functions

Several SuperTalk functions are used for determining the number of windows currently open or in the current project. Other functions allow you to refer to those windows without specifying them by name.

The topWindow Function

topWindow( )

This function returns a phrase completely describing the window currently active: the window on top of the others. Note that unless palettes are the only windows visible on the screen, palettes are never treated as the top window.

The phrase that this function returns looks like the following.

window "About..." of Project "Disk:SuperCard:About SuperCard"

This phrase constitutes a *window descriptor,* as the term is used in this chapter. A window descriptor should include the name of the window, and if the window to which you are referring is not in the current project, the descriptor must include the full pathname of the project containing the window. Likewise, *project descriptors* contain the full pathname of the project to which you are referring.

Note that when you are using commands to manipulate windows and the topWindow function, you don't need to use the word *window* in the command. For example, to close the top window, use the form

    close topwindow()

If you use the form

    close window topwindow()

you will get an error alert stating that SuperCard cannot find the window. This is because the phrase returned by *topwindow( )* contains the word "window" as its first word, creating a duplicate. The line above is interpreted by SuperTalk as:

    close window window "opening" of project "hard disk:test project"

Using the topWindow function is a way to create generic tools for working with windows. An example is in the Window Styles palette that is part of the Runtime Editor. In essence, this palette consists of seven buttons, one for each style of window. The script for each of these buttons sets the style of the top window to the style indicated by that button. For example, the script of the Scrolling button in that palette could be as simple as

    set the style of topwindow() to scrolling

The Number of Windows

the number of windows {of projectDescriptor}

This function returns the number of windows contained in the specified project. If you do not specify a particular project, it returns the number of windows in the currently open project.

In simplified form the Set Up Windows menu item in the File menu of the Runtime Editor uses the Number of Windows function to discover the names of each of the windows in the current project and to place those window names into a scrolling list. A function to return a list of all the windows in the current project is shown in Script 7-1.

The Number of Current Windows

This function returns an integer specifying the number of windows that are currently open. Since SuperCard quits when all windows are closed (see the Close All Windows command discussed earlier in this chapter), at least one window is always open, even if you do not see it. As mentioned, an open window can be hidden or located beyond the boundaries of the monitor. For example, the Runtime Editor keeps a small window open at all times and locates that window at the -1000, -1000 location—well to the left and top of the screen boundaries. This allows you to have an environment in which you can open and close windows at will without unintentionally quitting SuperCard.

The currentWindow Function

currentWindow(integer)
the currentWindow of integer

This function returns a phrase describing the window identified by the number. Like the topWindow function, you can use the currentWindow function to refer to any window on the screen, provided you know its number.

```
function getWindowNames
  repeat with x = 1 to the number of windows
    put the short name of window x into
    line x of theWindows
  end repeat
  return theWindows
end getWindowNames
```

Script 7-1. This function returns a list of all the currently open windows

Unlike the topWindow function, the currentWindow function counts floating palettes. If you have a window open on the screen with a floating palette on top of it, the floating palette will be current-Window(1), and the other window will be currentWindow(2). If several floating palettes are opened, the palette you opened most recently will be numbered 1; next recently number 2, and so on. Clicking on a palette to bring it to the front will make the number of that palette 1, and the other palettes will be numbered accordingly.

In numbering windows, the top window is always window 1 — the currentWindow of 1. Successive windows are numbered in layers below the current window. Figure 7-1 illustrates this layering with the windows named after the function that would return their name. The floating palette cannot be named, but it is currentWindow(1). In this case, the currently active window is currentWindow(2), and the overlapping of currentWindows 3 and 4 illustrates their numbering.

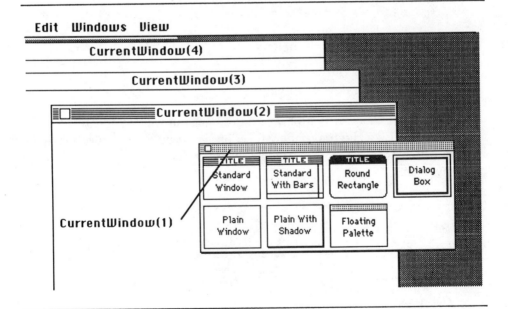

Figure 7-1.   Window numbering with the currentWindow function goes from the top card to the bottom

This function is useful for situations in which you want to perform the same operation on all the currently open windows. For example, Script 7-2 contains a handler that sets the style of all the currently open windows (except for palettes) to scrolling.

Window Properties

As with other objects in SuperCard, a set of properties defines the appearance of windows, and how you refer to them from within scripts. Some of the window properties can be set or queried even if the window is not currently opened.

The Name, Number, and ID Properties

Windows, like most objects in SuperCard, have three identifiers: their name, number, and ID. When referring to windows in scripts, you must be sure to include a *complete* descriptor of that window. If you use a statement such as **close window "about..."**, SuperCard assumes that you are referring to a window that is in the current project. When referring to windows, then, you must use a statement such as **close window "about..." of project "hard disk:about supercard"**. Later in this chapter you will learn how to use built-in functions when referring to windows.

```
on setEm
   repeat with x = 1 to the number of current windows
     if the style of currentWindow(x) is not "palette" then
        set the style of currentWindow(x) to scrolling
     end if
   end repeat
end setEm
```

Script 7-2.   This handler sets the style of all currently open windows to scrolling

Windows can have names, short names, and long names. For a window named "DIALOG" in a project called "ABOUT SUPERCARD," here are its name, short name, and long name:

name: window "dialog"
short name: dialog
long name: window "dialog" of project "hard disk:about supercard"

The short name of a window is also the name that appears in its title bar (if the style of window includes a title bar). Window names are limited to 255 characters and can include virtually any acceptable characters (though for clarity's sake, you should not include quotes in the names of windows).

The ID number of a window is assigned to that window when it is created and it is not changed except when the window is copied and pasted into another project.

A window's number is an ordinal, indicating its position within the project, that is, its number in SuperEdit's Project Overview window.

You can also refer to the top window by calling it **this window**. This is useful for such commands as **Close this window**, or **send "mouseUp" to this window**.

The Visible Property

get the visible of window windowDescriptor
set the visible of window windowDescriptor to true | false

The visible property of a window determines whether the window is visible, not whether it is open. In other words, a window can be opened, but still hidden. You can send messages to a hidden window with the Send command but it will not receive mouse messages and you cannot type into any fields on that card.

You can also use the Hide and Show commands to set the visible property of a window, as with lines such as **Hide this window** or **hide topwindow( )**.

Hiding windows can be useful when you need to scan quickly through a large number of cards in a window. Cards with large bitmaps on them—particularly if they are color bitmaps—can be slow to display on the screen; if the window is hidden, the process of moving through the cards is accelerated.

You cannot specify in SuperEdit that a window is hidden; you must use the SuperTalk language to hide or show a window.

If a window is closed, the visible property of that window is always set to "false." You cannot change the visible property of a window that is not currently open.

The zoomBox Property

set the zoomBox of window windowDescriptor to true | false
get the zoomBox of window windowDescriptor

This property determines whether or not a scrollable window displays a Zoom box in its upper-left corner. The Zoom box is discussed later in this chapter under "Types and Styles of Windows."

While you can get or set this property for any type of window, the Zoom box is only displayed and active in scrolling windows.

You can query with the Get command or set the zoomBox property of a window that is not currently open.

The closeBox Property

set the closeBox of window windowDescriptor to true | false
get the closeBox of window windowDescriptor

This property determines whether Standard, Scrolling, or Rounded Rectangle windows have a Close box displayed in their upper-left corner. Close boxes are discussed later in this chapter.

While you can get or set this property on any type of window, it has no effect on plain or Dialog Box windows.

You can query or set the closeBox property of a window that is not currently open.

The Draggable Property

set the draggable of window windowDescriptor to true | false
get the draggable of window windowDescriptor

This property determines whether or not you may move a window on the screen by dragging on its title bar. If the property is set to "false," clicking and dragging on the title bar of a window does nothing; if it is set to "true," clicking and dragging on the title bar of a window displays a rectangle that moves with the mouse—when you release the mouse button, the window is moved to the new location. When you drag a window, the dragWindow message, discussed later in this chapter, is sent to that window.

Macintosh users are accustomed to dragging windows on the screen: in general, if a window has a title bar, you can drag it. Before you make a window so it cannot be dragged, always consider very carefully why you are doing so. You should also consider changing the style of a stationary window to the Plain or Shadow styles (discussed later): since these windows do not have title bars, users will not attempt to drag them.

You can query or set the Draggable property of a window that is not currently open.

The Style Property

**set style of window windowDescriptor to
    standard | scrolling | roundRect | dialog | plain | shadow | palette
get the style of window windowDescriptor**

This property determines the appearance, and consequent behavior of the window. Window styles are discussed in detail later in this chapter. You can query or set the Style property of windows not currently open.

The Scroll Property

**set the scroll of window windowDescriptor to integer,integer
get the scroll of window windowDescriptor**

This property contains the number of pixels that a scrolling window has been scrolled. The property consists of two integers separated by commas. The first number indicates the number of pixels from the left edge of the card the window has been scrolled; the second number indicates the number of pixels from the top of the card the window has been scrolled.

With the mouse, you can change the scroll of scrolling windows only. With scripts, you can change the scroll of any type of window. Generally, Macintosh applications do not scroll the window for you unless you do so with the mouse; therefore, you should set this property with care under script control.

When a window is scrolled, the scrollWindow message, discussed under "Window-Related Messages," is sent to the window.

When a window is first opened, its scroll is automatically set to 0,0. Therefore, you cannot query or set the scroll of a window that is not currently open.

Size Properties

A number of window properties can be used to determine or set the location of various corners or edges of the window. The window shown in Figure 7-2, is 200 pixels on a side and is displayed at the center of a Macintosh Plus or SE screen that has a width of 512 pixels and a height of 342 pixels.

Use the Get command to determine the current values of these properties and the Set command to change any of them. Changing any

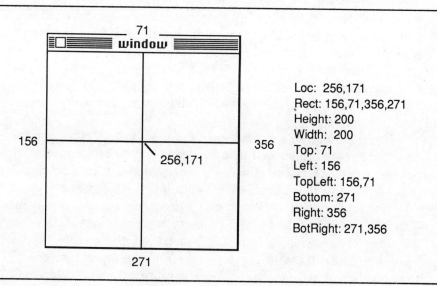

Figure 7-2.   The various properties of a window 200 pixels on a side and located in the center of a Mac Plus or SE screen

of these properties can change other properties as well. For example, changing the loc property of a window will change the properties that define the corners of that window.

SuperCard remembers the location and size of the windows on the screen; when you open a window in SuperCard, that window will have the same size and location it had when it was last closed. Resizing the windows to fit the current screen size is discussed later in this chapter, in the section dealing with screen properties.

The loc property determines the location of the center of the specified window, and it is this property you implicitly change when you drag the window on the screen. The property contains two numbers separated by commas. The *loc* of the window shown in Figure 7-2 is 256,171. The first number indicates the distance of the center of the window from the left edge of the screen. The second number indicates the distance of the center of the window from the top of the screen.

Changing the loc property affects all the other location and size properties of the window, with the exception of the height and width properties.

The left, top, right, and bottom properties each contain a single quantity, which represents the distance of the specified side of the window from the edge of the monitor: left and right represent the distance of these respective edges from the left edge of the screen. Top and bottom represent the distance of these edges from the top of the screen. Changing these properties does not *move* the window in question, but rather resizes the window, affecting certain other properties. For example, when you increase the top property 20 pixels (that is, move it 20 pixels down the screen), the left, right, and bottom properties remain unaffected.

If you attempt to set a property to a nonsensical value, you receive an error alert informing you that you "can't specify an empty rectangle." An example of a nonsensical value is when you try to set the right edge of a window to a value that is less than the left edge.

The topLeft and botRight properties each contain two numbers. The first number of the topLeft property represents the distance of the left edge of the window from the left side of the screen; the second represents the distance of the top edge from the top of the screen. The first number of the botRight property represents the distance of the bottom edge of the window from the top of the screen. The botRight property, along with the bottom and left properties, are changed when you resize a window with its Size box.

The width and height properties each contain one quantity that represents the size of the window. Both the height and width of the window in Figures 7-2 are 200.

When you use the Set command to alter the width and height of a window, certain other properties will be affected, leaving the loc property in its original state. For example, if you set the width property, the left and right properties will also be affected, but the loc, top, and bottom properties will remain the same.

The rect property contains four quantities: the left, top, right, and bottom properties. When you use the Set command to change the rect property of a window, you must specify all four new values.

Types and Styles of Windows

SuperCard offers the standard set of Macintosh window styles, as described in *Inside Macintosh* and in Apple's *Human Interface Guidelines*. When designing a project, pay special attention to the styles of the windows you create: the appearance of a window is a signal to your users as to the window's function.

As mentioned earlier in this chapter, you can change the style of a window by using the Set command to alter the style property of a window. In SuperEdit, you can also use the Window Info dialog box to set the style of a window. You can also change the style of a window by using the Runtime Editor's Window Info dialog box.

The Standard Window

The Standard window is shown in Figure 7-3. At the top of the window is a title bar which displays the name of the window. At the left of the title bar is a Close box (if the closeBox property of the window is set to "true").

Standard windows cannot be resized or scrolled with the mouse. If the draggable property of the window is set to "true," the window may be moved on the desktop by clicking and dragging on the title bar. When a window is dragged, the message dragWindow is sent to that window; see the "The dragWindow Message" section later in this chapter.

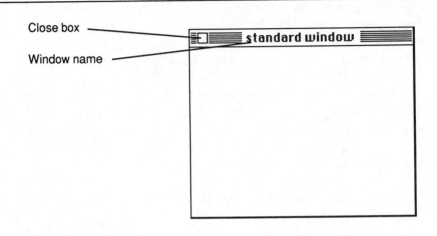

Close box

Window name

Figure 7-3. The Standard window features a title bar and an optional Close box

Since this window cannot be resized by the user, it is best that you use it for windows that can be displayed on the standard Macintosh screen. If you create a Standard window on a Macintosh with a larger screen, a person using a smaller screen will not be able to resize it.

The Scrolling Window

Most Macintosh users will think of the Scrolling window as the Standard window, since it is the type of window most applications provide for most purposes. A Scrolling window is shown in Figure 7-4.

Besides having a title bar, window name, and Close box, Scrolling windows possess all the accoutrements necessary for viewing different parts of the window and for resetting the size of it.

There are two ways to manually set the size of a Scrolling window. Clicking on the Zoom box expands the window to the full size of the current monitor. Clicking and dragging on the Size box allows you to size the window as you wish. As discussed later in this chapter, when a scrolling window is resized by the mouse, the resizeWindow message is sent to that window.

The scroll bar, Scroll box (also sometimes called an "Elevator box"), and the scroll arrows bring different parts of the card into view. These tools work in SuperCard windows in the same manner as they work in

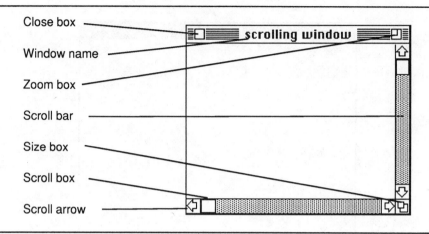

Close box

Window name

Zoom box

Scroll bar

Size box

Scroll box

Scroll arrow

Figure 7-4.   The Scrolling window includes standard Macintosh window sizing and scrolling objects

standard Macintosh applications, such as the Finder. When a window is scrolled with the mouse, the scrollWindow message is sent to that window.

The RoundRect Window

RoundRect windows have a black title bar, an optional Close box, and rounded corners. As Figure 7-5 shows, they have neither scroll bars nor a Size box.

This type of window is not often used in Macintosh programs. Most programs use the Standard or Scrolling style of windows, one of the few places that can use this type of window. The standard Calculator desk accessory is accessory. Following the lead of the Calculator, you can use this window to indicate a "control device," something like a floating palette. An example is Apple's CD Remote desk accessory, which plays music on the Apple CD-ROM drive. This RoundRect window feels like a remote control device for a CD music player.

The Dialog Box Window

A dialog box is a Macintosh device that allows a command (usually a menu item but sometimes a button) to query you for more information before the command is carried out. An example is the standard Print

Figure 7-5.   The RoundRect window includes a title bar, an optional Close box, and rounded corners

command in most Macintosh applications. This command usually presents a dialog box asking you what pages of the current document to print, how many copies of it to print, and the like. These dialog boxes usually feature OK buttons that proceed with the action, and Cancel buttons that let you change your mind.

A SuperCard dialog box is shown in Figure 7-6. This dialog box has no buttons or fields in it. SuperCard's dialog boxes have a thin line at their boundary and a thicker line just inside the thin line. Dialog boxes cannot be moved, resized, or scrolled using the mouse, and they include no Close or Zoom boxes.

SuperCard's dialog boxes are modal: while a dialog box is the active window you may not click outside that window to do such things as execute menu commands. Only under the following conditions can you work with objects that are not part of the dialog box:

1. If the project has the Runtime Editor installed, you may press COMMAND-M to summon the Message box, or COMMAND-Q to quit Super-Card.

2. If a floating palette is visible on the screen, you may click on buttons in that palette.

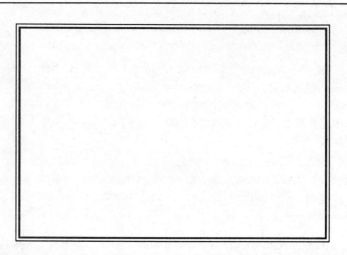

Figure 7-6.   An empty SuperCard dialog box

3. If the Message box is open, you may execute menu commands, or type into the menu box.

Note that the existence of these safeguards means that dialog boxes in SuperCard are not truly modal: if the Runtime Editor script is installed into the current project, it is almost always possible to work around a dialog box, and defeat its modal purpose. This was done intentionally. Otherwise, you could completely lock up or freeze your system by summoning a dialog box lacking buttons to close it.

Here are some rules for creating dialog boxes:

1. If a menu item summons a dialog box, include an elipsis (...) after its name to indicate to the user that a dialog box is coming.

2. Always include a Cancel button that allows your users to change their minds (and acts as an escape valve for closing the dialog box). Place and label the Cancel button so it is easy to locate in the dialog.

3. If the "standard" action that the dialog box is to perform is not destructive to data, include an OK button that has its default property set to "true" (see Chapter Ten), so that your user can execute this button by hitting the RETURN key.

4. If the dialog box is complex, that is if it contains a number of buttons and fields, put the name of the dialog box at the top left, to reinforce its purpose.

5. As *The Human Interface Guidelines* states, the most important information in a dialog box should be at the top left of the box, with items of decreasing importance following to the right and bottom. At the lower-left corner of the dialog box are the Cancel and OK buttons.

6. Finally, keep dialog boxes to a minimum. Since dialog boxes are modal, they limit the user's choice while they are on the screen, and in a sense violate the nonmodal nature of the ideal Macintosh program.

Note: The Ask and Answer commands, which in HyperCard automatically display a small dialog box, work in SuperCard as they do in HyperCard.

The Plain and Shadow Windows

The Plain window is simply a rectangle with a thin line around its border; it has no title bar, Close box, Zoom box, Size box, or scroll bar. It is similar to a dialog box in appearance, but does not have the heavier interior line. The Shadow window is the same as the Plain window, except it has a shadow two pixels wide around it. Unlike many other SuperCard objects, you cannot change the depth of the shadow around a window.

When using these windows in a project, you must make sure that you position them on the screen correctly for the screen your users are using. This must be done under script control, as there is no title bar to allow you to position them manually.

Generally, these types of windows are a good way to present images; cards full of clip art, for example, would be a good candidate for this type of window. Another good use is in a presentation, where you want to hide the nature of the windows. In some applications, the presence of a title bar and other window accoutrements is a distraction.

The Palette Window

Floating palettes, sometimes called "windoids," are unique types of windows; they are exceptions to many of the functions that deal with windows, such as the topWindow function (but not the currentWindow function). Floating palettes are always in front of all other windows on the screen (excluding the Message box), but messages are not sent to them unless you actually click the mouse in them. Floating palettes have a distinct, thin title bar (with no title displayed), and also have an optional Close box.

You should use floating palettes to contain tools that can work on other windows, cards, or objects as does the Runtime Editor (and HyperCard).

Window-Related Messages

As with all messages, the window-related messages are first sent to the current card in the window.

The openWindow Message

The openWindow message is sent to the first card in a window when that window is opened. An openWindow handler is the way to set up any conditions that a window might require to operate. For example, a window might have a menu that is associated with it, but is not normally inserted. You can use a handler similar to the one shown in Script 7-3 to discover if the menu is inserted, and insert it if it is not:

In this case, the window needs to have a menu called "Tools" inserted into the menu bar. The repeat loop checks each of the current

```
on openWindow
  -- check to see if the required menu is there
  repeat with x = 1 to the number of current menus
    if the short name of currentmenu(x) is "tools" then
      -- it's there, so we can exit
      exit openWindow
    end if
  end repeat
  insert menu "tools"
end openWindow
```

Script 7-3.   When placed into the script of a window, this handler displays a specified menu when that window is opened

menus (these functions are discussed in Chapter Eight), and if the repeat loop finds the menu in question, the handler is terminated. If the repeat loop finishes without an exit, the Tools menu is inserted into the menu bar.

An alternative method of displaying a specific menu when a window is displayed is discussed later in this chapter in the "The updateWindow Message" section.

The closeWindow Message

This message is sent to the currently displayed card in a window when that window is closed. As with the openCard message, this message can be used to dispose of any resources the window might have installed.

Script 7-4 is a closeWindow handler that removes the menu installed with the openWindow handler discussed in the previous section.

The deleteWindow Message

This message is sent to a window when it is being deleted with the Delete Window command. You cannot delete a window by deleting the last card in the window with the Delete Card command; an alert will warn you to use the Delete Window command.

The dragWindow Message

This message is sent to a window whenever you use the mouse to move the menu on the screen. More precisely, the message is sent to the window whenever you click on the window's title bar. The updateWindow message, discussed later in this chapter, is sent after the dragWindow message.

The newWindow Message

This message is sent to a new window whenever it is created. Since you cannot automatically put a handler in a new window to intercept this

```
on closeWindow
  remove menu "tools"
end closeWindow
```

Script 7-4.   This handler removes the window installed by Script 7-3

```
on newWindow
  ask "What do you want to name this window?" with "Untitled"
  set the name of topwindow() to it
end newWindow
```

Script 7-5.   This handler asks you to name a new window when you create it

message, the most useful place to put such a handler is in the project script or in the script of the SharedFile.

In one use this handler, shown in Script 7-5, prompts you to name a new window at its creation. Script 7-5 shows a handler that does that. This handler could also be modified to set various properties of a new window, such as its style, the background size, and more.

The resizeWindow Message

This message is sent to a window whenever it is resized, using either the Size box at the bottom right corner of the window, or the Zoom box in the window's title bar.

```
on resizeWindow
  set lockscreen to true
  put the topleft of this wd into temp
  if the width of this wd >
  item 1 of the backsize of this bg then
    set the width of this wd to
    item 1 of the backSize of this bg + 15
  end if
  if the height of this wd >
  item 2 of the backsize of this bg then
    set the height of this wd to
    item 2 of the backsize of this bg + 15
  end if
  set the topleft of this wd to temp
  set lockscreen to false
end resizeWindow
```

Script 7-6.   This handler prevents a window from being resized to a size
                    larger than the background

Script 7-6 shows a resizeWindow handler that effectively prevents you from resizing a window so that it is larger than the current background. It uses the backSize property of backgrounds, discussed later in this chapter, as well as the top, bottom, left, and right properties of windows to do so.

This handler first stores the topLeft of the window into the variable *Temp*. The handler next checks the width of the window, to see if it is greater than the width of the background (the first item of the backSize). If this is so, the width of the window is then set to the width of the background plus 15 (the width of the scroll bar). The same checks are made with the height of the window. Finally, the topLeft of the window is set to its original value, to keep the window in the same location as it was before you resized it.

This useful handler can make a window more aesthetic as it is resized; it obscures the unsightly pasteboard from you as you are using the window, and with a large screen you can be assured that you are seeing the entire card and nothing more than the card.

The scrollWindow Message

This message is sent to a scrolling window when you use the scroll bar to change the part of a window that is displayed on the screen.

The updateWindow Message

This low-level message is sent to the current card of a window whenever changes to the screen cause the window to be redrawn. This message is therefore sent when events such as the following occur:

- The window is obscured by another window being opened in front of it, or when a window is moved to obscure the target window.

- The target window is brought to the front when it is opened, or when you click on it.

- The window is redrawn on the screen after a dialog box that obscured the window is closed. This includes all of SuperCard's dialog boxes, floating palettes, and the Message box. The message is sent when the obscuring object is moved so that it no longer obscures the window, or is closed.

• The window is dragged or resized with the mouse. In these cases, the appropriate dragWindow, scrollWindow, and resizeWindow messages are sent to the window before the updateWindow message.

• You switch to another program in MultiFinder or, while in Multi-Finder, you resize a window that is on top of the current menu, causing a new part of that window to be redrawn.

• When running MultiFinder, if you switch back to SuperCard, even though no other window obscured the target window, the update Window message is sent to the top SuperCard window.

One use for the updateWindow message is to determine whether a specific window has been moved to the top of the stack of windows. Earlier in this chapter you saw how a window can insert a specific menu when the window is opened and remove that menu when the window is closed. Script 7-7 contains a suite of handlers that insert the menu when the window is brought to the top of the other menus and remove the menu when the window is sent to the back.

The first handler, for the updateWindow message, calls the onTop function to determine if the window containing this handler has been moved to the front or if it is in back of other windows. The onTop function compares the name of the window that received the updateWindow message with the long name of the top window: if the two are the same, the menu in question has been moved to the top. The updateWindow handler then uses the Installed function to discover whether the desired menu (in this case, "test" and part of the same project that contains the window) is on the menu bar. (For details on the menu functions that this function uses, see Chapter Eight.) The same thing happens if the window in question has been placed behind other windows. In that case, the "test" menu is removed.

These handlers are designed to be placed into the script of the window that needs to remove and insert the menu in question. By using the target function, you can generalize them, and place into the script of a project.

The updateWindow message is sent more often than you think, so it is a good idea to keep handlers for this message short. You should especially avoid handlers that place dialog boxes on the screen when a window is updated: as soon as the dialog box clears the screen, the

```
on updateWindow
  if onTop(the long name of this window) is true then
    if installed(the long name of menu "test") is false then
      insert menu "test"
    end if
  else
    if installed(the long name of menu "test") is true then
      remove menu "test"
    end if
  end if
end updateWindow

function onTop windowName
  if the long name of topwindow() = windowName then
    return true
  else
    return false
  end if
end onTop

function installed theMenu
  repeat with x = 1 to the number of current menus
    if the long name of currentMenu(x) = theMenu then
      return true
    end if
  end repeat
  return false
end installed
```

Script 7-7.   These handlers work together to display a menu when the window
is brought to the front, and remove it when the window is sent to
the back

updateWindow message is sent to the window again, and you fall into a
loop that you can only exit by pressing COMMAND-PERIOD.

The Screen

HyperCard regulars with large-screen Macintoshes find that moving to
SuperCard is a joy: the extra real estate you paid all that money for can
finally be used. However, as you are developing projects, especially
those that will be used by others, you must take responsibility for using
that real estate wisely. One of your tasks is making sure that your
projects can be used by those who have screens of different sizes.

SuperCard gives you two functions that you can use to determine the size of the current monitor.

The screenRect Function

the screenRect
screenRect( )

This function returns a set of four items (integers separated by commas) describing the rectangle of the current screen. The first two items will almost always be 0. The third item indicates the width of the current screen, and the fourth the height of the current screen.

You can use the screenRect function (when a window is open) to check the size of the window and make sure it fits on the screen. Since windows remember their own size and location, if a window is opened on a Mac Plus or SE after it was used on a Mac with a larger monitor, it is possible that the window will be opened beyond the boundaries of the current screen.

The screenLoc Function

the screenLoc
screenLoc( )

This function returns two integers separated by commas describing the center of the screen. The first integer specifies the horizontal center of the screen. The second integer specifies the vertical center of the screen.

This function is useful for centering windows on the screen. Rather than hardwiring locations for windows into your scripts, you can use the screenLoc function to center a window on the screen. Dialog boxes, for example, always look better when they appear centered.

If you are using a menu item to open a window, you can set the location of the window on the screen *before* it is opened. The benefit of doing this is that you will not first see the window opened, then see it move across the screen. Script 7-8 takes care of that.

Note: SuperCard also extends HyperCard's Ask and Answer commands to allow you to specify the locations at which these dialogs are shown on the screen. To specify the location, simply add "at" followed by two integers to the end of the command. For example, to center the

```
on itemSelect
  set the loc of window "about" to the screenLoc
  open window "about"
end itemSelect
```

Script 7-8.   This handler demonstrates how a menu can locate a window
before opening that window

dialog box on the screen using the Ask command, you would use a
command such as:

```
ask "what is your name" at the screenLoc
```

Backgrounds

Backgrounds in SuperCard work in much the same way as backgrounds
in HyperCard: Whatever is part of the background will appear on all the
cards that share that background, unless it has been hidden with the
Hide command or obscured by a card object that is located on top of it.

As mentioned at the beginning of this chapter, the size of a window
is independent of the size of the card it shows, and vice versa. Card size
is not controlled by the size of the window, but by the size of the
background. Therefore, you can have cards of different sizes in the same
window.

Generally, when referrring to backgrounds, you will type **this background** to refer to the current background in the current, or top,
window. You can, however, refer to backgrounds in other windows or
projects, even if those windows or projects are not currently open.

For example, you might need to know how many cards are contained in a specific background in a different project. If the project is
called "books," you could use a statement such as this:

the number of cards of bg 1 of window 1 of project "books"

Of course, the project descriptor—in this case, "books"— should include the full pathname for the project in question.

The backSize Property

backSize(backgroundDescriptor)
the backSize of backgroundDescriptor

The backSize property determines the size of the specified background. The property is expressed as two integers separated by commas. The first item determines the width of the background, the second determines the height of the background. In either case, the maximum value to which you can set these numbers is 32767—the limit defined by the Macintosh's QuickDraw ROM routines, and represents a potential card size of about 37 feet on a side, or some 1400 square feet of card size.

Cards

Card navigation in SuperCard works the same way as it does in Hyper-Card. One distinction is that you can use either the Go or Open commands to display a different card.

While SuperCard, like HyperCard, is constantly saving changes to your project (see Chapter Two), SuperCard does not actually save changes to a window or card until you close that window or card. Indeed, SuperCard gives you two commands that you can use to save cards.

The Save Command

Save

The Save command saves the current window, including any changes you have made to the current card since you last opened it.

Use this command while you are working on a card to make sure any changes you have made to that card are preserved on disk, in case of a system error.

The Revert Command

Revert

The Revert command, in effect, reloads the current card from disk, restoring it to the condition it was in when you last opened it or used the Save command to save it.

The Revert command, then, causes you to lose *all* changes to a card. This includes any new card objects you may have created on the card and any new text you may have typed into its fields.

You can use this command to have SuperCard stop and ask you if you want to save a card before going to a different card. Script 7-9 is a closeCard handler that accomplish this.

When you close a card, by going to a different card or closing the window containing this card, the closeCard message is sent, and this handler is triggered. It causes the Answer dialog box to be shown and asks if you want to save the card. If you click on the No button, the Revert command loads the last saved version of the card from disk, causing your changes to be lost. Since cards are automatically saved when you close them, the handler does nothing if you click on the OK button.

```
on closeCard
  answer  "Save this card?" with "No" or "OK" at screenLoc()
  if it is "No" then revert
end closeCard
```

Script 7-9.   This handler asks if you want to save a card when you leave that card

Menus

Menus are an important part of the Macintosh user interface. They provide a standard means of accessing commands and take up only a small amount of room on the screen. Menus also provide an overview of the functions or capabilities of an application. SuperCard's menu support is flexible, allowing you to do virtually everything with SuperCard menus that is done in traditional applications.

Menus are composed of two hierarchical parts: the menu itself, and the items it contains. The name of the menu appears on the menu bar, and the items appear when you hold down the mouse button on the menu name.

Remember that you can insert menus from any project on disk—whether or not that project is open. This is the case with the Runtime Editor. Whenever you are using a project with the Runtime Editor installed the menus are visible. This means that it is easy to create toolboxes of menus that you can use with all of your projects.

You should also remember that closing an individual project only closes the windows associated with that project—it does *not* close any of the menus you might have installed from that project. For that you should use a closeProject handler, which will be discussed later in this chapter.

E
I
G
H
T

Creating Menus

For the most part, SuperEdit is the only place you can create, copy and paste, or delete menus. Creating and copying menus and menu items is covered in Chapter Three.

Even though you cannot create, copy, paste, or delete menus or items from within SuperCard, you *can* edit the script of a menu item. To do so, simply hold down the SHIFT key as you choose any menu item, and the Script editor will be opened with the script of that item. There is no Menu Info dialog box available for menus in SuperCard or the Runtime Editor, though you could create one. (The problem is, if you put a Menu Info item on the Objects menu, how you do you specify which menu to get Info on?) You can edit the script of any menu by typing a command such as **Edit script of menu "File" of Project "Runtime Editor."** You can also use the currentMenu function, discussed later in this chapter, to facilitate the specifying of menus.

Managing Menus

Menus are not installed automatically when you open a project, nor are they automatically removed when you close a project. Both of these actions must be handled by explicit commands.

The Insert Command

Insert menu *menudescriptor* **before** ⦙ **after** *menudescriptor*

The Insert command makes the specified menu visible on the menu bar. Typically, the new menu will be installed as the last menu on the menu bar, to the right of the other menus. A command such as:

```
Insert menu "objects"
```

does this, assuming the menu "objects" is part of the current project. If you want to insert the menu elsewhere in the menu bar, you can do so with a command such as

```
Insert menu "objects" after menu "edit" of project "runtime
editor"
```

Note in this case that when you are specifying the menu that will precede the new menu, you must include a complete descriptor of the new menu, or use the currentMenu function discussed later in this chapter. Similarly, you must use a complete descriptor for the menu to be inserted. If you are inserting a menu that is not in the current project, you need to specify the project that owns the menu as in the following:

```
insert menu "palettes" of project "runtime editor"
```

If you use the Insert command on a menu that is already installed on the menu bar, that menu will be moved to the new location—either to the last spot on the menu bar (if you don't specify a place to insert the menu) or to the new specified location.

Remember that menus are not inserted automatically when you open a project. You must install your own menus when the project is opened in an openProject handler. One thing to beware of, though, is repeating some of the menus that are already on the menu bar. If the Runtime Editor is running, it does not make any sense to insert your own Apple, File, and Edit menus. Those are already handled.

The Remove Command

Remove Menu *menudescriptor*

This command removes a menu from the menu bar. Remember that the *menudescriptor* must include the complete address of the menu in question, or you can use the currentMenu function, discussed shortly, to refer to a menu.

Because a project's menus are not removed automatically when you close the project, you should use a closeProject handler, such as the one discussed later in this chapter.

The Number of Current Menus

This function returns the number of menus currently visible on the menu bar. It is similar to the currentWindow function, which returns the number of windows currently open. This will be discussed further in Chapter Seven.

The currentMenu Function

currentMenu*(integer)*
the currentMenu of *integer*

The currentMenu function allows you to get information about any menu currently installed, without requiring that you know which project that menu belongs to. It works in the same manner as the currentWindow function discussed in Chapter Seven. The function returns a phrase in this form:

```
menu "Apple" of Project "Hard Disk:sc:Runtime Editor"
```

This line was returned by typing **put currentMenu(1)** into the Message box with the Runtime Editor open. It gives you a "menudescriptor" that tells the name of the menu, and the name (including full pathname) of the project to which the menu belongs. This menuDescriptor is used with all the commands that relate to menus, and precisely describes the menu.

If you refer to a menu by name only (such as **Menu "Apple"**), SuperCard will assume that you are referring to a menu that is in the current project.

Cleaning Up After Yourself

Occasionally, you may create a project that uses its own menus, and, while it is designed to be used within the Runtime Editor, you do not want Runtime Editor windows to appear when your project is opened.

The solution is to remove all the Runtime Editor menus when the project is opened. The openProject handler shown in Script 8-1 takes care of that.

This handler first declares a global variable, *runTimeMens*, to contain the list of currently installed menus from the Runtime Editor. It then saves the long name of each of these menus into this variable, one menu to a line. This is handled by the first repeat loop. The second repeat loop removes the menus, and the final repeat loop installs all the menus from the project containing the script.

When the project is closed, the menu bar should be restored to show the menus that were visible before the project was opened. The closeProject handler shown in Script 8-2 takes care of that.

This handler is called when the project is closed. It first closes all the menus that were installed from the project, and then opens the menus listed in the global variable runTimeMens.

These two handlers are presented more as illustrations of techniques for managing Menus than as desirable solutions. One problem with using techniques such as these to open and close menus is that there might be several projects open in SuperCard when the project containing these handlers is opened, so that every project's menus are

```
on openProject
  global runTimeMens
  put empty into runTimeMens
  set lockMenus to true
  -- what menus are currently installed?
  -- save their names into a variable
  repeat with x = 1 to the number of current menus
    put the long name of currentMenu(x) into line x ¬
    of runTimeMens
  end repeat
  -- now kill the menus
  repeat with x = 1 to the number of lines in runTimeMens
    remove line x of runTimeMens
  end repeat
  -- now open my own menus
  repeat with x = 1 to the number of menus
    insert menu x
  end repeat
  set lockMenus to false
end openProject
```

Script 8-1.   This handler removes the Runtime Editor menus when the project is opened

```
on closeWindow
  global runTimeMens
  set lockMenus to true
  -- first, get rid of all my menus
  repeat with x = 1 to the number of menus -- in this project
    remove menu x
  end repeat
  -- now put the runtime Menus back
  repeat with x = 1 to the number of lines in runTimeMens
    insert line x of runTimeMens
  end repeat
  set lockMenus to false
end closeWindow
```

Script 8-2.   This handler installs the Runtime Editor menus that were removed by Script 8-1

removed by the handler. If that is the case, the user can simply switch to the other project by clicking on its window, at which time he or she might want to use the standard runtime menus. You could solve this problem by using the number of windows function discussed in Chapter Seven to determine if other projects are opened, and change the actions of this handler accordingly.

A Handler to Remove Menus

The closeMyMenus handler in Script 8-3 can be called in a closeProject handler, and is designed to be used when your project has installed menus along with the Runtime Editor menus. It removes any of the menus in the current project when that project is closed. closeMyMenus first builds a list of the menus that are in the current project, and places that list into a variable called *listOMenus*. This is handled by the first repeat loop.

The second repeat loop uses the functions number of current menus and currentMenu to cycle through each of the currently installed menus. If one of the currently installed menus is in the list of menus in the project, that menu descriptor is saved into a variable, *menusToKill*. The final repeat loop simply cycles through each of the lines in this final variable, and removes those menus.

```
on closeMyMenus
  put empty into listOMenus
  put empty into menusToKill
  -- first, find out which menus are mine
  repeat with x = 1 to the number of menus
    put return & the long name of menu x after listOMenus
  end repeat
  -- now find out which of mine are installed
  repeat with x = 1 to the number of current menus
    if currentMenu(x) is in listOMenus then
      put return & currentMenu(x) after menusToKill
    end if
  end repeat
  -- now actually kill them
  repeat with x = 1 to the number of lines in menusToKill
    if line x of menusToKill is not empty then
      remove line x of menusToKill
    end if
  end repeat
end closeMyMenus
```

Script 8-3.   This handler removes a project's menus when the project is closed

Menu Messages

The message itemSelect is sent to a menu item when the mouse button is released on an enabled menu item. As will be explained later in this chapter, this process is different than the one in HyperCard, in which the doMenu message is sent to the current card whenever a menu item is selected.

The itemSelect message is sent first to the menu item selected, then to the menu itself, then to the current card on the screen, and on up the hierarchy. This allows you to create an itemSelect handler in the script of the menu itself using the target function to determine which of the menu items was selected.

The standard message hierarchy works with menus a little differently than you might expect. If an itemSelect message is not intercepted by either the menu item or the menu itself, that message is sent to the current card instead of to the script of the project that contains the menu. Remember this when you are creating menu scripts. You should not refer to other handlers that reside in the project script. SuperCard might not find those handlers when the menu is actually used.

Menu Properties

Menus themselves have only one property: disabled. Menu items have the disabled property, as well as two others: style and checkmark. Two global properties, lockMenus and editMenus, determine basic things about the workings of menus.

The Disabled Property

When a menu is disabled, the name of that menu appears in grey at the top of the menubar. When you click on a disabled menu and hold down the mouse button, the names of the menu items appear below the menu. But because they are also greyed out, when you drag the mouse pointer over those items, they are not selected. No messages are sent to disabled menus.

In effect, the disabled property of a menu is inherited by each of the items on that menu, though it will not appear to be so by checking the disabled property of any of those items. Figure 8-1 shows a menu that has been disabled.

Menus are disabled to prevent users from getting error messages when they attempt to choose a menu command, and then find that the command is not appropriate. The Copy or Cut commands are examples. They are usually not enabled unless something has been selected.

Figure 8-1.   This greyed-out sample menu appears when you click the mouse button on it, but none of the items highlight

```
on setMenus newValue
set lockMenus to true
repeat with x = 1 to the number of current menus
   set the disabled of currentMenu(x) to newValue
end repeat
set lockMenus to false
end setMenus
```

Script 8-4.   This handler locks the menu bar, then disables all of the menus

Another example is the dialog box. You cannot click outside a dialog box while it is on the screen. This also means that you cannot choose a menu command. When you open a dialog box, you can disable menus to prevent user confusion. Script 8-4 shows a handler that serves the double purpose of enabling and disabling all the menus on the menu bar.

This handler takes one parameter: the value to which the disabled property of the menus should be set. This will be either "true," to disable a menu, or "false," to enable a menu. Note that it uses the function number of current menus to count the menus and determine how many times to execute the repeat loop. Inside the repeat loop, it uses the currentMenu function to allow it to set the disabled property of a menu without having to know which project that menu belongs to. Script 8-5 contains two handlers that you can use when opening and closing a Dialog Box window.

Menu items can be disabled individually, with a command such as Set the disabled of item "paste" of menu "edit" to true. Disabling menu items works the same way as disabling menus: the item becomes grey, it

```
on openWindow
   -- disable all the menus
   setMenus true
end openWindow

on closeWindow
   -- enable all the menus
   setMenus false
end closeWindow
```

Script 8-5.   These open- and closeWindow handlers enable and disable all the current menus

does not highlight as the mouse is passed over it, and it receives no messages. A menu with one item disabled and one item enabled is shown in Figure 8-2.

The CheckMark Property

set the checkMark of menudescriptor to true ¦ false
get the checkMark of menuDescriptor

This property determines if a check mark is placed in front of a menu item or not; if the value of the property is "true," a check mark is in front of the menu and if it is "false" one is not. A menu with one item checked is shown in Figure 8-3.

Check marks on menus are usually used to indicate the value of a menu item that is a toggle. Choosing the menu item one time turns the toggle on (and displays the check mark); choosing it again turns it off. Examples of this are in the Font, Size, and Style menu items in the Runtime Editor. Each of these items displays a new menu on the menu bar, and checks the item. Choosing the menu item again removes the menu and unchecks the item.

Script 8-6 is an example of a script that does this for a Font menu item. There is a hidden problem in this script, however. If you quit the project with this item checked and the Font menu visible, the next time you start the project, the Font menu will generally not be displayed properly. The Font menu item, however, will still have the checkMark property set to true, and that item will be checked. Worse yet, selecting the menu item will not work—when it sees that the checkMark property is true, the script will attempt to remove a menu that is not visible, yielding an error alert. You can fix this by writing a closeProject handler to clean up the menu.

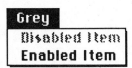

Figure 8-2.   Individual menu items can be disabled

```
┌─────────────────────┐
│ Singers             │
├─────────────────────┴──┐
│  Merle Haggard         │
│  Bob Wills             │
│  Bill Monroe           │
│  David Byrne           │
│ ✓Bob Dylan             │
│  Hank Williams         │
│  Roy Orbison           │
│  Placido Domingo       │
└────────────────────────┘
```

Figure 8-3.   If the checkMark property of a menu item is true, a check is placed in front of the name of that item

The Style Property

set the style of menuItemDescriptor to
{bold | italic | underline | outline | shadow}
get the style of menuItemDescriptor

The style property of a menu item determines which text style will be used to display that menu item. The styles are self-explanatory. The font used for the menu and items is always the Chicago system font. A menu item may have only one of these styles at a time—for example, one entity may not be both bold and italic. The five styles are shown in Figure 8-4.

Menu item styles are typically used on a *Style menu*, which is what sets the style of selected text (or a selected field or draw text object) to

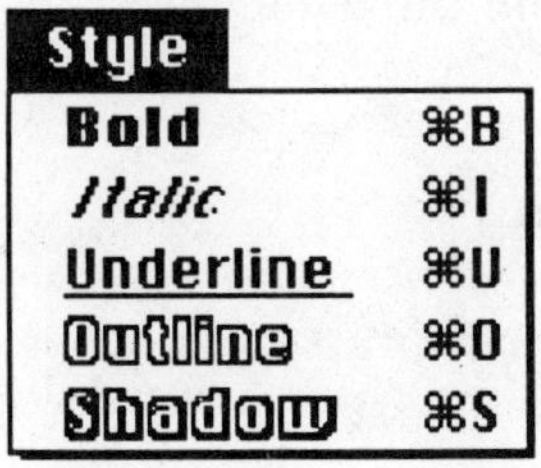

```
┌─────────────────┐
│ Style           │
├─────────────────┴─┐
│ Bold        ⌘B    │
│ Italic      ⌘I    │
│ Underline   ⌘U    │
│ Outline     ⌘O    │
│ Shadow      ⌘S    │
└───────────────────┘
```

Figure 8-4.   This menu shows the five possible menu item styles

```
on itemSelect
  if the checkMark of the target is false then
    insert menu "Fonts"
    set the checkMark of the target to true
  else
    remove menu "Fonts"
    set the checkMark of the target to false
end if
end itemSelect
```

Script 8-6.   This script for a Fonts menu inserts a menu called "Fonts" and places a checkmark before its name

a new value. Including the actual style as part of the menu item provides excellent feedback to your users as to the effects of the menu command. Using these styles in other menus should be handled with restraint.

The LockMenus Property

set the lockMenus to true ¦ false

This property governs whether changes to the menu bar are visible to the user or not. If it is "true," as the menu bar is changed, those changes are not presented to you until the property is set to "false" again.

Use this property when you are making wholesale changes to the menu bar. Since changes do not appear on the menu bar when the lockMenus property is true, changes go a little faster and prevent user confusion when the menu bar is changing. The lockMenus property was used in the setMenus handler presented earlier in this chapter, which disables all the menus on the menu bar.

The EditMenus Property

set the editMenus to true ¦ false
get the editMenus

This property governs whether or not you will be able to edit the script of a menu or menu item. If editMenus is false, holding down the SHIFT key while choosing a menu item simply executes that menu item instead of opening the script editor with the script of that item. EditMenus does *not* govern your ability to change the menu bar in other ways, such as adding and removing menu items.

The doMenu Command

doMenu *menuItem*

SuperCard's doMenu command works in exactly the same manner as HyperCard's. To call a menu item from within a script, use the doMenu command, including the text of the menu item in quotes. Make sure to include three dots within the quotes of the menu if the menu item has three periods after it. This indicates that the menu will summon a dialog box.

If you misspell a menu command or attempt to use the command with a menu that does not exist, you will receive an error message indicating that SuperCard cannot find the menu item.

Script 8-7 shows a handler for the doMenu message that is sent when the doMenu command is executed.

One difference between SuperCard and HyperCard is that in HyperCard the doMenu message is usually used to handle cases where the programmer does not want the user to use a certain menu item. Any time a menu item is chosen in HyperCard, the doMenu message, followed by the name of the menu item, is passed up the hierarchy. This

```
on doMenu whatCommand
  if whatCommand is "Cut Card" then
    answer "Please don't cut this card" with "OK"
  else
    pass doMenu
  end if
end doMenu
```

Script 8-7   This doMenu handler prevents you from cutting a card

does not happen in SuperCard; choosing a menu item does not send the doMenu message. Instead, as you have seen, the itemSelect message is sent to the menu item itself. If you want to disable menu items in SuperCard, you should set the disabled property of the menu item (or menu as a whole) to "true" to prevent users from selecting it. This is a more "Mac-like" solution, as it gives your users feedback on what menu items they can choose *before* they try to execute the command, and not after the fact. Some stacks that you have imported from HyperCard might need to be changed in this regard.

Special Menus

As you saw in Chapter Three, SuperCard defines two special menus, the Apple menu and the Fonts menu, which provide standard services that would be difficult to handle in SuperTalk alone.

Apple Menu

If you create a menu in SuperEdit named "Apple," that menu, when displayed, will automatically list all the Desk Accessories (DAs) that are available to SuperCard. This includes, of course, DAs installed by Suit-Case or Font/DA Juggler, as well as the MultiFinder menu that appears below the list of Desk Accessories and allows you to switch between programs. Further, you don't need to do any scripting to launch the Desk Accessory that is selected with this menu—SuperCard takes care of that for you.

You can include other menu items in the menu simply by adding them to the menu in SuperEdit. Typically, the first item will be an "About" item that tells the user something about your project. A second item might summon a Help window. For the sake of clarity on the menu, if you add new menu items to the Desk Accessory menu, make sure you insert a dividing line after the new items to separate them from the list of DAs.

Font Menu

Like the Apple menu, a Font menu will automatically display a list of all the fonts available to SuperCard, including those opened by utilities such as SuitCase or Font/DA Juggler.

Unlike the Apple menu, the Font menu does require that you do some scripting to make it work. The Font menu also does not work exactly the same as other menus in SuperCard. When you choose an item from most menus, the itemSelect message is sent up the hierarchy. You can trap that message either in the script of the menu item itself, in the menu itself, or anywhere up the hierarchy. Since you cannot edit the script of any of the items in the Font menu, however, you cannot intercept the messages in those items.

This might lead you to believe that you need to use the target function to discover the name of the font from the name of the menu item. This isn't the case. The Font menu automatically sets the value of the global property *textFont* to the name of the font chosen from the menu. When you choose a font from this menu, the target simply becomes the Font menu itself, and does not include the name of a menu item. You then need to determine the value of that property, and set the font of the selected object to the textFont. The script of the Font menu included in the Runtime Editor is an excellent example of how to do this. Setting the font of fields and of words in fields is discussed in Chapter Eleven.

As with the Apple menu, you can include your own items on the Font menu, and those items will appear before the list of fonts that is inserted automatically. These items behave just as they should—the itemSelect message is sent to that item, and you can handle that message in the script of the item just as you do with other menus. Again, for the sake of clarity, if you add your own items to the Font menu, include a dividing line after them to separate them from the automatic list of fonts.

Menu Tips

After five years of using the Macintosh, some standards have emerged for creating menus. Following these standards will give your project a professional look and feel, which will give your users confidence in the program and make it more accessible to them.

Always remember that the main purpose of the Macintosh menu bar is to present clearly the set of commands that are currently applicable. Do not defeat this purpose by creating obscure, randomly placed menus.

Group Menu Items by Function

Beyond the standard File and Edit menus, you should group the menus you have created so that all items that perform related actions appear on the same menu. This makes it easier for users to find commands. One example is the Palettes menu in the Runtime Editor. That menu is clearly labeled, and the type of menu items it contains is clear from its name.

Within the structure of each menu, you should further organize your menu items, grouping related items together and separating them with a dividing line. The standard File menu, for example, includes commands for printing, and these printing commands are always shown together and separated from the other commands with dividing lines.

Keep Menu and Item Names Short

The names of menus are always, in practice, one word, although Super-Card allows you to create menu names that are more than one word. Menu items themselves can be very long, but it is poor practice to use more than two or three words for the name of a menu item.

This seems obvious, but several commercial programs on the market have long menu or item names in them. One example is the Red Ryder program. Although from all reports this is a flexible, powerful, communications program, some of the menu items have very long names, as long as five or six words.

When a menu item appears as you click on the menu bar, you glance at it quickly to discover what it does. One or two words can be quickly assimilated by the eye; you may not even realize that you are "reading" the menu name. Longer item names, however, require conscious effort— effort that people do not want to expend. So, keep your item names as short and scannable as possible.

Use Standard Command Keys

Certain keyboard shortcuts have also become standard, and defying these standards invites user confusion and frustration. For example, the standard Macintosh keyboard shortcut for the Undo command is COMMAND-Z, but one filing program used this keyboard shortcut to delete the current field and shift the contents of the same field up one record, thus effectively destroying your data. If you ever made a mistake and used the COMMAND-Z keystroke—a natural thing to do—it was likely that you ruined the data in memory and, if you didn't notice it, possibly ruined the data on disk. Obviously, that software had many critics.

Program designers violate standards at their own risk, for software that behaves contrary to established custom and user expectation becomes frustrating, and most users would rather use software that does what they expect it to.

COMMAND-key equivalents for menu items virtually always appear in uppercase. Standard keyboard shortcuts for common menu items are shown in Table 8-1.

Write Transportable Menus

As mentioned earlier in this chapter, a menu can be on the menu bar even if the project of which it is a part is not open. For that reason, the scripts in your menus should make as few assumptions about the windows on which they will be operating as possible. If your menus *do* require a specific window or project, you should either close those windows when your project closes, or test when the menu item is selected to make sure that its necessary prerequisites have been met before it executes. It is better for your scripts to check this than for SuperCard to give a script error to your users. The menu scripts in the Runtime Editor provide excellent examples of techniques for writing transportable menus that check for errors before executing.

Use the Runtime Editor Menus

When you are creating a project that is to be used as part of the SuperCard environment (as opposed to a stand-alone application), there is no need to reinvent the wheel. The menus, palettes, and windows that

Menu Command	COMMAND-**key Equivalent**
Cut	X
Copy	C
Paste	V
*Clear	BACKSPACE
*Undo	Z
Select All	A
Open	O
New	N
Print	P
Quit	Q
Close	W
Get Info	I
Duplicate	D
Save	S
Find	F

*Not Supported by SuperCard

Table 8-1.   Keyboard Shortcuts for Standard Commands

are built into the Runtime Editor are fast, elegant, and tested. For standard services, use those menus, or allow users of your program to install the Runtime Editor into the projects themselves. You will certainly save yourself a lot of time and work, and your users will find themselves in a familiar environment.

Menus You Should Include

When you are building projects to be used in the SuperCard environment—that is, with the Runtime Editor, and allowing the user to open and close projects at will—the only menus you need to include as part of your project design are the menus that provide special services unique to your project.

However, if you are creating an application that is to be run in a stand-alone mode, the services of the Runtime Editor will not be available, and you should include in the project at least a minimal set of menus. A minimal set of menus could include the following.

Apple Menu

Virtually all well-behaved Macintosh programs include an Apple menu. The only exception that springs immediately to mind is Apple's Font/DA Mover, and that program can at least modify the Apple menu. Your users will expect to have Desk Accessories available to them when they are running your program, and the appearance of your project as a quality application is enhanced by their availability.

File Menu

Most programs include a File menu that has at least one item on it, Quit, and usually other standard items, such as opening, closing, and printing of files. These latter functions might not be applicable to your program, but you should always include the Quit item as a standard method of leaving the application. Implementing the Quit menu item is very easy. Simply create the Quit menu item, assign COMMAND-Q to it, and use this script:

```
on itemSelect
   close all windows
end itemSelect
```

The close all windows command causes SuperCard (or your application) to quit, because SuperCard cannot run with no windows opened. (The Runtime Editor may appear to not have any windows open, but that project opens a small window, sets its visible property to "false," and locates it off screen.) This will be discussed further in Chapter Nine.

Edit Menu

All applications should include an Edit menu for two reasons. First, your users will expect it. Programs that don't have an Edit menu look strange on the screen. Second, you should include an Edit menu for the instances when your program is running on a machine without MultiFinder. When SingleFinder is running, the Edit menu of the application itself is used to provide cutting, copying, and pasting functions for

Desk Accessories, so if you don't provide those functions in your program, the Desk Accessories will not have them either. This is definitely nonstandard practice for Macintosh applications.

To implement standard Cut, Copy, and Paste functions, you only need to create these menu items (be sure to include the standard COMMAND-key shortcuts) and put a handler for the itemSelect message into each one. Only one command is necessary in the itemSelect handler for each of these menus, and that command is as simple as Cut, Copy, or Paste. For example, to implement a Copy menu item, simply create the item and include this script in it:

```
on itemSelect
  Copy
end itemSelect
```

Do the same for the Cut and Paste menu items. When it is this easy to implement menus, there is no excuse not to do it.

Unfortunately, SuperCard does not include support for that other standard of the Edit menu—the Undo command. For more details about creating stand-alone applications with SuperCard, see Chapter Sixteen.

Resources

Standard Resources Versus SuperCard Resources
No Resource Forks Open
The SharedFile: A Place to Put Resources
Importing Resources
Icons
Cursors
Sounds
Cluts
Windows
Menus
Fonts
External Commands and Functions

Resources are an integral part of the Macintosh "identity." Resources on the Macintosh were created to make such things as changing the text of menu items relatively easy. For example, a developer does not need to rewrite and recompile an application to change a program so that it works in a foreign language. Instead, only text needs to be changed in the menu resource. Resources on the early Macintosh were also used to separate the program into small chunks that could be loaded into RAM when needed, and discarded, or purged when no longer required. This was necessary in the days of the 128K machine.

Standard Resources Versus SuperCard Resources

Many Macintosh files consist of two parts, or forks. The *data fork* contains the data portion of the file, such as the text of a word processing document. The other part, the *resource fork*, stores the program's resources, such as the text of menu items, icons, fonts, cursors, the text and appearance of dialog boxes, and program code.

Resources in Macintosh applications are handled by a set of tools in the Macintosh ROM and System file called the Resource Manager, which is essentially a small librarian that keeps track of the resources in resource forks of files. When a program needs to retrieve a resource, it sends a message to the Resource Manager asking for that resource. The Resource Manager is limited and somewhat outdated, but it has not been replaced because so much depends on its current architecture.

The Resource Manager does have its limitations. Apple's technical documentation states that the Resource Manager is not designed to work with files that contain more than about 2727 resources, and performance deteriorates considerably before this figure is reached. In most cases, this is not much of a problem. HyperCard, for example, has a limited number of possible resources (and HyperCard does slow down with large numbers of resources).

In SuperCard, however, the 2727 resource limit could have been a very serious limitation. SuperCard's creators wanted to design a program with few, if any, limitations to the number of projects, windows, cards, and menus open at any one time. In that environment, you could be pushing the limits of the Resource Manager very quickly.

Consider a project full of color graphics. On the Macintosh, information about which colors any graphic uses are stored in a resource called a "clut," for color lookup table. It is possible, even likely, that each card in a project would have its own clut. If you have a project of 1000 cards, you have 1000 cluts in the resource fork of the file. Clearly, if you open another project at the same time, you will need to have fewer than 1700 color cards in that project, or you will have trouble with the Resource Manager. When you consider that projects could also have external commands and functions, icons, cursors, and sounds as part of their structure, you can see that the limitations of the Resource Manager are profound.

No Resource Forks Open

In SuperCard, the problem with the Resource Manager was solved by nearly doing away with resource forks altogether. Instead of keeping them in the resource fork of a project, SuperCard maintains its resources as part of the data fork, and provides its own tools for managing resources.

In SuperCard, only two files have traditional resource forks: the SharedFile and SuperCard itself. Neither of these files is likely to include a large number of resources (such as cluts), and, while you can add your own resources to SuperCard itself, it would be wrong.

The SharedFile: A Place to Put Resources

In HyperCard, the Home stack is the central storage place for traditional resources and common scripts. In SuperCard, the SharedFile is used for this purpose.

As mentioned, the SharedFile is the only SuperCard project with a resource fork that is open. Therefore, any *real* resources you need (that is, any resources that cannot be imported and transformed into Super-Card's special format) can be stored in the SharedFile.

The only time that the SharedFile is not used to store resources is when you have built a stand-alone application of one of your projects. In this case, the application *does* have its resource fork open, and traditional resources can be stored there. Also, when you are building such an application, you need to remember to use SuperEdit to copy any SuperCard-style resources into your project. To copy traditional resources into your project, you need to use a utility such as ResEdit.

As you will see later in this chapter, when you are converting a HyperCard stack with resources, you can specify in advance whether you want those resources to be placed into the current project or into the SharedFile. When importing resources from another type of file, you need to first import them into a new project, and then use SuperEdit to copy them into the SharedFile. For resources of a type that SuperEdit cannot convert, you need to use Apple's ResEdit, or a similar program, to install them into the SharedFile.

The SharedFile Function

put the sharedFile
put sharedFile( )

This function returns the pathname of the currently active SharedFile.

If your project is running as a stand-alone application, this function returns "None."

You should note that this is a function and not a property, meaning that you can use it to discover the name of the current SharedFile, but you cannot use it to *change* the name of the SharedFile. The full pathname of the SharedFile is stored in the file SUPERCARD PREFS on your disk. This file is usually contained in a folder called SC POUCH, which is, in turn, contained in your SuperCard Folder. When you start SuperCard or SuperEdit for the first time, it asks you for the location of this file and remembers it.

Importing Resources

You use SuperEdit to import resources into SuperCard. To do so, choose the Import Resources menu item from SuperEdit's File menu. You will be shown a list of only those files with resource forks.

When you have chosen the file whose resources you wish to import, SuperEdit will then prompt you to name the new project. The new project will be created on disk, and an alert will tell you the progress SuperEdit is making in importing the resources.

SuperEdit can import these types of resources: icons, cluts, XCMDs and XFCNs, menus, cursors, sounds, and windows.

Importing Resources from HyperCard Stacks

You can import resources from HyperCard stacks using the Convert Stack menu item, or using the Import Resources menu item. The Convert Stack command gives you more control over how resources are imported.

When you convert a stack, if that stack has resources, SuperCard will present you with the dialog shown in Figure 9-1. If you click the Cancel button on this dialog box, the stack is not converted. If you click

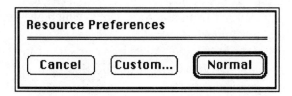

Figure 9-1.   The Resource Preferences dialog box appears when you convert a
HyperCard stack that includes resources

the Normal button, all resources in the stack are converted and placed
into SuperCard's resource structure, as normal. SuperCard ignores resources it cannot deal with.

If you click on the Custom button, you get the dialog box shown in
Figure 9-2. This allows you to specify whether each type of resource is
installed into the new project, into the resource fork of SharedFile, into
both, or not installed at all. Click on the checkbox to the left of the
resource name to install it into the new project, or on the checkbox to its
right to install it into the SharedFile. If you don't want a certain type of
resource to be converted at all, make sure neither checkbox is checked.
You can install the resource into both the current project and into the
SharedFile by clicking on both buttons.

The final checkbox at the bottom of the dialog box tells SuperEdit
what to do with resources of a different type. Since the resource fork of
the current project is never opened, it doesn't make any sense to install
resources into that project (unless you are making a stand-alone Super-
Card application). You can elect to install them into the SharedFile, or
not install them at all.

Icons

If the file has icons in it, SuperEdit will import those icons and place
them into the list of SuperCard resources. Once the icon has been
imported, you can edit it using the Icon editor built into SuperEdit (see
Chapter Three).

Note that these icons are different from the icons displayed for files on the desktop. These icons, denoted as ICN# in ResEdit and other programs, are distinct from standard icons, which are denoted by ICON. SuperEdit cannot import ICN#s.

Once installed into SuperCard, icons are used in the same manner as they are used in HyperCard. Use the Set Icon command to specify the icon for a particular button.

Cursors

Cursors are imported into SuperCard in a straightforward manner, and once they have been imported, can be edited in the manner discussed in Chapter Three. In ResEdit, cursor resources are of the CURS type.

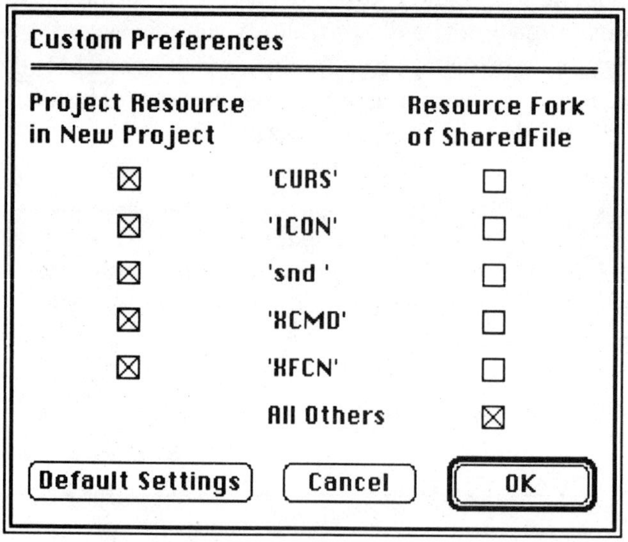

Custom Preferences

Project Resource in New Project		Resource Fork of SharedFile
☒	'CURS'	☐
☒	'ICON'	☐
☒	'snd '	☐
☒	'HCMD'	☐
☒	'HFCN'	☐
	All Others	☒

[Default Settings]   (Cancel)   (OK)

Figure 9-2.   When you convert a HyperCard stack with resources, you can specify where standard resource types are to be placed

You should note that not all programs use CURS resources to create their mouse pointers. HyperCard, for example, uses a special *font* for many of its cursors; only the Browse cursor or pointer is defined as a CURS resource.

Once a project has cursor resources, SuperCard works with those cursors in the same manner as HyperCard. The Set Cursor command can take either the name or ID number of the cursor you want to use as the standard cursor. Remember that cursor changes are in effect only *so long as the handler that changed the cursor is executing.*

Sounds

SuperCard imports sound resources that have the signature "snd_" (the underscore represents a space). This is the same type of sound resource that HyperCard uses. Therefore, some sounds that are stored as different types of resources or files will not be directly imported into SuperEdit.

The best way to import sounds of a different type into SuperEdit is to use Farallon's SoundEdit program (part of the MacRecorder package) or other similar software. SoundEdit can read files and resources of the type created by most programs, and can in turn save them into other formats. In this case, you might create a HyperCard stack, use SoundEdit to save sounds into that stack, and then convert the Hyper-Card stack to SuperCard or use SuperEdit's Import Resources command to import those sounds. Silicon Beach is making tools available to developers that allow them access to SuperCard's "data" style of resource management, so it is likely that future versions of such programs as SoundEdit and HyperSound, Farallon's HyperCard sound stack, will directly support SuperCard resources.

Sounds in SuperCard are played using the Play command. It will play sounds that are in either the standard resource fork of the Shared-File, or are part of the current project.

Cluts

The following are two ways to import cluts into SuperCard.

1. When you use the Import Graphics command in SuperEdit to import a color PICT file or other type of file that contains colors, SuperEdit will ask you if you want to add the new clut to your project.

2. When you use the Import Resources menu command in Super-Edit to bring in resources, SuperEdit will convert any clut-type resources in the Source file to SuperCard clut resources.

In the former case, it is interesting to note that PICT files do not contain cluts as separate resources. Instead, PICT files are stored as data (they don't always have resource forks), and the colors used by the files are part of the data fork. In this case, SuperEdit scans the data to discover which colors are used, and then creates a clut based on those colors.

In SuperTalk, the clut is a property of either cards or backgrounds. In SuperEdit, you control which clut is associated with a card or background using the Set Colors command. In SuperCard, management of cluts as you change from card to card is handled automatically, or you can use the Set Clut command to switch cluts under script control. For more details about cluts, see Chapter Fourteen.

Windows

Most Macintosh programs use a WIND resource to define their windows. This resource defines the size and location of the window on the screen. If a file from which you are importing resources contains WIND resources, SuperCard will create windows in the new project that match the specifications of the windows in the file. Use standard SuperEdit and SuperCard window editing techniques to alter the windows.

As with the other types of resources discussed here, not all programs use this resource to define their windows, so you will not be able to import the window designs from all files.

Menus

Most programs use a Menu resource to contain the definitions of the items on their menus, along with such things as the style of the menu item and the command key that activates the menu. If a file that you are importing contains such a resource, SuperEdit will import that resource and create SuperCard menus based on what it finds in those resources. You can use standard SuperCard and SuperEdit techniques to manage the menus once they have been imported.

Fonts

Many applications use their own fonts for special purposes. As was mentioned earlier in this chapter, HyperCard uses a font for many of its mouse cursors. Many developers have installed custom fonts while creating HyperCard stacks to assure the right size fonts in fields, and for more exotic purposes such as quick animation.

When importing resources, SuperCard ignores fonts, and does not install them into a project. Only by using the Custom Preferences dialog box, discussed above, can you install the font into the SharedFile.

SuperCard does not provide support for fonts for several reasons. The first reason is that in order to maintain the same user interface as it does for icons and cursors, a font editor would have to be provided. Font editing is complex, and for those who need to create fonts, specialized programs are available (or you can use Apple's ResEdit).

Secondly, in order to allow you to use the fonts that might have been converted to SuperCard, Silicon Beach would have had to provide SuperCard with the abilities to use those fonts. Since the Font Manager that is part of the Macintosh already does a fairly good job of this, there is no need to duplicate that function.

Finally, using customized fonts as part of a project is probably not the best idea. Those who have machines with a large number of fonts installed have several problems relating to fonts. In order to rectify these problems, Apple is changing the ways that fonts are managed on the Macintosh. It is likely that the format for fonts will change in the near future. If you really need fonts in your project, you can install them into the SharedFile. If you need to deliver projects that contain specialized fonts, you should build a stand-alone application out of your project, and include the font as part of its resource fork.

External Commands and Functions

SuperCard manipulates external commands (XCMDs) and functions (XFCNs) much as other resources do. You can import these from HyperCard stacks using the Convert Stack or Import Resources command, and they are converted to SuperCard's resource format.

SuperCard's formats for externals are the same as HyperCard's, and the vast majority of existing externals work in SuperCard as they do in HyperCard. However, you need to ask a few questions before importing externals into SuperCard:

- *Do you really need the external?*   Some externals allow Hyper-Card to perform such functions as display color PICT files on the screen or copy resources between HyperCard stacks. Since Super-Card supports color, and SuperEdit allows you to copy and import resources, these externals are not really necessary.

- *Does the XCMD or XFCN work by itself?*   If the external is a stand-alone external, it is probably going to work in SuperCard. However, some externals use other types of resources as they are operating. Steve Maller's ResCopy is an example of an XCMD that uses other resources—DLOG and DITL resources—to display its dialog boxes. If the other resources are of types that SuperCard cannot convert to its data structure, you must install those other resources into the resource fork of your SharedFile. If you do not, the external will likely crash your system.

- *Does the XCMD or XFCN obey the rules?*   This is a difficult question to answer, and you may find your system crashing or hanging as you attempt to use certain externals. Some external commands and functions attempt to work directly with HyperCard data structures in RAM. These externals will not work with Super-Card, and they probably will not work with future versions of HyperCard. Unfortunately, it is not always possible to tell which externals work before you try them.

In general though, most external functions work in SuperCard as they do in HyperCard. At this time, SuperCard has had few problems with externals and has successfully used a number of standard Hyper-Card externals, as well as a few created using the script compiler CompileIt!

At first SuperCard's new way of handling resources might seem a nuisance. However, when you consider the tools that SuperEdit gives you for manipulating resources, as well as the probable side effects of working in the standard manner, the nuisance value decreases, and the performance improves.

Objects, Buttons, and Tools

Objects
Buttons
Tools

Objects, buttons, and tools are crucial features of SuperCard. Objects are containers for information, which might be text in a field, a picture in a graphic object, or a script in a button. Tools are used to click on buttons, create new objects, select menu items, and for many other tasks.

The first part of this chapter discusses objects in general, followed by a discussion of buttons in particular. Field, Draw, and Paint objects, and the particular tools with which you work with them, are discussed in succeeding chapters.

Objects

Objects are the "raw material" of the Macintosh user interface, and you use them every time you use the Macintosh. Icons on the Finder's desktop are objects that represent disks or files. Buttons are objects that cause things to happen. Fields are objects that contain text. The menus you use to send commands to programs are objects. Even the text you select in a word processor or in a SuperCard field is an object (though the commands you use to manipulate that class of object are different than the commands you use to manipulate other objects). In SuperCard, as in many other programs, graphics are objects that you can manipulate in various ways.

SuperCard gives you tools to manipulate most of these kinds of objects. SuperCard's objects, however, are slightly different from some of the other objects in the Macintosh world. For example, menus in

SuperCard are not really objects, or rather they are a different *class* or type of object that is handled differently from the other classes of objects discussed here.

SuperCard's objects are all part of cards and appear only within the card environment. There are three general classes of objects in Super-Card: the button, the field, and the graphic. The graphic class is further divided into two separate subclasses, bitmap and draw graphics.

The card-based objects in SuperCard have properties and charac-teristics that are logical extensions of the properties of HyperCard's buttons and fields.

SuperCard's objects have these features:

• *They receive messages.* Mostly these messages are sent in re-sponse to events generated by the mouse. The mouseDown mes-sage, for example, is sent to an object when you place the mouse cursor over the object and depress the button. Mouse messages are sent to objects in SuperCard and are handled by those objects in the same manner in which they are sent and handled in HyperCard.

• *They can contain scripts.* In HyperCard, both buttons and fields can contain scripts, allowing you to control how they react to events. In SuperCard, graphics objects can also have scripts in them and can react to mouse events.

• *Properties determine their characteristics.* A suite of properties determine such things as what messages are sent to an object (or whether they are sent at all), if the object is visible, and how it appears on the screen.

Kinds of Objects

There are three kinds of objects in SuperCard—buttons and fields (both also present in HyperCard), and graphic objects (which are not present in HyperCard).

Some of SuperCard's objects can also be polygonal—that is, they may be irregularly shaped. If you have worked much in HyperCard, you have probably been frustrated by its inability to create buttons that have shapes other than rectangles. For example, creating a map of the world using Rectangular buttons for each of the countries becomes quite annoying; there are very few rectangular countries in the world.

SuperCard buttons and draw graphics can be polygons that have an almost unlimited number of sides. You can even use the AutoTrace tool (discussed in Chapter Four) to instruct SuperEdit to create a Polygonal object for you, based on the outline of an object in a painting.

Referring to Objects

Objects have names, numbers, and ID numbers. You can use any of these identifiers to refer to an object. When referring to an object, you need to specify the type of object, as well as its name, number, or ID number.

When referring to *card-level buttons*, you do not need to include the word *card* when referring to the button, as the default for buttons is the card level. The situation is reversed when referring to fields. When referring to fields, the default is the background level. When referring to graphics, you always need to use the card or background descriptors.

Here are some sample object descriptors:

```
card graphic ID 101
background graphic "weasel"
button "next"  -- if "next" is a card button
background button 6
```

SuperCard also features names, short names, and long names for each of its objects. The long name of an object includes a complete descriptor of it. For example, suppose you have a button called "test" on a card called "firstCard" in a window called "test" in a project called "home" on a hard disk called "hard disk". The long name of that button then is

```
card button "test" of card "firstCard" of window "test" of
project "hard disk:home"
```

The short name of an object consists of an identifier followed by its name (or ID number if it has no name). The button mentioned in this example, then, would have a short name of

```
card button "test"
```

In any case where the object, card, or window has no name, the ID number of that object is used instead.

SuperCard, like HyperCard, allows you to abbreviate many of its terms. "Graphic" can be abbreviated as "grc" and "window" as "wd."

The Exists Function

exists(objectDescriptor)

This function returns true if the specified object exists, and false otherwise. You can specify any type of SuperCard object, including Resources, Menus, Windows, Cards, Buttons, Fields, and Graphic objects. Here are some samples of its use:

```
exists(card ID 100) — check for a specific card
exists(icon "next")
exists(menu "file")
exists(clut "grayscale")
exists(card grc "sun")
exists(card button "OK")
```

This function always refers to the current project, that is, the one containing the card that is currently on top. If you want to check, a script for objects in a different project, use the setWindow command, discussed in Chapter Seven.

Object Properties

As previously mentioned, all objects have a suite of properties that govern how they function and appear on the screen. This section discusses those properties that are common to one or more classes of SuperCard objects. The chapters on fields, draw, and paint objects (Chapters Eleven, Twelve, and Thirteen, respectively) discuss properties relevant to those classes of objects only.

The Selected Property
set the selected of objectDescriptor to true¦false
get the selected of objectDescriptor

When you click on an object with the Pointer, Universal, or Object-specific tools (discussed later in this chapter), the selected property of that object is set to true, and selection rectangles appear at each corner of the object if it is a rectangle or if it is a polygon, at each corner of a rectangle that would contain the object.

An object can be selected even if you are using the Browse tool and not the Pointer tool. In this case, the only way to select it is from a script or the Message box. When an object is selected, and you are using the Browse tool, the selection handles at the objects corners will *not* appear. However, the Cut and Copy commands will work on the selected object.

To see how the selected property of objects is used, look at the scripts of the menu item Select All in the Edit menu of the Runtime Editor. This script loops in turn through all the fields, graphics, and buttons on the current card and simply sets the selected property of each object to true.

If you have an object selected on a card when you quit SuperCard and then edit that same card in SuperEdit when you open the card, you will find that object still selected. You can also select objects using the Select command, discussed later in this chapter.

The Disabled Property
get the disabled of objectDescriptor
set the disabled of objectDescriptor to true¦false

This property determines whether an object will receive and respond to mouse messages. If it is true, all messages are sent to the object. If it is set to false, messages will pass through the object and go directly to the card containing the object.

If the disabled object is a button and the button's showName property is true, that name will be greyed out, indicating to you that the object is not receiving messages. You can manipulate this property with the Disable and Enable commands, discussed later in this chapter.

Location and Size Properties

As with HyperCard buttons and fields, all SuperCard objects have a set of properties that determine their location and size on the card. All these properties are expressed as integers and are relative to the left edge and top of the card, which are always 0.

Loc

get the loc of objectDescriptor
set the loc of objectDescriptor to horizontal,vertical

The loc property contains two integers separated by commas. The first describes the distance of the center of the object from the left edge of the card. The second describes the distance of the center of the object from the top of the card.

Height

get the height of objectDescriptor
set the height of objectDescriptor to integer

The height property contains a number that specifies the height of the object in pixels. If the object is a polygon, this property contains the number of pixels that separate the topmost point on the polygon and its bottommost point.

When you change the height of an object, the loc property of that object is left alone. The top and bottom properties will be adjusted to accommodate the new height. If you attempt to set the height of an object to a number less than zero, you will receive an alert indicating that you cannot specify an empty rectangle.

Width

get the width of objectDescriptor
set the width of objectDescriptor to integer

This property contains a number that specifies the width of the object in pixels. If the object is a polygon, this property contains the number of pixels that separate the leftmost point on the polygon and its rightmost point.

When you change the width of an object, the loc property of that object is left alone. The left and right properties will be adjusted to accommodate the new width. If you attempt to set the width of an object to a number less than 0, you will receive an alert indicating that you cannot specify an empty rectangle.

Left

get the left of objectDescriptor
set the left of objectDescriptor to integer

This property contains one integer that specifies the distance of the left edge of the object from the left edge of the card. If the left portion of the object lies to the left of the card (you can position it there with the Pointer tool), you will not be able to see the part of the object that lies off the card, and the left property will contain a negative number.

Top

get the top of objectDescriptor
set the top of objectDescriptor to integer

The top property contains the number of pixels from the top of the card to the top of the object. The top portion of an object can be above the top of the card; if this is so, the top property will contain a negative number, and you will not be able to see the part of the object that is off the card.

Right

get the right of objectDescriptor
set the right of objectDescriptor to integer

This property contains the number of pixels from the left edge of the card to the right edge of the object. If the right part of the object lies beyond the right edge of the card, that part will not be visible in SuperCard. Later in this chapter, in the "Tools" section, a handler is described that prevents an object from being dragged beyond the boundaries of the card.

Bottom
get the bottom of objectDescriptor
set the bottom of objectDescriptor to integer

This property determines the distance of the bottom of the object from the top of the card. If the bottom part of the object is beyond the boundaries of the card, that part will not be visible in SuperCard.

TopLeft
get the topLeft of objectDescriptor
set the topLeft of objectDescriptor to integer

This property contains two integers separated by commas. The first is the same as the left property, the second the same as the top property.

Note: The order of the integers is the *opposite* of the order indicated in the name of the property (as it is with the botRight property, discussed next). The standard on the Macintosh is that the width always comes before the height, but in naming these properties, for some reason the height comes before the width!

BotRight
get the botRight of objectDescriptor
set the botRight of objectDescriptor to integer

This property contains two integers separated by commas. The first is the same as the right property, the second the same as the bottom property.

Rect

get the rect[angle] of objectDescriptor
set the rect[angle] of objectDescriptor to left,top,right,bottom

The rect property contains four integers separated by commas. The first describes the distance of the object's left edge from the left side of the card, the second describes the distance of the object's top edge from the top of the card, the third describes the object's right edge, and the fourth describes the object's bottom.

Fill and Pen Properties

These properties control the patterns used to fill buttons and draw objects. You can use different methods to change these properties. First, you can select the object and use the Patterns and Colors palettes in the Runtime Editor to change the appearance of the object. Second, you can set one of these properties for a specified object from a script or from the Message box (which amounts to the same thing except that the scripts are written for you). Third, you can set these properties without referring to a specific object by setting a global property—new objects will take on these properties.

The fill properties include fillBack, fillFore, fillPat, and showFill. The pen properties, which work in much the same way as the fill properties, affect the *lines* that form an object. They include penBack, penFore, penPat, penHeight, and penWidth. All of these properties are discussed in detail in Chapter Fourteen.

The Points Property

get the points of objectDescriptor
set the points of objectDescriptor to listOfPoints

Only Polygonal Draw objects and Polygonal buttons have this property. It contains a list of paired integers separated by commas, which describe each of the points on the polygon.

Though you do not see them explicitly, the points are a set of paired numbers. In each pair, the first number describes the distance of the point from the left edge of the card, and the second describes the distance of that point from the top of the card.

The Move command, discussed in Chapter Fifteen, can be used with the points property to create simple animations.

The Shadow Property
get the shadow of button ¦ field
set the shadow of button ¦ field to integer

This property of buttons and fields determines the *offset value* of the shadow of an object. The offset value is the number of pixels that separate the shadow of the object from the object itself. If you set the shadow of a button to 10, that shadow will appear 10 pixels below and 10 to the right of the original object.

You can use the Button or Field Info dialog boxes in the Runtime Editor to change this property interactively.

The Style Property
get the style of objectDescriptor
set the style of objectDescriptor to style

This property determines the style, including the appearance, of objects. Different types of objects can have different styles. The various styles of different kinds of objects, including windows, are shown in Table 10-1.

The style characteristics of each type of object are discussed in different locations in this book. Button styles are discussed later in this chapter; window styles are discussed in Chapter Seven; field styles are discussed in Chapter Eleven; and graphic styles are discussed in Chapter Twelve.

Text Properties

Fields, buttons, and draw text objects have text properties that determine the appearance of text in those objects. These properties affect

Window	Button	Field	Graphic
standard	checkbox	opaque	roundRect
scrolling	opaque	rectangle	oval
roundRect	radioButton	scrolling	line
dialog	retangle	shadow	polygon
plain	roundRect	transparent	bitmap
shadow	transparent		text
palette			arc
			group

Table 10-1.   Each SuperCard Object Has Its Own Style Properties

all the text of buttons — you cannot mix text styles within buttons. You can mix text styles within draw text objects while in SuperEdit, but not within SuperCard. You can, however, select draw text objects in Super-Card and change the style of all the text in that object. When you change these properties for fields, they affect only the selected text in fields.

Text properties also have current or global values that affect all new text created with the Paint Text tool, or newly created text with that tool. See Chapter Thirteen for a more detailed discussion on paint objects.

textAlign

get the textAlign [of button ¦ field ¦ drawObject]
set the textAlign [of button ¦ field ¦ drawObject] to left ¦ center ¦ right

This property determines whether text will be aligned with the left or right edge of the object to which it belongs, or centered within that object.

The textAlign property of buttons is normally center of the field. The textAlign of fields and draw text objects is normally to the left.

textFont

get the textFont [of button ¦ field ¦ drawObject]
set the textFont [of button ¦ field ¦ drawObject] to fontName

The textFont property determines the name of the font used for displaying the text of an object. FontName should be the name of the font as it appears on a standard Font menu. If you use a font name that is not currently available to SuperCard, the font will be set to Chicago.

The textFont of a button is normally Chicago unless that button also has an icon associated with it, in which case it will be Geneva. You can control the default textFont for other objects by using the Preferences dialog box in SuperEdit.

textHeight

get the textHeight [of button | field | drawObject]
set the textHeight [of button | field | drawObject] to integer

This property determines the number of pixels between one line of text and the next. It is usually the integer closest to 20 percent greater than the textSize (discussed next).

The minimum value for the textHeight is 5. If you try to set the textHeight to a value smaller than this, it will be set to 5 anyway (except for buttons). The maximum textHeight is 200.

You can set the textHeight for a button, but it has no effect; the textHeight of a button is always 0.

textSize

get the TextSize [of button | field | drawObject]
set the TextSize [of button | field | drawObject] to integer

This property determines the size of the text of the specified object. The size is expressed in points, just as it is in the Style dialog box of SuperEdit, and in most other Macintosh programs.

The minimum value for the textSize is 5. If you try to set the textSize to a value smaller than this, it will be set to 5 anyway. The maximum textSize is 127.

The default textSize of a button is 12. You can use the Preferences dialog box in SuperEdit to set the default textSize for other objects.

textStyle

get the textStyle [of button | field | drawObject]

set the TextStyle [of button ¦ field ¦ drawObject] to
   bold ¦ condense ¦ extend ¦ italic ¦ outline ¦ plain ¦ shadow ¦ underline

This property determines the style of text in the specified object. When setting this property, you can include multiple styles by separating the different styles with commas, as in the line:

   set the textStyle to bold,italic

If you use the Get command to determine the textStyle of an object, it will, in turn, return a list of all the styles of that text separated by commas.

The Visible Property

get the visible of objectDescriptor
set the visible of objectDescriptor to true ¦ false

This property determines whether or not an object is visible on the screen. If the property is true, the object is visible; if it is false, it is not visible. Invisible objects receive no messages. You can also use the Hide and Show commands, discussed later in this chapter, to set the value of this property.

The Script Property

get the script of objectDescriptor
set the script of objectDescriptor to container
edit [the] script of objectDescriptor

All SuperCard objects can contain scripts, which are actually properties of objects. You can use SuperTalk to modify the script of an object.

   Buttons and fields always receive messages, whether or not they contain scripts. Graphic objects, however, do *not* receive messages if they do not contain scripts. Mouse messages sent to those objects— mouseDown, mouseUp, and the others—are sent to the *card* containing an object, if the object itself does not contain a script.

Object Commands

Several commands operate on objects and in essence provide automatic tools, which allow you to change values of various properties.

Select
Select objectDescriptor

This command selects the specified object, causing handles to appear at its four corners. This command also causes the tool to be changed to one of the universal tools for selecting objects. For example, if you use a statement such as "select background graphic 1," that graphic will be selected and you will be switched to the Graphic tool. You cannot use this command to select multiple objects.

Hide/Show
Hide objectDescriptor
Show objectDescriptor

This command changes the visible property of the specified object. Visible objects appear on the screen. Invisible objects neither appear on the screen nor receive mouse messages.

Enable/Disable
Enable objectDescriptor
Disable objectDescriptor

This command sets the disabled property of the object to true or false. Disabled objects do not receive messages. If the mouse clicks on the objects, messages are sent directly to the card, whether or not a handler for that message appears in the script of the object.

When buttons are disabled, the text of the name of the button is greyed out to show that it is disabled.

BringFront/SendBack
BringFront
SendBack

The BringFront command brings all selected objects to the front of the card. It is equivalent to the Bring To Front command in SuperEdit. Since the "stacking order" of the object reflects the number of the object, this has the effect of changing the number of the selected object to match the number of objects on the card as shown in Figure 10-1. At the top of the figure, Object 1 is behind Object 2. If you select Object 1, executing the BringFront command will produce the effect shown at the bottom of the figure. The object with the cross-hatching is now in front of the object with the grey pattern, and the numbers of the objects are changed.

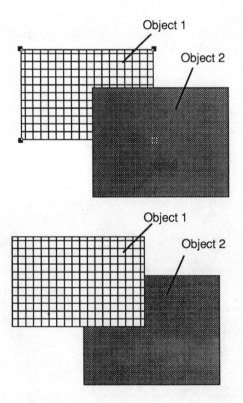

Figure 10-1.   The BringFront command brings the selected object or objects to the front

If multiple objects are selected when this command is executed, the order of those objects is preserved by the command. The SendBack command works in the same manner as the BringFront command but has the opposite effect.

The Intersect Function
put intersect(objectDescriptor, objectDescriptor)

This function returns true if the outlines of the two specified objects overlap one another. It is useful in situations where you need to have some sort of "collision-detect" mechanism, such as games or animations. Suppose you want to move one graphic across the screen until it hits another graphic and then stop. You could put a handler such as the one shown in Script 10-1 into the script of card graphic 1.

This simple script is initiated when you click on card graphic 1. The repeat loop simply tests to see if the two card graphics intersect one another. As long as they do not intersect, card graphic 1 moves to the right across the screen and stops moving when it "hits" card graphic 2; that is, when the Intersect function returns "true."

Buttons

In general, buttons are screen devices that perform some action when you click on them. As a Macintosh user, you are no doubt familiar with

```
on mouseUp
  repeat until intersect(card grc 1, card grc 2) is true
    get the loc of cd grc 1
    add 1 to item 1 of it
    set the loc of cd grc 1 to it
  end repeat
end mouseUp
```

Script 10-1.   This handler moves one graphic across the screen until it collides, or intersects, with another

the buttons in dialog boxes, such as the OK and Cancel buttons that confirm or cancel your changes. Much of the Macintosh user interface is built around buttons.

Because Supercard's graphic objects can also be active areas that respond to mouse clicks, confusion has arisen over the difference between graphic objects and buttons. What, then, *are* the distinctions between SuperCard's graphic objects and buttons?

> • *Buttons have styles that determine their appearance.*   The style property of SuperCard's buttons provide support for a number of standard Macintosh button styles, such as Rounded Rectangle, Checkbox, and Radio buttons. These are handled automatically for you. If you were to try to use graphics for these types of devices, you would end up doing more work than you need to do. A suite of other properties differentiates buttons from draw objects in such areas as editing and colors and pattern display.

> • *Buttons hilite.*   The Hilite and AutoHilite properties of buttons allow you to blacken (highlight) and unblacken (de-highlight) the button as it is clicked. Graphic objects do not have this capability.

> • *Buttons can have names and icons.*   You cannot automatically display the name of a graphic object or associate an icon with it.

> • *Buttons always receive messages.*   Graphics with no handlers in their scripts *do not receive mouse messages* when you click on them. Buttons receive messages even if there is no handler for that message in the button's script.

Many times, you will not need to worry about the distinction between the button and the graphic. You can use the object that meets the design criteria of your card. However, before you use one type of object over another, you should consider what that object is doing and how it is to behave on screen.

Button Tools

There are three button-specific tools for use in SuperCard.

The Button Tool

choose button tool
set the tool [of windowDescriptor] to button

This universal tool allows you to select and edit buttons. If the editBkgnd property is set to true—that is, if you are in Background Editing mode—you can select only Background buttons with this tool. If you are in Card Editing mode, you can select buttons on either the card or background layers. See "The Pointer Tool" and "The Universal Tool" sections later in this chapter.

You can control this tool with a handler like the one shown in Script 10-2, which is a trivial handler that moves a button when you click on it.

The Button Polygon

choose button polygon tool
set the tool [of windowDescriptor] to button polygon

When you choose this tool, the mouse pointer turns into a small circle with cross hairs in it. Click where you want the polygon to start, release the mouse button, move the pointer to the next point on the polygon (a rubber band line will follow the mouse), and click again. When you click at the original starting point to close the polygon, the button will be created. If you double-click at another point, a line will automatically be drawn to the original point, and the button will be completed.

When you have finished creating the new button, the message newButton is sent to the current card. If you have the Runtime Editor installed in your project, you will be switched to the Pointer tool, and the button will be selected.

You can reshape Polygonal buttons by using the Reshape Poly command (or by using the Reshape Polygon item on the Objects menu). When you do so with a Polygonal button selected, handles will appear at each of the corners of the polygon. Clicking and dragging on one of these points moves that point to the location at which you release the mouse.

```
on mouseUp
  choose button tool
  click at the loc of card button x
  drag from the mouseLoc to 100,100
end mouseUp
```

Script 10-2.   This handler moves a button when you click on it

For all practical purposes, you cannot use this tool to create Polygonal buttons under script control. When you choose this tool under script control, the tool is in effect until you double-click the mouse, at which time the rest of the handler is executed.

The Button Rectangle Tool

choose button rectangle tool
set the tool [of windowDescriptor] to button rectangle

This tool allows you to create Rectangular buttons, which include all types of buttons except for Polygonal buttons. Use the style property to set the type of button you created.

To use this tool, click to specify the location of one corner of the button, drag to make a rectangle, and release the mouse at the other corner of the rectangle. You can also hold down the OPTION key while you click with this button, and a new button will be created that is 60 pixels wide and 20 pixels tall.

When you have finished creating the new button, the newButton message is sent to the current card. If you have the Runtime Editor installed in your project, you will be switched to the Pointer tool, and the button will be selected.

This tool can be used under script control to create new buttons, as the handler in Script 10-3 shows. This handler simply chooses the Button Rectangle tool, and then uses the Drag command to draw a rectangle with its upper-left corner located 50 pixels from the left of the window and 50 pixels from the top, and the lower-right corner 100 pixels from the left and top edges of the window.

```
on mouseUp
  choose button rectangle tool
  drag from 50,50 to 100,100
  choose browse tool
end mouseUp
```

Script 10-3.   This handler creates a new button

Button Properties

Buttons have the same properties in SuperCard that they do in Hyper-Card, with some additions.

The Style Property

get the style of buttonDescriptor
set the style of buttonDescriptor to checkBox | opaque | radioButton | rectangle | roundRect | transparent

The style of a button determines its appearance on the screen. You should use the style of a button to signal to users which functions the button performs. Button styles are discussed later in this section.

The AutoHilite Property

set the autoHilite of buttonDescriptor to true | false
get the autoHilite of buttonDescriptor

When this property of a button is set to true, highlighting of the button as you click the mouse on it is handled automatically. If the button is a Checkbox or Radio button, the hilite property of the button is set to the opposite value of what it was before it was set; otherwise, the button briefly blackens as the mouse is depressed, and then reverts to its previous color when the mouse is released.

Highlighting sets buttons apart from graphic objects, since graphic objects and fields do not highlight as they are clicked.

The ShowName Property

set the showName of buttonDescriptor to true | false
get the showName of buttonDescriptor

If this button property is true, the name of the button appears in the center of the button (centered about its loc property). For Polygonal buttons, this can lead to some strange effects. In Figure 10-2, Button A is a Rectangular button. Notice that its name appears at its center. In

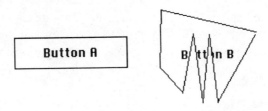

Figure 10-2.   Showing the name of a Polygonal button can give some unusual effects

contrast, since Button B is a Polygonal button, the center of the button is not entirely within the rectangle that defines the extent of the button. As a result, the button's name does not appear in its entirety.

The Icon Property
set the icon of buttonDescriptor to *number* ¦ *name*
get the icon of buttonDescriptor

This property determines which icon is displayed for buttons. The *number* corresponds to the number of the icon selected. You can also use the name of the icon.

Icons can be located in two places — as part of SuperCard's resource structure and thus part of the current project, or as part of the resource fork of the SharedFile project.

As with the showName property, if you use this property to display an icon with a Polygonal button, part of the icon may not show due to the irregular shape of the polygon.

Note: You can set this property within SuperCard, but you *cannot,* with version 1.0 of SuperCard, automatically display a scrolling list of icons as HyperCard allows you to do from the Button Info dialog box.

The Default Property
set the default of buttonDescriptor to true ¦ false
get the default of buttonDescriptor

If this button property is set to true, Rounded Rectangle buttons will have an added border three pixels thick outside its normal one-pixel-wide border. You can set this property for any kind of button, but it affects the appearance of only Rounded Rectangle buttons.

You should note that a heavy border does not necessarily a default button make. When you hit the RETURN or ENTER key on a card with a default button, messages are not sent to that button automatically. Instead, when you press the RETURN key, the ReturnKey message is sent to the current card, and when you press the ENTER key, the EnterKey message is sent to the current card. Therefore, you must create a handler for the ReturnKey and EnterKey messages *in the script of the current card.* This script should simulate the automatic highlighting of the default button so that you know the message has been received, and then send the mouseUp message to the button directly.

Suppose you have a default button called "Default" on a card and want to implement that default. In the script of the *card* you should include handlers similar to those in Script 10-4. Then, in the script of the button itself, you should include a handler for the mouseUp message, just as you do with most buttons.

Default buttons are commonly used only in dialog boxes and alerts—they are out of place in nonmodal windows. Further, Apple's *Human Interface Guidelines: The Apple Desktop Interface* (Reading, Mass.: Addison-Wesley, 1987) specifies that the action performed by the default button should be the "preferred (safest) button to use in the current situation." Do *not* create a dialog box such as the one in Figure 10-3, which will certainly cause you to lose data.

```
on returnKey
  click at the loc of cd button "default"
end returnKey

on enterKey
  click at the loc of cd button "default"
end enterKey
```

Script 10-4.   These two handlers are needed to fully implement a "default" button on a dialog box

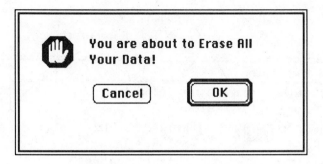

Figure 10-3.   Do *not* create dialog boxes with default buttons that cause destructive actions

The Styles of Buttons

As mentioned earlier in this chapter, different styles of buttons are used for different purposes. Their appearance on the screen should indicate to your users what function the button performs.

When you are using SuperEdit, you use different tools to create the different styles of buttons. In SuperCard, you change the style of a button by changing its style property.

Checkbox Buttons

The Checkbox button is a simple true/false button. When the button is highlighted, a small x appears in the checkbox. If the element that the button is controlling is true, the x appears, but if it is false, no x is shown.

Checkbox buttons often come in groups, as in the Page Setup dialog box shown in Figure 10-4. The checkboxes appearing at the bottom of the dialog box control certain facets of printing. Note that none, some, or all of these checkboxes can be checked at the same time; the setting of one of these boxes does not affect the settings of others. If a checkbox is not applicable in a certain situation, it should not have an x in it, and it should be disabled.

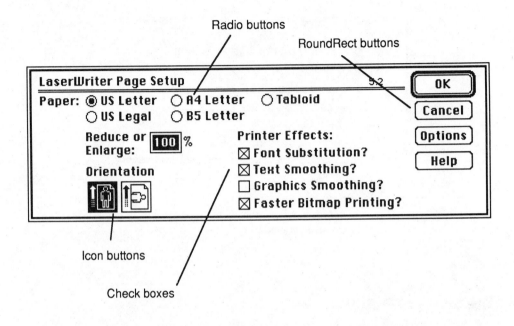

Figure 10-4.   The LaserWriter Page Setup dialog box provides examples of several styles of standard buttons

Checkbox buttons cannot have fill patterns, colors, or a shadow. They are always rectangular.

Radio Buttons

The name "radio buttons" derives from car radios: You select one station at a time by pushing the button corresponding to that station in, at which time the button for the previous station pops out. Radio buttons work the same way. When you click on one button in a set, that button highlightes and the button that was previously highlighted becomes de-highlighted (pops out). Dialog boxes may contain several sets of Radio buttons, but those sets should be clearly delineated from one another, usually by a box around each set. Silicon Beach provides a palette called Link Radio Buttons that allows you to select a group of Radio buttons and link them together to provide the automatic highlighting and de-highlighting of buttons you click on.

The Page Setup dialog box shown in Figure 10-4 features Radio buttons to indicate paper sizes. This is appropriate because you can only have one paper size at a time.

As with Checkboxes, Radio buttons may not contain fill or line patterns, colors, or shadows.

Opaque and Transparent Buttons

The names of these buttons indicate what they do. Opaque buttons are Rectangular buttons that obscure anything that lies underneath them. Transparent buttons allow whatever is underneath them to show through.

When you create a new Opaque or Transparent button, it normally has no border line (the only difference between an Opaque button and a Rectangular button). You can change this by changing appropriate properties of the button or by using the Line and Pattern palettes in the Runtime Editor. You can set the fill pattern and colors of Opaque buttons, but not, of course, of Transparent buttons.

Transparent buttons are normally used to create buttons or hot spots on the screen that are sensitive to mouse clicks, but not necessarily apparent as buttons. Transparent buttons are carryovers from HyperCard where using a Transparent button is the only way you can make a graphic, or a portion of a graphic, appear to be sensitive to mouse clicks. Transparent buttons are not needed for this purpose in SuperCard, so they will not be used as often.

Transparent buttons are distinct from hidden buttons. Although neither kind of button appears on the screen, hidden buttons do not receive messages when you click on them, and transparent buttons do.

Rectangle Buttons

Rectangular buttons are standard rectangles and feature right angles at their corners. The Button Rectangle tool in SuperCard creates this type of button.

Rounded Rectangle Buttons

Most Macintosh buttons, including the OK and Cancel buttons that appear in the Page Setup dialog box in Figure 10-4, are Rounded Rectangle buttons.

Dialog boxes should always include OK and Cancel buttons, and the one that performs the least destructive action should be the default button.

Polygon Buttons

Polygon buttons can have any shape. They are a significant enhancement over HyperCard and have a wide variety of uses. Figure 10-5, shows two examples of Polygon buttons. The button in the shape of Africa was made using the AutoTrace tool in SuperEdit; the irregular star button was made with the Button Polygon tool.

At first glance, the function of Polygon buttons might appear to be close to the function of Polygon draw objects. Buttons, however, can do three things that draw objects cannot do—they can AutoHilite, display their name, and display their icon. If you need any of these capabilities, use Polygon buttons instead of Draw polygons. Polygon buttons can be created in SuperEdit using the AutoTrace tool (see Chapter Four), or in SuperCard using the Button Polygon tool.

You can change Rectangular buttons into Polygons and vice versa by changing the style property of the button. When you change a Polygon button into a Rectangular button, that new button has the size of a rectangle that would enclose all the points of the polygon. When you change a Rectangular button into a Polygon button, each of the four corners becomes a point of the new Polygonal button, and you can use the Reshape Polygon menu item to alter its shape.

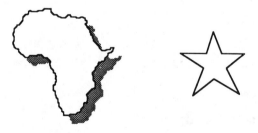

Figure 10-5.   Polygonal buttons can be used for a wide variety of purposes

Tools

Many Macintosh users take tools for granted. For example, you are probably accustomed to the changing nature of the mouse pointer as you point to different types of objects on the screen. In the Finder, the pointer has its traditional form of an arrow pointing to the left. When you move the pointer over text, it generally turns into an I-beam shape, indicating that you can click to select text. When you are using the Macintosh, you don't always consider these different shapes as tools. When you are creating applications for the Macintosh, however, you need to consider tools carefully.

Given its expanded capabilities, managing tools is quite different in SuperCard than in HyperCard. There are two main differences:

• *SuperCard has an extended set of tools.* Just as SuperCard offers a significant number of new objects beyond HyperCard's buttons and fields, it also provides new tools that allow you to create these new objects, and new tools that allow you to select only certain types of objects.

• *Tools are set for specific windows.* When you use the Choose or Set command to select a specific tool, it affects *one window only*. As long as a window is open, it remembers its tool, and only the Set or Choose command will change the tool of that window. When you bring a different window to the top of the stack of windows, the tool is switched to the current tool for that window.

When a window is first opened in SuperCard, its tool is always the Browse tool. In SuperEdit, you use the palettes at the left of the Card editor to change tools. In SuperCard, you can use the Choose command to change tools. The palettes that are part of the Runtime Editor also allow you to switch between the various tools.

The Choose Command

choose toolName tool

The Choose command switches the tool of the top window (the window specified by the topWindow( ) function) to the specified tool. You must use the trailing word "tool".

Valid toolnames are shown in Table 10-2. Note that to maintain HyperCard compatibility, the word paint is optional for all painting tools. The words "button", "draw", and "field" are not optional for those tools. Paint tools are discussed in more detail in Chapter Thirteen.

The Tool Property

get the tool [of windowDescriptor]
set the tool [of windowDescriptor] to toolName [tool]

The tool is a property that contains the name of the current tool of a specific window. You can use the Get command to determine which tool is selected for a specific window and the Set command to switch the tool of a specific window to a different tool.

If you do not specify a window when using either the Get or Set commands, the window referred to will be the top window. Note that unlike the Choose command, the use of the word "tool" is optional for the Set command.

browse	**[paint] bucket**
button	[paint] curve
button polygon	[paint] eraser
button rectangle	[paint] lasso
button roundRect	[paint] line
draw arc	[paint] oval
draw curve	[paint] pencil
draw line	[paint] polygon
draw oval	[paint] rectangle
draw polygon	[paint] regular polygon
draw straight	[paint] roundRect
draw straight line	[paint] select
field	[paint] spray [can]
field rectangle	[paint] text
field scroll	pointer
graphic	universal
[paint] brush	

Table 10-2.   The Full Complement of SuperCard's Tools

The Browse Tool

The Browse tool works in SuperCard just as it works in HyperCard. You use it to click on buttons, fields, and other objects, and standard messages are sent to those objects. When you move the Browse tool over an unlocked text field, the mouse pointer turns into a text-editing I-beam and you can select text in that field or click to enter new text. Otherwise, the Browse tool appears as a small hand with a pointing finger.

The Pointer Tool

The Pointer tool is used to select any type of SuperCard object. When this tool is in effect, the mouse pointer becomes an arrow, and you can select any object. When an object is selected, black handles appear at each of its four corners. Clicking and dragging on one of the handles resizes the object; clicking and dragging on the object itself moves the object on the card. You can select multiple objects by holding down the SHIFT key as you click on objects. (Note that selecting an object manipulates a property of that object. This will be discussed later in this chapter.)

When you use the Pointer tool, you can only select objects on either the background or card layer of the card. If the editBackground property (set and determined the same way that it is in HyperCard, or by using the appropriate item on the Runtime Editor's Edit menu) is true, you can select background objects only. Otherwise, you can select card objects only.

When using this tool, normal mouse messages—mouseEnter, mouseDown, mouseUp, and so on—are *not* sent to the object you click on. Instead, when you click on an object, the selected property of that object is set to true. Rather than the standard mouse messages, a new set of messages are sent to an object when using the Pointer tool. These messages are shown in Table 10-3.

The CardClick Message

The cardClick message is sent to a card when you click on it with the Universal or Pointer tool, or when you click on an object with one of

cardClick	dragButton	resizeButton
doubleClickButton	dragField	resizeField
doubleClickField	dragGraphic	resizeGraphic
doubleClickGraphic		

Table 10-3. A Unique Set of Messages Is Sent to Objects When Using the Pointer and Universal Tools

these tools without dragging. For this message, you can write a handler, as shown in Script 10-5, that makes it easy to edit the script of a card.

If this handler is placed either in the script of a card or up the heirarchy when you click on a card with the OPTION key held down, then you will enter the Script editor with the script of the card you clicked on.

Double-Click Messages

Double-click messages are sent to the appropriate object when you click the mouse button with the Pointer tool twice in succession on that object. Note that these double-click messages are the only messages of their type in SuperCard or HyperCard—most messages are sent with *one* action (such as mouseDown, mouseUp, and others) while these are sent with *two* actions.

In the scripts of the Runtime Editor that is installed in your projects, handlers for these messages are used to allow you to double-click on an object to get information on that object. Consequently, you

```
on cardClick
  if the option key is down then
    edit the script of the target
  end if
end cardClick
```

Script 10-5. This handler edits a script of a card when you OPTION-click on the card with the Pointer tool

should include handlers for these messages in the scripts of objects only when you do not wish to permit this action.

Drag Messages

The drag messages are sent to an object after you have used the Pointer tool to select an object and move it on the screen. One use of the drag message is to implement a grid as in HyperCard or in many drawing or painting programs. A grid constrains placement of objects on the screen, permitting their locations to be separated only by specific intervals. Script 10-6 shows a pair of handlers that work together to check the new location of an object and align it to a grid 10 pixels wide.

The first handler is for the dragGraphics message. This handler simply calls the checkGrid handler and passes to that handler the name of the target—the graphic that was dragged with the Pointer tool. Place the dragGraphic handler either in the script of a graphic or anywhere in the hierarchy that you want this message to be intercepted.

```
on dragGraphic
  checkGrid the target
end dragGraphic

on checkGrid theObject
  put 10 into gridSize
  put the loc of theObject into theLoc
  -- check the horizontal location of the object
  if item 1 of theLoc / gridSize ≠ ¬
  round(item 1 of theLoc / gridSize) then
    put round(item 1 of theLoc / gridSize) * ¬
    gridSize into item 1 of theLoc
  end if
  -- now check the vertical location and fix
  if item 2 of theLoc / gridSize ≠ ¬
  round(item 2 of theLoc / gridSize) then
    put round(item 2 of theLoc / gridSize) * ¬
    gridSize into item 2 of theLoc
  end if
  set the loc of theObject to theLoc
end checkGrid
```

Script 10-6.   These two handlers partially implement a grid system for moving objects on a card

This handler uses the local variable GridSize to hold the value of 10, the spacing of the grid in this example. The handler first stores the location of the object that received the message — held in the variable *theObject* — into the *theLoc* local variable. The first loop simply checks to see if item 1 of *theLoc* is an exact multiple of 10, using the Round function. If it is not an exact multiple of 10, the nearest number that *is* an exact multiple of 10 is stored in the first item of the *theLoc* variable. The same process is repeated for the vertical location of the object. Finally, the location of the property is set to the new value.

You could also make this grid system work for all buttons and fields by including dragButton and dragField handlers that perform the same function as the dragGraphic handler in this example.

Resize Messages

The Resize Messages are sent to objects when you click on one of the handles that appear at the corner of a resized object and drag. These messages are sent *after* an object has been resized, so they are not useful for preventing a user from resizing an object.

The resize messages can be used to implement a grid system in the same manner as the drag messages. Script 10-7 shows a checkGridSize handler that adjusts the height and width of an object to make sure that it is aligned with the grid.

```
on checkGridSize theObject
  -- this makes sure the height and width of an object
  -- is aligned with the grid
  put 10 into gridSize
  if the width of theObject / gridSize ≠ ¬
  round(the width of theObject /gridSize) then
    set the width of theObject to ¬
    round(the width of theObject /gridSize) * gridSize
  end if
  if the height of theObject / gridSize ≠ ¬
  round(the height of theObject /gridSize) then
    set the height of theObject to ¬
    round(the height of theObject /gridSize) * gridSize
  end if
end checkGridSize
```

Script 10-7.   This handler makes sure the size of an object aligns with a grid

This handler works in much the same manner as the one in Script 10-6. It should be called from handlers for the resizeButton, resizeField, and resizeGraphic messages. Before using it, you should note that when bitmap objects are resized by altering their height and width properties, they will be distorted. For more details about bitmap or paint objects, see Chapter Thirteen.

The Universal Tool

The Universal tool is similar in many respects to the Pointer tool. It is used to select and manipulate objects. The Universal tool is different from the Pointer tool in two respects:

• *You can select background or card objects with the Universal tool.* With the Pointer tool, you are forced to work in one layer only. The Universal tool, however, allows you to select *any* object, whether or not it is on the background or card layer.

• *You can select only individual objects, not groups of objects with the Universal tool.* The Universal tool has the ability to select both background and card objects, but shift-selecting to select multiple objects does not work with the Universal tool, as it does with the Pointer tool.

The Button, Field, and Graphic Tools

These three tools work as Universal tools for their types of objects only. The Button tool allows you to select buttons on either the background or card levels, the Field tool allows you to select either background or card fields, and the Graphics tool allows you to select either background or card fields (of either the bitmap or draw variety).

The Grabber Command

The Grabber is not really a tool per se because you cannot choose it and manipulate it as you would a tool. Instead, it is a command that can only be used from within a handler.

```
on mouseDown
grabber
end mouseDown
```

The Grabber command needs to be called from within a handler or other event that is triggered when the mouse button is down. While it is in effect and the mouse button is held down, the mouse pointer turns into a small hand with the fingers splayed. Dragging the mouse at this point scrolls the window to allow you to view different areas of the card. The command needs to be called when the mouse is down—in handlers for the mouseDown or mouseStillDown messages—because the command has no effect if the mouse button is up when the command is called or once the mouse button is released.

Fields

Fields, one of the primary elements of SuperCard, hold text and receive messages. SuperCard, like HyperCard, has two kinds of fields. *Background fields* appear on every card that shares the background, though the text they contain varies from card to card. *Card fields* appear only on one card.

Referring to Fields

In this chapter, we use the term *fieldDescriptor* when specifying fields. When you refer to fields, the syntax is as follows:

[background | card] field {name | number | id} [of cardDescriptor]
[of windowDescriptor] [of projectDescriptor]

When referring to a field, you should distinguish between a background field and a card field, just as you do in HyperCard. (If you do not include a specific background/card descriptor, SuperCard will assume you are referring to a background field.) You can then reference either the name, number, or ID number of the field. If the field is on a different card than the one currently in the top window, you can specify the card (by name, number, or ID) that contains the field. If it is in a window other than the one currently on top, you can specify the name, number, or ID of the field. Finally, you can refer to fields in different projects by including the full pathname of that project. For example, you might need to get a value from a field called "update" on card 2 of a window called "preferences" of a project called "Home." To get this value, you would use this statement:

```
get cd field "update" of cd 2 of window "preferences" of project
"Home"
```

Note that the project called Home does not need to be open when this command is issued, nor does the window called preferences.

Field Tools

From the discussion of SuperEdit's Card editor in Chapter Four, you will remember that SuperEdit features four separate tools for creating different kinds of fields. Despite the appearance of the Field Tools palette in the Runtime Editor, SuperCard itself includes only two tools for creating fields; different kinds of fields are created by manipulating the style property of the field. A third field tool allows you to select fields. The various types of fields are created in the Runtime Editor palette by changing the style property of new fields.

The Field Tool

choose field tool
set the tool to field [tool]

This tool allows you to select fields—and only fields—on either the background or card layers of the current card. You cannot use the SHIFT key to select multiple fields, nor can you drag to draw a rectangle and select multiple fields. Otherwise, the Field tool works in the same manner as does the Universal tool, discussed in Chapter Ten.

The Field Rectangle Tool

choose field rect[angle] tool
set the tool to field rect[angle] [tool]

This tool creates rectangular fields. While all fields are rectangular, this field specifically creates nonscrolling fields.

When you select this tool, the pointer becomes a small circle with cross hairs in it. Click to create one corner of the field, and then drag to form the rectangle of the field. When you create a new field, the message newField is sent to the current card, and up the hierarchy of message handling, as long as no handler for that message is encountered. Once you have created the new field, you will be switched to the Pointer tool (if the Runtime Editor scripts are installed in your project or the Shared File), and the new field will be selected.

The Field Scroll Tool

choose field scroll tool
set the tool to field scroll [tool]

This tool works in the same manner as the Field Rectangle tool, with the exception that fields created with this tool automatically have their style property set to scrolling.

Field Properties

The properties discussed below are particular to fields. In addition to these properties, fields also have the same location and fill properties that are discussed in Chapter Ten.

The Style Property

set [the] style of fieldDescriptor to style
get [the] style of fieldDescriptor

The style of a field determines its appearance on-screen, as well as some of its behavior. You can set this property directly from the Message box or from a script. If you are working in SuperEdit, or in the Runtime Editor in SuperCard, you can use the Object Info command to set the style of a field.

Basically, there are two general styles of fields: scrolling and rectangle. However, there are variations within the rectangle style.

Scrolling

A scrolling field features a scroll bar at the right edge of the field allowing you to type and see text that extends beyond the lower boundary of the field. If text does not scroll beyond the bottom of the field, the scroll bar is not active—clicking on the up and down scroll arrows has no effect. If text *does* extend below the bottom of the field, the scroll arrows are activated, the scroll bar becomes grey, and the scroll box appears. Figure 11-1 contains examples of both scrolling fields with a lot of text and scrolling fields with little text in them.

Rectangle

All fields are rectangular, even scrolling fields. The distinction between the rectangular field and the scrolling field is that the rectangular field

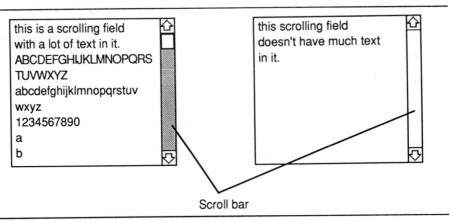

Scroll bar

Figure 11-1. When a text in a scrolling field does not extend below the boundaries of the field, the scroll bar becomes white and the scroll box disappears

does not scroll. However, rectangular field style has some variations. These variations are *opaque* and *transparent*. You can set a field to be opaque with a command such as

```
set the style of field 1 to opaque
```

Opaque fields do not permit objects that are beneath them to show through. Transparent fields *do* permit objects that are beneath them to show through.

Note: When you use the Get command to determine the style of a field, it will return either "Scrolling" or "Rectangle" only; while you can set the style of a field to "Transparent" or "Opaque," you cannot determine from SuperTalk whether a specific field is opaque or transparent.

Text Style Properties

Text in fields can be styled using a suite of properties that will be discussed later in this chapter.

Fill and Line Properties

Fill and line properties determine which patterns are used to control the appearance of fields on the screen. They are discussed in Chapter Ten.

The autoTab Property

set [the] autoTab of fieldDescriptor to true ¦ false
get [the] autoTab of fieldDescriptor

This property determines what happens when you strike the ENTER or RETURN key when the cursor is at the end of the text of a nonscrolling field. If the autoTab property is true, the next field will be selected. If it is not true, a Return character will be entered into that line, and the cursor will be moved to the next (hidden) line in the field.

The lockText Property

set [the] lockText of fieldDescriptor to true¦false
get [the] lockText of fieldDescriptor

If this property is set to true, when you move the mouse pointer over text in the field, the cursor will not turn into the text editing I-beam. You will not be able to select text in that field. If this property is set to false, you will be able to select text in the field.

When the lockText property is set to false (that is, when text selection is enabled), most mouse messages are not sent to that field. These messages are only sent when the field is locked; otherwise, you could have difficulty selecting text in fields. Mouse messages and fields will be discussed in more detail later in this chapter.

The showLines Property

set [the] showLines of fieldDescriptor to true¦false
get [the] showLines of fieldDescriptor

If this property is set to true, lines showing the baselines of text in the field will appear in the field. Figure 11-2 shows a rectangular field with the showLines property set to true.

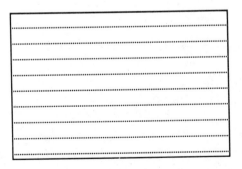

Figure 11-2.   When the showLines property of a field is true, baselines for text show in the field

The wideMargins Property

This field property, if set to true, adds extra white space between the top, horizontal edge of the field, and the text it contains. The amount of space added is determined by the textFont and textSize properties.

Figure 11-3 shows rectangular fields with the wideMargins property set to true and false.

Field Messages

Several messages are specific to fields.

The returnInField Message

This message is sent to a field when you have an insertion point or text selected in that field, and strike the RETURN key. If you have a handler for this message in the field script (or anywhere in the message hierarchy), the RETURN key is completely trapped making it impossible to enter a Return character into a field.

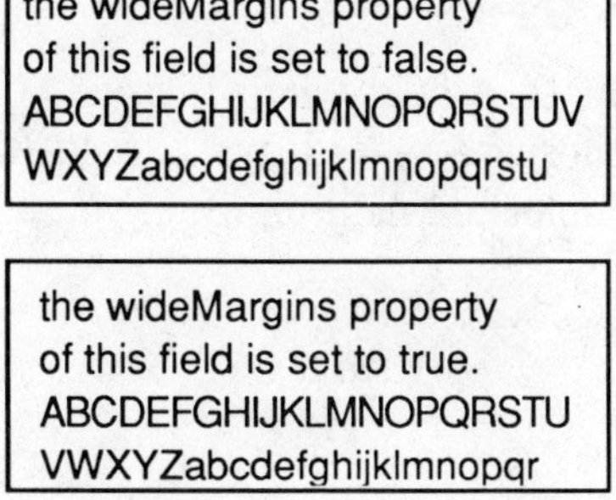

```
the wideMargins property
of this field is set to false.
ABCDEFGHIJKLMNOPQRSTUV
WXYZabcdefghijklmnopqrstu
```

```
the wideMargins property
of this field is set to true.
ABCDEFGHIJKLMNOPQRSTU
VWXYZabcdefghijklmnopqr
```

Figure 11-3. The wideMargins property adds white space at the left and right margins of a field

This message, for example, may be sent to a Default button in a dialog box. As discussed in Chapter Ten, Default buttons are executed when you hit the RETURN or ENTER key when the dialog box is visible. Commonly, you would create card-level handlers for the returnKey or enterKey messages. The problem with this solution is that it prevents you from typing characters into the Message box with the dialog box visible, because these handlers intercept the keystrokes and stop the message box statements from executing.

Instead, if your dialog box has only one field in it, you can install a handler for the returnInField (and enterInField) messages into the script of that field. This handler would then execute the Default button when you strike the RETURN key with the selection point in the field. Such a handler might read:

```
on returnInField
  click at the Loc of cd button "default"
end returnInField
```

The enterInField Message

This message is similar to the returnInField message previously discussed. It is sent to the field (and up the message hierarchy) if you strike the ENTER key when text is selected in a field or if the insertion point is in a field.

The openField Message

This message is sent to a field when text of a field is selected or the insertion point is otherwise placed into a field (that is, if you click the mouse button in an unlocked field or when you use the TAB key to select a field).

The closeField Message

This message is sent to a field after you have changed the contents of a field and then deselected the text of that field or moved the insertion point outside the field. For example, if you type some text into a field and then use the TAB key to select the next field, the closeField message is sent to the field you just left. It is also sent to the field if you click outside a changed field with the mouse button.

This message is useful for such things as verifying that the correct type of information has been entered into a field. For example, you might want a field to contain only numbers. You can write a closeField handler such as that shown in Script 11-1 to make sure that only numbers have been entered into the field.

The first two lines in this handler get the text contained in the target—the field that contains this handler is the one you want to check. These lines place the text entered into the field into a variable called *Temp*. Next the repeat loop checks each character to make sure it is a number (or a decimal point or a comma). If a character is not a number, SuperCard beeps to let you know that you have made an error and the text of the field is selected so you can correctly enter the number into the field.

Mouse Messages

As was mentioned earlier in this chapter, three mouse messages are not sent to fields when those fields are unlocked: mouseDown, mouseStill Down, and mouseUp. These messages are not sent to unlocked fields so that you can select text in those fields. Mouse Messages that *are* sent to unlocked fields are mouseEnter, mouseWithin, and mouseLeave.

```
on closeField
  put "put" && the target && "into temp" into theTask
  do theTask
  repeat with x = 1 to the number of characters in temp
    if char x of temp is not in "1234567890.," then
      beep
      select text of the target
      exit closeField
    end if
  end repeat
end closeField
```

Script 11-1.   This field handler makes sure that all the characters entered in a field are numbers

Styling Text in Fields

SuperCard fields can contain text of mixed fonts and styles. Within a SuperCard field, you can have text that is all of the same style or is of mixed styles. For example, a single word or group of characters in a SuperCard field can have its own font, style, size, or height characteristics, independent of other text in the same field.

Note that if you save the contents of a field to a text file, all the formatting in SuperCard fields will be lost. No standard method of storing formatted text on the Macintosh is available to all programs.

Each of the following properties can be changed with the Set command. As an example, here is the syntax for changing the textFont property:

```
set [the] textFont [of drawObject‖field] to fontName
```

If you specify the name of a drawText object or of a field when setting the property, and you have *not* selected any text in that field or object, all the text contained in that object or field is set to the new font. An example follows:

```
set the textFont of bg field 1 to "avant garde"
```

However, if you use a script command to change a text property of a field while you *have* text selected in that field, only the selected text is changed. By the same token, when you use the Get command to determine the style of text in a field, the style returned pertains *only* to the selected text, if any. In neither of these cases is this true of the textAlign property.

If you use this form to change the textFont,

```
set the textFont to "geneva"
```

the global property affects only new text created with the Paint Text tool (see Chapter Thirteen).

The ability to have different fonts, styles, and sizes of text in fields has some consequences. If you use the Get command to discover the font, style, or size of text in a field that has mixed styles, SuperCard returns "mixed." As mentioned earlier, you can use the Set command, with no text in a field selected, to affect globally all the text in a field. You cannot explicitly set properties to "mixed."

Background fields work a little differently because of SuperCard's ability to deal with mixed fonts. Even though a background field appears on all cards with a common background, text properties may be set separately for the background field on different cards. On one card, a specific background field might have the font of Geneva, and on a different card the same field may be in Chicago. When you create a new card in a background, the font of the background field will have the same property as the previous card (unless it is mixed).

The textFont Property

set [the] textFont [of drawObject ¦ field] to fontName
get [the] textFont [of drawObject ¦ field]

This property determines the actual font used for displaying text. The fontName can be any font currently available to SuperCard, including those installed directly into the System file, loaded with utilities such as SuitCase II, or installed directly into the SharedFile or the stand-alone application. If you specify a fontName that is not currently available, SuperCard will use the Chicago font.

If the fontName is comprised of two or more words (such as "Avant Garde"), then you should enclose the fontName in quotes. Otherwise the quotes are optional.

The textStyle Property

set [the] textStyle [of drawObject ¦ field] to styleList
get [the] textStyle [of drawObject ¦ field]

The styleList can contain any of these values: bold, condense, extend, italic, outline, plain, shadow, or underline. You can specify more than one of these styles by separating them with commas, as in the next line.

```
set the textStyle of bg field 1 to bold,italic
```

You cannot *add* styles. If a field is already bold, for example, you cannot also make it italic by setting the textStyle property to italic. You must set it to both bold and italic at the same time.

The textSize Property

set [the] textSize [of drawObject | field] to integer
get [the] textSize [of drawObject | field]

This property determines the size of the text in points. You can set the textSize to any value between 5 and 127. If you attempt to set it to a value less than 5, the textSize will be set to 5. If you attempt to set it to a value greater than 127, it will be set to 127.

As with the textFont property, if you set the textSize property of a field when text in that field is selected, only the selected text will be affected. Otherwise, all the text of a field is set.

The Get command works in a similar manner. If you use this command to determine the textSize of a particular field, the size of selected text will be returned. Otherwise, the textSize of only the selected text will be returned.

If a field or selection contains text of different sizes, the Get command will return "mixed," indicating that different sizes are represented. You cannot set the textSize of a field to "mixed."

The textHeight Property

set [the] textHeight [of drawObject | field] to auto | intger
get [the] textHeight [of drawObject | field]

This property determines the number of pixels between the baselines of adjacent lines of text. The baselines are the lines shown when the showLines field property is set to true. Figure 11-4 illustrates this property.

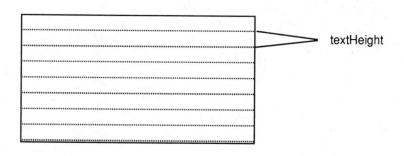

Figure 11-4.   The distance between baselines of text is controlled by the textHeight property

There are two ways to set this property. The first way is to set this property to Auto, which means that SuperCard will automatically determine the needed textHeight as you change the textSize property of text. If, for example, you have the textHeight property set to Auto and you change the textSize property, the textHeight will be adjusted accordingly to allow for the larger (or smaller) text.

The second way is to directly set the textHeight of a field to any integer between 5 and 200. In this case, the textHeight of the field becomes hardwired and will not automatically change as the textSize changes. This can lead to some unusual effects on screen, such as text being clipped off at the top of the line, so you should use this with care.

The textHeight property always affects *all* the text in a field, not just the selection.

The textAlign Property

set [the] textAlign [of drawObject | field] to left | center | right
get [the] textAlign [of drawObject | field]

This property affects how text aligns with the margins of the field. It always affects *all* the text in the field, not just a selection or a particular line.

Draw Objects and Tools

Draw Tools and Objects

The chief limitation of MacPaint and other paint-type programs (such as HyperCard) is that once you create a shape on the screen, it is very difficult to edit that shape. It becomes part of the array of pixels that make up the painting. You cannot edit the shape without painstakingly modifying each pixel that forms the shape.

MacDraw, in contrast, remembers the shapes you use. Each shape on the screen is defined by the program as a mathematical description of the shape. Instead of changing each pixel that comprises the shape, you can click on handles that define the shape and drag to change its size or form.

SuperCard gives you these MacDraw-type objects, which have four major advantages over paint objects:

- Since they are stored as mathematical descriptions of shapes, not as arrays of pixels, they can easily be reshaped, and many of their attributes—fill color, line width, and so on—can be easily changed.

- Because they are stored as mathematical descriptions, they take up less room on disk and in RAM than do bitmaps. This results in fewer memory requirements and greater display speed.

- Draw objects translate better between color and black-and-white environments than do bitmap objects. When a bitmap object is translated from color to black-and-white, or when it is displayed on a black and white screen, SuperCard must use different patterns to approximate the shades of the color bitmap. Draw objects, though, are translated in such a way that you can experiment with the fillFore and fillBack properties (discussed in Chapter Fourteen) to create objects that work effectively in both black and white and color.

• When you print a draw object, a mathematical description of the object instead of an array of pixels is sent to the printer. This means that draw objects print at the highest possible resolution, an especially important feature for laser printers, which print objects at a resolution of 300 dots per inch instead of at the screen resolution of 72 dots per inch.

In general, the advantages of draw objects over paint objects center around the fact that you can *alter* these objects once they have been created. You can resize, reshape, rotate, and change the patterns and lines that form the object, and more. For information about coloring and texturing objects, see Chapter Fourteen.

Draw Tools and Objects

SuperCard's Draw tools take advantage of tools and capabilities that are integral to the Macintosh toolbox. These graphic "primitives" are an inherent component of QuickDraw. This discussion of draw objects is based on the types of objects created.

Remember that when you use the Set or Choose command to choose a Draw tool, you must include the word *draw* as shown in the examples in this chapter. Since many of the Draw tools have direct counterparts when working with paint objects, and for the purpose of maintaining HyperCard compatibility, the "draw" identifier is necessary to specify a Draw tool.

Rectangles, Rounded Rectangles, and Ovals

These three types of draw objects work similarly. In SuperEdit, you can draw them by choosing the appropriate tool from the Draw Tools palette. In SuperCard, you can also choose from the Draw Tools Palette in the Runtime Editor, or you can use the Set Tool or Choose Tool commands to select the following tools.

choose Draw Rect[angle] tool
choose Draw RoundRect tool
choose Draw Oval tool
set the tool of windowDescriptor to draw Rect[angle] tool
set the tool of windowDescriptor to draw roundRect tool
set the tool of windowDescriptor to draw Oval tool

When you use one of these tools, you first click at the location at which you want to place one corner of the object, and then drag and release the mouse to define the opposite corner of the object. To constrain the shape to a perfect square or circle, hold down the SHIFT key as you drag.

When you draw a rectangle, the corners of the rectangle define the actual appearance of the shape. If you draw an oval, that oval will be the largest oval that will fit within the confines of the rectangle. Figure 12-1 shows a rectangle on the left, and on the right an oval that fits within the same rectangular area. You can see this in SuperCard by drawing a rectangle, and then typing: **set the style of card graphic 1 to oval**, where card graphic 1 is your rectangle. The rectangle will be transformed into an oval that fits exactly inside the rectangular area. If you click on the oval, handles will appear at the four corners of the rectangle. Clicking and dragging on one of these corners resizes the oval.

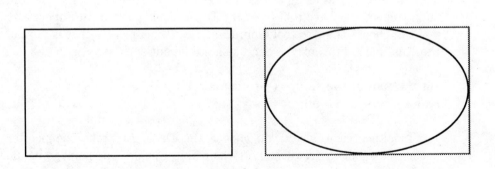

Figure 12-1.   An oval is defined by the points of a rectangle that contains the oval

Round rectangles are the same as normal rectangles, except that they have rounded corners. You can control the rounding of corners with the roundHeight and roundWidth properties.

The roundHeight and roundWidth Properties

set the roundHeight of objectDescriptor to integer
set the roundWidth of objectDescriptor to integer
get the roundHeight of objectDescriptor
get the roundWidth of objectDescriptor

These properties determine the degree of rounding of roundRect objects. Predictably, the roundHeight property determines the degree of vertical rounding of the corner, and the roundWidth property determines the degree of horizontal rounding.

As Figure 12-2 illustrates, you can visualize this rounding as a specification for an oval that would fit exactly in the corner of the rectangle. The roundHeight equals the height of such an imaginary oval, while the roundWidth equals the width of the imaginary oval.

Arcs

You can create arcs using either SuperEdit or SuperCard. In SuperEdit, simply choose the Arc tool from the Draw Tools palette. In SuperCard, you can choose the Arc tool from the Draw Tools palette that is part of the Runtime Editor, or you can use a statement such as:

set the tool of topwindow( ) to draw arc tool
choose draw arc tool

In either case, when you choose the Draw Arc tool, the pointer becomes a small circle with a cross hair in it. Click at one point to define the beginning of the arc, and drag to form the end of the arc.

The Arc tool always creates arcs that are 90-degree sections of ovals. If you want to draw a 90-degree section of a *circle*, hold down the SHIFT key as you draw the arc. When you draw a new arc, its starting point is always 0 degrees and its end point is always 90 degrees. You

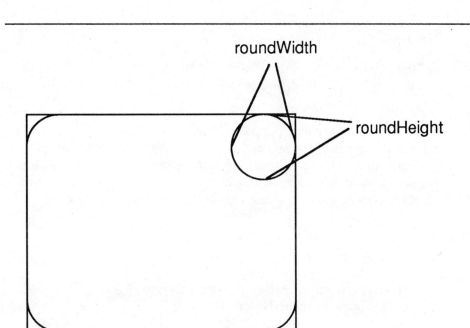

Figure 12-2.   The roundHeight and roundWidth properties are expressed in terms of the height and width of an oval that fits exactly into the corners of the rounded rectangle

can, however, set two properties of arc objects to control the size of the arc, its starting point, and its end point.

Note that when you select an arc, handles appear that define a rectangle so that it contains the entire arc. The upper-left corner of the rectangle is the arc's starting location; the lower-left corner is the center of the oval or circle that contains the arc; the lower-right corner is the ending point of the arc; and the upper-right corner completes the rectangle. Use the Reshape Arc command to change the arc itself. When you fill an arc, the entire area of the circle or oval that the arc contains is filled.

Arc Properties

Angles have two properties, startAngle and arcAngle, that allow you to control the orientation and shape of the angle.

The startAngle Property

set the startAngle of objectDescriptor to integer
get the startAngle of objectDescriptor

This property determines the point on a circle or an oval that represents the starting point of the angle. You can set this point at any number. If you set it to a negative number, the starting point will be set to 0; if you set it to a number greater than 359, it will be set to 359. Changing the startAngle of an angle does not change the arc that the angle subtends.

The arcAngle Property

set the arcAngle of objectDescriptor to integer
get the arcAngle of objectDescriptor

This property determines the arc of a circle or oval subtended by the arc. If you set the arcAngle to an angle less than 0 degrees, the angle is set to 0 degrees and effectively disappears from the screen. If you set it to a value larger than 360 degrees, the angle is set to 360 degrees. The arcAngle property does not affect the startAngle property of the arc.

Figure 12-3 shows two angles. The top angle is a standard 90 degree angle drawn with the Arc tool. Its startAngle is 0 degrees, its arcAngle is 90 degrees, and therefore its ending point (labeled endAngle) is 90 degrees. The second angle was formed with two actions. First, the startAngle was changed to 10 degrees with the statement **set the startAngle of cd grc "arc2" to 10**. Second, the statement **set the arcAngle of cd grc "arc2" to 80** produced an arc with a starting point of 10 degrees, an angle of 80 degrees, and an ending point of 90 degrees.

Though endAngle is not a property of arcs, you can derive the endAngle by adding the startAngle to the arcAngle.

You can create some interesting animations using the startAngle property. Create an arc on the screen and open its script. Type into it a script such as the following.

```
on mouseUp
  repeat 36
    get the startAngle of me
    if it > 358 then put 0 into it
    set the startAngle of me to it + 10
  end repeat
end mouseUp
```

When you click on the arc, it will "sweep" around the oval or circle it forms, adding 10 degrees to its startAngle each time. It will finish at the point where it started.

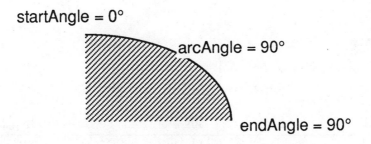

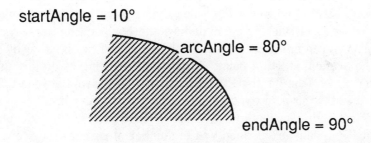

Figure 12-3.   Arcs have two properties: the startAngle determines the point on an oval at which the angle starts; the arcAngle determines the number of degrees the angle subtends

The Reshape Arc Command
Reshape Arc

In SuperEdit, you can reshape an arc by using the Reshape Arc command on the Objects menu, with an arc selected. In SuperCard, you can execute this command from the Message box or a script (as long as the Pointer or Universal tool is in use, and an arc is selected) receiving the same result.

When you reshape an arc, handles will appear at both ends of the arc. You can click and drag on a handle to change its location on the oval or circle.

Polygons

choose draw poly[gon] tool
set the tool of windowDescriptor to draw poly[gon] tool

In SuperEdit, you can choose this tool from the Draw Tools palette. In SuperCard, you can use it with one of the above statements, or choose it from the Draw Tools palette in the Runtime Editor.

When you use the Draw Polygon tool, clicking the mouse at one point defines the starting location for the polygon. When you release the mouse button, and move the pointer on the screen, a line follows the pointer around. Clicking again defines another point on the polygon, and so on. You can finish drawing the polygon in two ways: either by clicking at the original starting point, or by double-clicking at a different point. If you choose the latter method, a line will be drawn between that point and the starting point; you cannot have "open" polygons.

Rectangles, ovals, and arcs are defined with a limited number of points. Polygons are defined by the number of corners they contain (the points property will be discussed in the next section). For this reason, they are less efficient than the other objects, and complex polygons will take up more room than rectangles on disk and in RAM.

The points Property

get the points of objectDescriptor
set the points of objectDescriptor to list

The points property contains a list of numbers separated by commas. Each pair of numbers defines a corner of the object, with the horizontal location first, followed by the vertical location of that corner. The first and last sets of numbers are the same; that is, the starting point is the same as the ending point.

The points property has several uses. One is for animation, which is discussed in Chapter Fifteen. You can also use the points property to "smooth" an object; a palette for this purpose is included in the Palette Projects folder and is accessible from the Runtime Editor.

Note that SuperCard has no "Regular Polygon" tool to perform the function that tool has in HyperCard. Here is a short function that returns the number of sides of a polygonal object in SuperCard:

```
function countSides theObject
  if the style of theObject is "rectangle"¬
  or the style of theObject is "roundRect" then
    return 4
  end if
  if the style of theObject is "polygon" then
    return (the number of items¬
    in the points of theObject / 2) -1
  end if
end countSides
```

To call this function, type **countSides("Cd grc 1")** into the Message box. Note that you must enclose the objectDescriptor in quotes.

Aside from the points property, polygons also have rectangle properties, as discussed in Chapter Ten. You can see this when you select a polygon with the Pointer tool; handles appear at the corners of a rectangle that completely encloses all the points of the polygon. By clicking and dragging on one of these points, you can reshape the polygon and move all the points that comprise the polygon. The polygon can be scaled by scaling the rectangle that encloses it. The handler on the next page scales a specified object to a specified value.

```
on scaleIt theObject,theFactor
  set the height of theObject to¬
  round(the height of theObject * theFactor)
  set the width of theObject to¬
  round(the width of theObject * theFactor)
end scaleIt
```

You could use this command with a statement such as **scaleIt "card graphic 1",2**, which would double the size of the object in both its horizontal and vertical directions. If you want to make the object smaller, a value such as .50 would halve the size of the object.

The Reshape Polygon Command

Reshape Poly[gon]

In SuperEdit, you can reshape a polygon by clicking on that polygon and choosing the Reshape Polygon command from the Objects menu. You can do the same thing in SuperCard if you are using the Runtime Editor, or you can include this command in a script.

When the command is executed, handles appear at the points of all selected polygons. You can click and execute on one of these points and drag it to a new location. The command stays in effect until you click at a point on the card that is not a point of the polygon.

The Rotate Polygon Command

Rotate Poly[gon]

This command rotates a selected polygon 90 degrees. If several polygons are selected, all will be rotated. You can use the Rotate Polygon command on the Objects menu in SuperEdit or SuperCard, or issue this command yourself in a script or the Message box.

Curves

choose draw curve tool
set the tool of windowDescriptor to draw curve tool

Curves behave in much the same manner as polygons; they have the same points properties, and the Reshape Polygon and Rotate Polygon tools have an effect on them. Indeed, when you get the style of a curve object, the word *polygon* is returned.

Curves differ from polygons in the *way* that their tools work. In either SuperEdit or SuperCard, when you use the Draw Curve tool (called the "Freehand" tool in the SuperEdit documentation), new points are created as long as you hold down the mouse button. Click at the starting point of the curve, hold down the button, and trace a shape with the mouse. When you release the button, an enclosed polygon will be completed as it is with the Polygon tool, and the object will be created.

You can also use the AutoTrace tool in the Draw Tools palette of SuperEdit to trace bitmap graphics and make Polygon tools of them. Use of this tool is discussed in Chapter Four.

Lines

choose Draw line tool
choose draw straight [line] tool
set the tool [of windowDescriptor] to draw line
set the tool [of windowDescriptor] to draw straight [line]

Creating lines is simple. Choose the tool, click at the starting point of the line, and then drag. A line will follow your mouse around until you release the mouse button. If you are using the normal Line tool, you will be able to draw lines in any direction. If you are using the Straight Line tool, lines will be drawn only in horizontal or vertical directions.

The SuperEdit manual calls the Straight Line tool the "Perpendicular Line" tool, but SuperTalk refers to it as the Straight Line tool.

Text

Draw text has several advantages over text in bitmap objects or fields, but also one disadvantage. Draw text's advantages are

- If it is placed on a background, it appears on all the cards that share that background. This makes Draw Text useful for creating labels for fields and other functions.

- It prints as a "true" font, not as a bitmap version of the font. This means that if you are using a font designed for the LaserWriter, the text will be accurately scaled and positioned.

- It can be edited. Unlike paint text, draw text can be clicked on with the Draw Text tool and edited. You have the ability to mix text styles (including fonts, sizes, and styles) on a single line of text.

The main disadvantage of using draw text is that the Draw Text tool is not currently implemented in SuperCard, which means that, while you *can* edit the text, you can do so *only* when using SuperEdit, and not with SuperCard.

Painting

Although SuperCard's draw-type graphics boast a number of benefits, they also suffer from a number of drawbacks. Because they are generally composed of simple lines and patterns, it is difficult to generate subtle effects with them. Attractive illustrations, as well as accurate depictions of real world objects, require more flexibility than draw-type objects allow. SuperCard's paint tools let you create these effects. When you import images that were created by digitizers, these images are treated as bitmaps in SuperCard.

The Bit Box

SuperCard handles graphics differently than HyperCard. In SuperCard, all bitmap graphics are contained in rectangular objects. In HyperCard, all graphics are part of the card or background. As soon as you create a graphic on the card, the bits that comprise that graphic blend into the bitmap that composes the card picture.

A crucial difference between the way SuperCard handles bitmap or paint graphics and the way it handles draw-type graphics is that a draw-type graphic itself makes up the object. A bitmap graphic, on the other hand, always exists within a rectangle that encloses the painting.

T
H
I
R
T
E
E
N

275

You must create this rectangle, called the "bit box" or "bit bucket," before you can paint on a card. You can see this when using the Runtime Editor. Select "Paint Tools" from the Palettes menu, and the palette showing the Painting tools appears. Choose the paint brush or any other Painting tool, and click on an area of the card that does not contain a paint graphic. When you click, the mouse pointer turns into a crosshair and you can draw the bit box rectangle on the screen. When you release the mouse button, the rectangle is shown as a dotted line and you can then use the paint brush to paint within that bit bucket.

As soon as the bit box is created, the newGraphic message is sent to the current card and up the hierarchy of message handling.

Note: If, after creating the bit box, you do not actually paint within that bit box, the box disappears and, in effect, no new graphic object is created. A bit box only exists *as long as a nonwhite pixel is in that bit box.* This means that if you erase the contents of a bit box, you have, in effect, deleted that object. Note that when you do so, the deleteGraphic message is *not* sent to that object, even though it is deleted!

It is important to remember that even when you use SuperCard's paint tools under script control, you must first have a bit box in which to paint. Existing HyperCard scripts that draw on cards with no illustrations will have some compatibility problems with SuperCard, since there will be no bit box to hold the graphic.

When painting under script control, then, it is important to know whether the point *at which you start the painting* is within a paint graphic. Only the starting point is important. If you start painting at a point that is not within a bitmap object, your first step will be to create the bit box. If you start painting within an existing bitmap graphic, only the painting that falls within the rectangle of that graphic will appear on the card.

Script 13-1 shows a function that determines whether a given point falls within an existing bitmap object. This handler takes two parameters—the horizontal location of the point (theLeft) and its vertical location (theTop). It then places those two points, separated by a comma, into a local variable called *thePoints.* The handler contains two loops, one for background objects, and one for card objects. If the editBkgnd property is true, all new graphics will be placed on the background layer, so only those objects will need to be checked. If it is false, only card-level objects need be checked.

```
function inGraphic theLeft,theTop
  put theLeft & "," & theTop into thePoints
  if the editBkgnd is true then
    repeat with x = 1 to the number of background graphics
      if the style of bg graphic x is "bitmap" then
        if thePoints is within the rect of bg grc x then
          return true
        end if
      end if
    end repeat
  else
    repeat with x = 1 to the number of cd graphics
      if the style of cd graphic x is "bitmap" then
        if thePoints is within the rect of cd grc x then
          return true
        end if
      end if
    end repeat
  end if
  return false
end inGraphic
```

Script 13-1.   This function checks to see if a specified point lies within an existing bit box

The repeat loops simply check each object, first determining if the object is a bitmap object. If it is, the Is Within function compares the points passed to the function with the Rect property of the object in question. If the points are within the rectangle of the object, the function returns "true" to the statement that called it. Otherwise, after all the objects have been checked, the function returns "false."

Paint Tools

The Paint tools are used to create and modify bitmap or paint graphics. To use any of these tools, you must first use the Choose or Set commands to make the tool active. If the Runtime Editor is installed in the project you are using, you can also choose the tool you want from the Paint Tools palette.

The Set command and paint tools syntax is

Set the tool [of windowDescriptor] to [paint] toolName

where toolName is one of the valid tools listed in this chapter. Chapter Ten discusses the Set command in more detail.

The Choose command has this syntax,

Choose [paint] toolName tool

where toolName is one of the tools listed below. Note that in the discussions of the following tools, the word *Paint* precedes each tool name. When using the Choose or Set commands to select a different tool, this word is optional.

Remember that you cannot alter bitmap graphic objects in the same way you can edit draw-type objects. To change a shape on the screen you have to redraw the object. For example, if you draw an oval that is filled with solid black, you cannot simply select the object and choose a different pattern from the Patterns palette to alter the fill pattern.

Most of these tools work in SuperCard in the same manner in which they work in SuperEdit's Card editor. Exceptions are noted throughout this chapter.

Using the Paint Tools Under Script Control

Using the Paint tools under manual control (that is, with the mouse) is straightforward. Most of the tools work the same way in SuperCard that they do in SuperEdit.

Under script control, you use the Drag or Click command, which simulates the physical activity of the mouse.

The Drag Command

Drag from *location1* to *location2* [with keyModifier]

The Drag command simulates pointing to one location (location1), holding down the mouse button, dragging the mouse to another location (location2), and releasing the button. The variables *location1* and *location2* are sets of two integers separated by a comma. In each set, the first number indicates the number of pixels from the left edge of the card, and the second number indicates the number of pixels from the top of the card.

The optional keyModifier allows you to specify a modifier key to be used with the drag command. Allowable modifiers are shiftKey, commandKey, and optionKey. You can use several key modifiers by separating them with a comma. For example, when you hold down the SHIFT key while using the Rectangle tool, a perfect square is drawn. The Super-Talk statement for handling this is

drag from 10,10 to 100,100 with shiftKey

Since you use the Paint Bucket and Paint Text tools by clicking at a location, don't use the Drag command when using these tools.

The Click Command

Click at location

The Click command simulates pointing at a specific location and clicking the mouse button. As with the Drag command, location is a set of two integers separated by a comma. The first integer is the horizontal location; the second is the vertical location.

Using the Click command with the Paint Curve, Polygon, Oval, Lasso, Line, Rectangle, and Select tools has little effect because these tools require dragging.

The Paint Brush Tool

With the mouse held down, the Paint Brush tool paints using the current fillPattern, fillFore, and fillBack properties if you move it within an existing or new bit box. You can change the shape of the brush by using the brush property discussed later in this chapter, or with the Brushes palette in the Runtime Editor. You can change these properties under script control (see Chapter Fourteen) or by using the Patterns and Colors palettes in the Runtime Editor.

The Paint Bucket

The Paint Bucket pours paint of the current fill pattern into an *enclosed space,* which is a space that is completely surrounded by nonwhite pixels. If the outline you are filling has a gap of even one pixel, the paint will flow out of the enclosed space and fill the entire bit bucket. In SuperEdit, you can use the Undo command to rectify this disaster. As SuperCard has no Undo command, you can use the Revert command, which reloads from disk the last version of the card you saved (use the Save Card command, discussed with the Revert command in Chapter Seven, to save the card before using the Paint Bucket).

The Paint Curve, Paint Polygon, and Paint Regular Polygon Tools

You can choose any of these tools under script control, but only one of them—the Paint Polygon tool—is available on the Paint Tools palette, even though they all behave the same way. The Paint Polygon tool works in the same manner as the Draw Polygon tool: click at a starting point in a bit box, move the mouse pointer, click again, and repeat the process. When you click at the starting point or when you double-click the mouse, the polygon is closed and filled with the current pattern.

The Paint Eraser Tool

The Paint Eraser tool simply erases all pixels it passes over while you hold the mouse down. It erases a square 16 pixels on each side.

Remember that if you erase all the pixels in an existing bit box, you have, in effect, deleted that bit box.

The Paint Lasso Tool

The Paint Lasso tool is used to select nonwhite pixels in an existing bit box. It works in the same manner as it does in SuperEdit: hold down the mouse button while you drag to encircle an area of a graphic. When you release the button, the lasso will "shrink" to select only the nonwhite pixels in the area enclosed. You can then Cut or Copy this selection, or hold down the mouse button and drag to move it.

The Paint Line Tool

This tool creates lines of the current pen and line settings in a new or existing bit box. You can use the lineSize, penBack, penFore, penHeight, penPat, and showPen properties to control the type of line drawn. If you are using the Runtime Editor, you can then use the Lines, Patterns, and Colors palettes to control these properties.

The Paint Rectangle, RoundRect, and Oval Tools

These tools work in SuperCard in the same manner as they work in SuperEdit: they create new shapes filled with the current patterns.

The Paint Pencil Tool

The Paint Pencil tool works in the same manner in SuperCard as it does in SuperEdit, with one exception. In SuperEdit, you can hold down the OPTION key while clicking and enter the Zoom Bits mode for magnified editing of a bitmap. SuperCard has no Zoom Bits mode, so OPTION-clicking with the Pencil tool has no effect.

The Paint Select Tool

The Paint Select tool selects rectangular areas of bitmap graphics. With the pointer at one corner of the area you want to select, hold down the mouse button and drag to define the rectangle. Once an area is selected, you can Cut or Copy it. You can also click and drag within it to move it within the bit object, or you can hold down the OPTION key and drag the selection to duplicate it.

The Paint Spray Can Tool

When using a script to select this tool, the words *paint* and *can* are optional. This tool works in SuperCard as it does in SuperEdit.

The Paint Text Tool

With this tool you can type text into a new or existing bit box. The text will have the font, size, and style of the current global properties controlling text appearance. These properties are discussed later in this chapter, and in more detail in Chapter Eleven.

Paint Properties

Most of the properties that affect SuperCard's other objects (buttons, fields, and draw objects) also affect paint objects. The crucial difference is that with these other types of objects, you can change the properties *after you have created the object*. You cannot do so with bitmap objects. Instead, global properties affect all *new* paintings created in bit boxes.

Brush

set the brush to integer

SuperCard supports 40 different brush shapes, which are easily visible using the Brushes palette in the Runtime Editor. You can use this palette to choose a particular brush manually, or you can set this property under script control.

Legal brush values range from 1 to 40. If you attempt to use a number smaller than 1, the brush will be set to 1; if you set the brush to a number greater than 40, the brush will be set to 40.

Using SuperEdit, you can modify brush shapes. Modifications you make will affect the project, and modified brushes will be available in SuperCard. However, you cannot modify brush shapes in SuperCard, nor does the Brushes palette display modified brush shapes.

Fill Properties

The fill properties govern the patterns that are used by the Paint Brush, Bucket, Oval, Polygon, and Rectangle tools. They are: fillBack, fillFore, and fillPat. These properties are discussed in Chapter Fourteen.

Pen and Line Properties

The pen and line properties control the lines drawn by the Line, Rectangle, Oval, RoundRect, and Polygon tools. These properties are discussed in Chapter Ten.

Text Properties

The text properties control the appearance of text created by the Paint Text tool. These properties are discussed in Chapter Ten.

There are two ways of setting the text properties of bitmaps. First, you can set the global properties. These settings affect *all new text* created with the Paint Text tool. Second, you can change *existing* paint text, providing you do so *immediately* after you create it—that is, before you click the mouse anywhere else. For example, if you type **SuperCard** into a bit box, you can then use the Font, Style, and Size menu items on the Runtime Editor's Objects menu to change it. However, once you click elsewhere on the card, the new text you have typed becomes "frozen" into the array of pixels that comprise the bitmap object and you cannot change that text.

The Reset Paint Command

The Reset Paint command sets all painting properties to their default values. The defaults are shown in Table 13-1.

Resizing and Cropping Paint Objects

You can resize and crop a graphic object or bit box with the Pointer, Universal, or Graphic tools. To resize a graphic, click on the graphic

Property	Default Value
Brush	1
fillBack	1
fillFore	256
fillPat	22
lineSize	1
penFore	256
penHeight	1
penPat	12
penWidth	1
showFill	true
showPen	true
textAlign	left
textFont	geneva
textHeight	16
textSize	12
textStyle	plain

Table 13-1.   The Values to Which Painting Properties Are Set by the Reset Paint Command

object with the tool and four handles will appear at its corners. Click on one of the handles and drag to reshape the bit box. If you hold down the SHIFT key while resizing the bit box, you will be constrained to horizontal or vertical resizing only.

If you make the bit box smaller, any painting obscured by the smaller bit box will be lost. This is called *cropping*. In SuperEdit, you can use the Undo command to prevent cropping. In SuperCard, however, you should use the Save Card command before resizing the graphic and then use the Revert command to reload the last saved version of the card from disk.

If you hold down the OPTION key while you resize the object or bit box with the mouse, the painting within the bit box will be resized along with the bit box itself. If you change the rect properties of a bitmap object, the painting it contains is scaled automatically.

Paint Messages

Only one message specific to painting is sent in SuperCard. For messages that are sent to all types of graphics (such as deleteGraphic, doubleClickGraphic, and dragGraphic), see Chapter Twelve.

Graphic objects, including both draw and bitmap objects, do *not* receive mouse messages unless their scripts actually contain something (as was discussed in Chapters Ten and Twelve). As little as a single character qualifies a graphic object to receive messages. This means that functions, such as Me and the Target, do not work with graphic objects that do not contain scripts.

The CardPaint Message

This message is sent to the current card whenever a paint tool is changing a bitmap object. It is *not* sent when a paint tool is creating a new bit box. For example, if in a card script you have this handler

```
on cardPaint
  beep
end cardPaint
```

and you use the Paint Brush tool to create a new bit box, SuperCard will allow you to create the bit box. When you release the mouse button *after* painting with the brush, SuperCard will beep.

The CreatePaint Property

set the createPaint to true | false
get the createPaint

This global property determines whether or not a Paint tool is permitted to create a new bit box. When the createPaint property is set to "true," new bit boxes are permitted, otherwise they are not allowed. Even if the property is set to "false," you can still modify existing paintings.

If the createPaint property is set to "false," nothing happens when you attempt to use a Paint tool: moving it around the card with the mouse down has no effect unless you go into an existing bit box.

Because createPaint is a global property, it is not set for a particular card, background, or window. If you want to set it to "false" to prohibit creation of new bit boxes on a particular card, you need to set it when that card is opened. Script 13-2 shows openCard and closeCard handlers that take care of this.

When the card containing the openCard handler is opened, the current state of the createPaint property is saved into a global variable, paintDefault, and the createPaint property is then set to "false" to prohibit creation of a new bit box on the card. When you close the card (either to move to another card or to close the window containing the card), the createPaint property is set to the value it had before it was set to "false" for this card.

One problem with this approach is that you might want to prohibit creation of new bit boxes in a certain card that is open at the same time other windows are open. This handler would also prohibit creation of new bit boxes on those other cards. You can use the group of update-Window handlers shown in Chapter Seven to set and reset this property when a card is brought to the front of the stack of windows or sent behind other windows.

```
on openCard
  global paintDefault
  put the createPaint into paintDefault
  set the createPaint to false
end openCard

on closeCard
  global paintDefault
  set the createPaint to paintDefault
end closeCard
```

Script 13-2.   These handlers set the createPaint property when the card containing the handlers is opened and closed

Color and Ink Effects

F O U R T E E N

In the early 1960s when color television first came along, television producers were obsessed with the new tools at their disposal. The name of Walt Disney's show was changed from "The Wonderful World of Disney" to "The Wonderful World of Color," and had a theme song with the lyrics "the world is a carousel of color, color, color." Such is the novelty of new toys.

SuperCard users will likely feel the same way at the start: the color tools SuperCard gives you are such an advance over HyperCard's, the temptation is to use them extensively. In many situations, these tools are appropriate—color carries a lot more information than does black and white. However, you must pay a price for color—both in disk space and speed.

Color takes up a lot more room on disk and in memory than does black and white. And because it occupies so much room, it takes longer for SuperCard to display a color image to display a black-and-white one. For large color bitmap images, you can lose a great deal of performance.

Also, if you are developing applications for others, you should consider whether these users will have color. Many users have Mac Pluses or Mac SEs, which cannot display color. If this is the case, you have two solutions. One is to use color, and notify potential purchasers or users that color graphics will not look right on their machine. The other solution is to create two versions of a project: one that uses color and one that does not.

Nevertheless, color has its appeal. If pictures convey information that words cannot, so does color convey information that black and white cannot. In this chapter, when we speak of color, we mean 8-bit color *or shades of grey*. When we speak of black and white, we mean 1-bit graphics, as on the Macintosh Plus and SE screens.

Color and the Macintosh

The Macintosh was originally capable of displaying only two colors on its screen: black and white. A pixel or picture element on the screen could be either black or white with no other choices. Each pixel on the screen was represented by a single bit in memory. (A bit is the smallest unit of computer memory; it can have a value of either 0 or 1, "true" or "false.") If the bit had a value of 0, the pixel associated with that bit was white; if it had a value of 1, the pixel was black. Programs were able to work with these black-and-white graphics using QuickDraw, built into the Macintosh.

Color is more complicated. Instead of using just one bit per pixel, more bits are allowed for each, depending on the capabilities of the interface board that controls your monitor. A board that supports two bits per pixel has 2^2, or 4 colors available. A board that supports four bits per pixel has 2^4, or 16 colors available. Most color interface boards for the Macintosh II are capable of 8-bit color: 256 colors on the screen at any one time. This capability is determined by the amount of RAM memory residing on the interface board that controls the monitor. When Apple produced the Macintosh II, the first of the line with color capabilities, QuickDraw was extended into Color QuickDraw.

Color QuickDraw is theoretically capable of working with as many as 2^{48}, about 281 trillion colors. This limit is not implemented; instead, Color QuickDraw is "limited" to 24 bits or 16.7 million colors. This is true even with the recently announced "32-bit" color; the remaining 8 bits are reserved for other uses.

The remainder of this discussion assumes 16.7 million colors as the maximum color universe for the Macintosh. Because SuperCard is designed to work with 8-bit color, the color we discuss will actually be the 256 colors available for display at any one time as a subset of the 16.7 million possibilities.

Red, Green, and Blue

How are the numbers for 16.7 million colors "mapped" to the actual on-screen colors? How does the Macintosh convert numbers to colors? The Macintosh, like most other personal computers, uses three primary colors, red, green, and blue (sometimes called "RGB color"). Three signals for the monitor are generated for each pixel on the screen. The signal tells the monitor how much of each color to blend in each pixel. Each color in the mix is represented by a number, which can have any value between 0 and 65535.

Figure 14-1 illustrates what Apple calls "RGB space," which you can think of as a three-sided pyramid representing all the possible values each color can have. Pure black, in which the color has a zero value for each of its red, green, and blue portions, is at the apex of the pyramid. The bottom corners represent pure red, green, and blue. Pure white, in which the value of all three elements of a color is the maximum, is at the middle of the base of the pyramid. A line drawn from that point to the apex of the pyramid represents shades of grey.

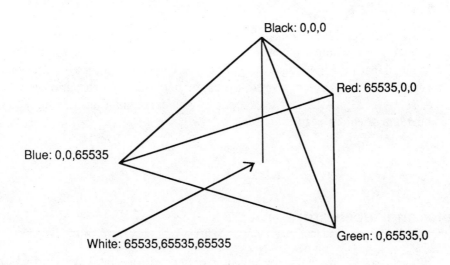

Figure 14-1.   RGB space takes the form of a pyramid, in which black is at the apex, and red, green, and blue are at the corners

Color Lookup Tables

At any one time, the Macintosh can display 256 colors out of about 16.7 million. These 256 colors are contained in color lookup tables, or *cluts*. Each color in a clut is assigned a value from 0 to 255. A table in memory maintains a record of the various red, green, and blue values that are assigned to each of the 256 colors. For example, a clut with a pure, bright blue has three values assigned to it: one for the red portion of the color, one for the green, and one for the blue. In this case, assume that the value for the blue is 65535 (the maximum), and the value for the red and green colors is 0. The color might be number 64 on the clut; when the Macintosh wants to display this color, it looks up the number 64 on the table and finds the values for red, green, and blue that are contained in that color. The Macintosh then instructs the video circuits to display a particular pixel with the values of 65535 for blue, and 0 for green and red.

You can directly manipulate these cluts with SuperEdit, which allows you to create new cluts or edit existing ones.

Additive Colors

Macintosh colors are *additive*, which means that different colors are combined to produce mixes of colors. Because the Macintosh produces light instead of reflecting it, mixing equal values of red, green, and blue results in a white color; *no* red, green, or blue results in black. Colors on a real paint palette are *subtractive*, which means that mixing equal portions of colors results in dark colors.

Color and SuperCard

SuperCard 1.1 works in either of two modes: one-bit black-and-white graphics (of the type supported by the standard Mac Plus and SE monitors), and 8-bit color or grayscale (of the type supported by Apple's

Enhanced Graphics Adaptor and compatibles). When you start Super-Card or SuperEdit, it determines what kind of system you are using and adjusts accordingly. If you are using 2- or 4-bit color monitors, Super-Card acts as if you were running on a 1-bit black-and-white monitor.

SuperCard determines whether or not you are using color *when the program starts*. That means, if your monitor is set for less than 8 bits per pixel when you start SuperCard and you use the Monitors section of the control panel to change the monitor to 8-bit color, you're out of luck. You will need to quit SuperCard change the Monitors setting, and then restart SuperCard.

If you use the control panel to switch from 8 bits per pixel to fewer, SuperCard presents you with an alert requesting that you quit Super-Card and start again.

The ColorWorld Property

the colorWorld

Your scripts can use this property to determine whether or not the machine on which they are currently running is using color (8-bit color or grayscale) or not. As mentioned, the colorWorld property is set when SuperCard starts—you cannot change the color state of the monitor in midstream and expect SuperCard to notice it.

One use of this function is to notify users that your project requires color. A small handler for this purpose is

```
on openProject
  if the colorWorld is "false" then
    answer "This project requires color!"¬
    with "Drat!"
  end if
end openProject
```

Working with Cluts

As discussed, the Macintosh and SuperCard use cluts to determine which 256 colors are displayed on the screen at any one time. In SuperEdit, you can control which colors are part of any one clut.

Creating and Editing Cluts

In SuperEdit, you create a clut by clicking on the Resource icon in the project Overview. Then, double-click on the Resource icon, and a dialog box will ask you what kind of resource you want to create. Click on the clut Radio button and then on the OK button. When you open the new resource by double-clicking on it, you are presented with a dialog similar to the one shown in Figure 14-2.

This dialog box shows all the colors in the standard system clut supplied by Apple. The right portion of the dialog box displays the 256 colors that comprise the clut.

To pick a different color out of the 16.7 million available to you, double-click on the color you want to replace, or click on that color and then on the Pick button above the OK button. You will be taken to the Color Picker, which is a part of the Macintosh system to be discussed in the next section.

You can use the Copy button to copy the selected color and the Paste button to paste it into a different location on the clut. This is

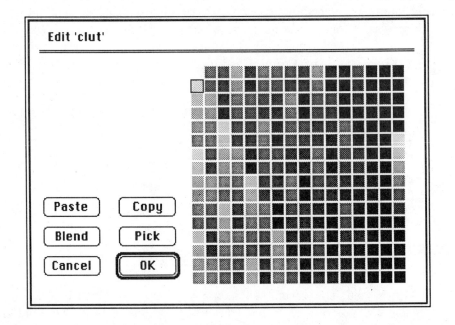

Figure 14-2.   SuperEdit's Edit Clut dialog box

useful for the Blend function. To blend two colors, first select one color and then a second color a few positions away. When you click on the Blend button, all the colors between the two positions are assigned values that are equally far apart. For example, if you want to create a set of even grey colors, first click on a white color and then on a black one. When you use the Blend button, the intervening pixels are assigned grey levels.

SuperCard reserves two colors; that is, you cannot edit the colors at the top-left of the clut (white), nor those at the bottom right of the clut (black).

The Color Picker

The Color Picker, shown in Figure 14-3, is a standard tool accessible from most programs that work with color. It provides a mechanism that allows you to pick any of the Macintosh's 16.7 million colors. In Super-Card, you will use the Color Picker to select new colors for your cluts.

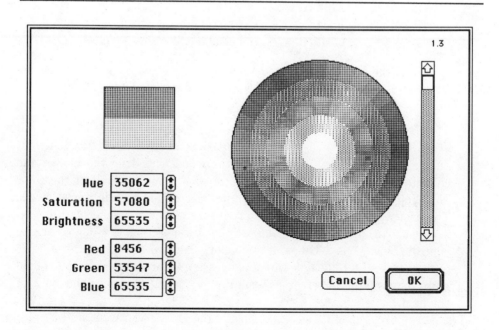

Figure 14-3.   The Macintosh Color Picker

The Color Picker has three basic parts.

1. The box at the top-left shows two colors in it. At the bottom is the color you double-clicked on in the Edit Clut dialog box and the color you will be replacing. As you choose a new color, it is shown in the top half of this box. With over 16.7 million colors from which to choose, it is practical to be able to compare the new color with the old one (shown in the bottom half of the box).

2. To the right of this box is the color wheel, which shows all the colors available at the current brightness level. The scroll bar to the right of the color wheel controls the brightness level. The currently selected color is shown as a small box in this wheel.

You can think of the Color Picker as a cylinder, as shown in Figure 14-4. The brightness control to the right of the Color Picker allows you to view different brightness "slices" from the cylinder. When the scroll bar is at the top, brightness is at a maximum; when it is at the bottom, brightness is at a minimum and most of the colors are indistinguishable from black.

The different pure colors are at three points of the color wheel. Green is at the eleven o'clock position on the wheel, red at about the three o'clock position, and blue at about the seven o'clock position.

3. At the bottom-left corner of the dialog box are a series of fields that allow you to control precisely the numeric values of any color.

Using this dialog box, you have two ways to select the color you want. The first way is by using the mouse to point to the color you want on the color wheel. As you click on the wheel and drag the mouse, the color to which you are pointing will appear in the top half of the color box. You can slide the scroll box to select different brightness levels. The best way to understand this procedure is to experiment with it.

You can also use the fields at the lower-left of the dialog box to control the various settings of any color. The two groups of these fields each represent a different way of expressing color. You can select a field and type a new number or use the up and down arrows to the right of the field.

The first set of these fields include the Hue, Saturation, and Brightness controls. *Hue* is a value that determines which color appears. A

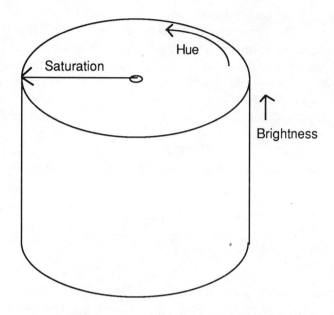

Figure 14-4.   The Color Picker is a cylinder, and the brightness control
determines which "slice" of the cylinder you are viewing

Hue of 0 is a red color, green is 21845, and blue is 42690. Increasing the Hue level moves you counterclockwise around the color wheel. The Hue setting "wraps around;" that is, after reaching the maximum value of 65535, the Hue then resets to 0.

Saturation is the amount of color chosen by the Hue versus the amount of white that is mixed with the color. A saturation of 0 means that it has none of the actual Hue and so is white or grey (depending on the brightness), and a saturation of 65535 contains no white. As the saturation is increased, the color becomes deeper and the indicator moves from the center of the wheel to the edge.

Finally, the Brightness field controls the amount of *black* that is mixed with the color. At a brightness level of 65535, the color contains no black and so is very bright. A brightness level of 0 indicates no color mixed with the black.

Notice that as you change any of these values, the pointer moves around the color wheel and the scroll bar changes to reflect the current brightness. The red, green, and blue fields also change.

These red, green, and blue fields represent another way of expressing a color on the Macintosh. As mentioned earlier, the Macintosh uses this RGB manner of displaying colors with additive techniques. You can use these fields to directly control the amount of each primary color that is mixed to compose the new color. For example, to choose the bluest blue color, set the blue level to its maximum value of 65535 and the red and green fields to 0. You mix colors by setting different values for each color. For example, you can create a yellow by making the values for red and green the same: the larger the value, the richer the yellow.

Importing Cluts

Aside from manually creating cluts, a sometimes tedious process, you can also import cluts from other files. There are two ways to do this. The first is to use SuperEdit's Import Resources item on the File menu. If a file from which you are importing resources contains any resources of the clut type, SuperEdit will translate these cluts into SuperCard-type cluts. You will then be able to rename and edit these cluts.

The second way to import a clut is to use the Import Graphics item on the File menu. This item is only available when you are actually editing a file. The command places the contents of the file onto the clipboard, allowing you to paste it onto the card.

When you paste the imported image onto a card, if that image contains colors, SuperEdit presents you with the alert shown in Figure 14-5, asking if you want to add the new clut. Note that SuperEdit does not check to see if the clut of the image you are pasting is different than the current clut; it asks whenever you paste a color image.

If you decide to add a clut to the resource list, you are presented with the dialog box shown in Figure 14-6, which allows you to name and number the clut. Generally, it is a good idea to assign a name to the clut that is the same as the card or background with which it is associated.

If, when pasting a graphic, you click on this dialog box's Cancel button, the clut will not be created, but the image will be pasted anyway using the current clut.

The clipboard picture has its own color look-up table. Would you like to add this "clut" to the resource list?
No
Yes

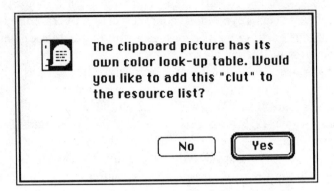

Figure 14-5. When you paste a color graphic onto a card, this dialog box asks if you want to add a clut for that graphic

Selecting a Clut

You can assign cluts to either backgrounds or cards, or to both. If a card has no clut assigned to it, it will use the clut assigned to its background.

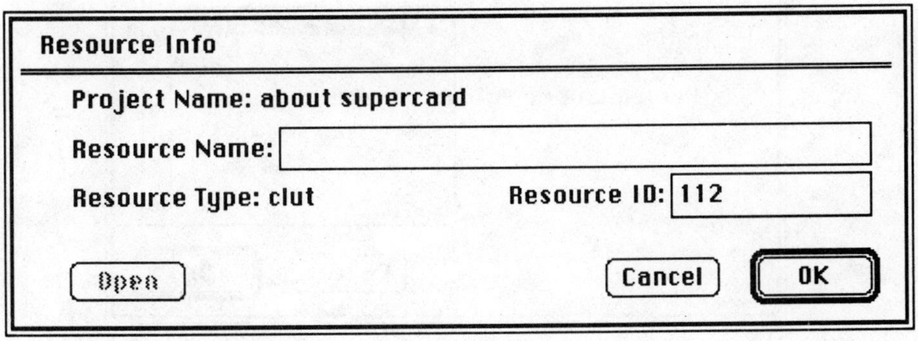

Resource Info
Project Name: about supercard
Resource Name:
Resource Type: clut
Resource ID: 112
Open
Cancel
OK

Figure 14-6. This dialog box allows you to name and number the new clut

In SuperCard, as you move from card to card, the clut used by the next card to which you are going is loaded slightly before the new card is displayed. This might cause some distortion to the colors displayed on the current card. Some techniques to minimize this distortion are discussed later in this chapter.

To select a clut for a card or background, use the Select Colors menu item on the Object menu when you are editing a card or background in SuperEdit. You will be presented with a dialog box similar to the one shown in Figure 14-7. This dialog box contains two parts. The first part consists of a set of radio buttons that allow you to set the color matching the color SuperCard will use for that card; this color matching is discussed in the next section. The scrolling list box on the right of the dialog box presents the cluts that are part of your project. The System clut is the standard clut used by the Macintosh. Grayscale and Rainbow are standard cluts supplied by SuperCard. Other cluts that you have added to the project (such as "my clut") will also be listed. To assign a

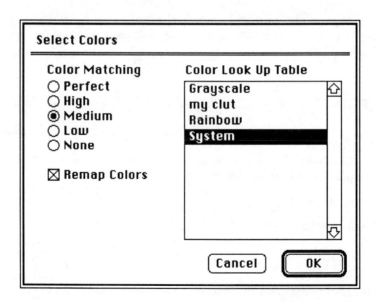

Figure 14-7.   The Select Colors dialog box

new clut to the current card, click on the clut you want and then on the OK button at the bottom-right corner of the card.

Note the Remap Colors checkbox below the Color Matching radio buttons. If this box is checked when you switch colors, SuperEdit will attempt to match any current colors on the card with those in the new clut you select. This matching will be accurate, although it will usually be less than 100 percent accurate with complex bitmaps. However, if this box is checked when you are selecting colors, any bitmaps on the card will be significantly modified; you will not be able to go back to the original colors.

If the Remap Colors box is *not* checked, the new colors will not be matched as precisely; some color bitmaps might be distorted. However, you *will* later be able to reselect the original clut and return to the original colors of the bitmap. This box is normally checked—be sure to examine it before clicking on the OK button. Remap Colors is useful for determining if a color picture can use a different clut effectively.

Color Priority

The Color Matching radio buttons control how precisely SuperCard will map colors when displaying a clut. If you set Color Matching to "None," SuperCard will not change cluts at all when a new card is displayed; instead, it will use whatever colors are available *in the current clut* (that is, the clut that was used to display the previous card) to display the new card.

The None option has two benefits and perhaps one significant drawback. The first benefit is that when SuperCard changes cluts, the monitor (and any images displayed on it) flashes colors slightly as the new clut is loaded. This flashing can be disconcerting so setting the Remap Colors property to "None" reduces the flash. The second benefit is speed. Though loading cluts takes little time, this can add up if you are moving through a number of cards. The drawback to the "None" option is that the appearance of the card might not exactly match the appearance you wanted: some of the colors used on the card might not be available on the current clut. This can cause some image degradation, especially if you are displaying high-quality scanned color bitmaps.

When Color Matching is set to "Perfect," SuperCard almost always loads the new clut associated with a card to display the image on that card. This has the advantage of assuring you the best quality possible in displaying a card. However, this option has a price. Suppose a card on the screen displays a rich color bitmap and you are going to a card also featuring a rich color bitmap with Color Matching set to "Perfect." In this case, the new clut will be loaded *while the current card is still on the screen,* and then the new card will be displayed. This will cause a momentary distortion to appear on the first card. Later in this chapter, you'll see some techniques for minimizing this effect. You can consult the Tips and Techniques project included with SuperCard for an illustration of this effect.

The Clut Property

**set the clut of [cardDescriptor ¦ backgroundDescriptor] to
    clutDescriptor
the clut of [cardDescriptor ¦ backgroundDescriptor]**

In SuperEdit, this property is set using the Select Colors dialog box discussed earlier. In SuperCard, you can use this property to determine which clut is used for a particular card or background or to set the clut used by a card or background.

The clutDescriptor can consist of either the ID number of the clut or its name. When you get this property, it is always returned in the form of its ID number, never its name.

When changing the clut, the new clut *must* be in either the project to which the card or background belongs or in your SharedFile. Unfortunately, SuperTalk has no way to determine the names or ID numbers of all the cluts that are part of a specific project.

The Cycle Command

cycle {all ¦ number1 to number2}[step\speed [number times]]

This command cycles the current clut causing the colors to shift, and each color pixel with each color from the clut shifts in turn. For example, a pixel that is colored with the color 1 from the clut will in turn be colored with the colors 2,3,4, and so on to 255.

Cycle all

Cycle all causes each of the pixels to be colored with all the other colors of the clut in turn.

Cycle all step

Each color is replaced by the color above it.

Cycle integer1 to integer2

Cycle integer1 to integer2 cycles the colors between the first and second integers. Integer1 must be less than integer2, or SuperCard will give you an error message. This variation is used to cycle only specific colors in the current clut.

Speed variations

The standard HyperCard speed keywords (*very fast, fast, slowly,* and *very slowly*) determine the delay between each cycling of the clut.

Number times

If you provide a number, you must use the word *times* after it. This specifies how many times the complete cycling occurs.

Here are some examples:

Cycle all very fast 10 times   Cycles all the colors in the clut through every other color in the clut very fast, and does it 10 times.

Cycle 10 to 20 very slowly   Cycles *only* colors 10 to 20.

Cycle 2 to 6 step   Cycles *only* colors 2 through 6. The step option causes the cycling to occur only once.

The following table shows the effect of repeated iteration of this command.

Starting	2	3	4	5	6
First	3	4	5	6	2
Second	4	5	6	2	3
Third	5	6	2	3	4
Fourth	6	2	3	4	5
Fifth	2	3	4	5	6

Color cycling affects the appearance of the screen only. It does *not* alter any colors in the objects themselves. When you next open the current card, colors will be as they were when you created it. This is a nondamaging change to the screen.

Color and Objects

All the objects that reside on SuperCard backgrounds or cards can be colored. This includes draw and paint objects, buttons, and fields. For paint objects you have already created, you cannot change the properties mentioned below; you must paint over them. For other objects, however, you can change any of these properties once the object has been created.

Properties

Two sets of properties determine the appearance of objects. The fill properties determine the pattern and color that fills or comprises the interior of an object. The pen properties determine the pattern and color of the line that defines the object.

The fill and pen properties essentially have two components: pattern and color. Figure 14-8 shows the standard patterns available in Super-Card. On the left are the actual patterns; on the right are the numbers that correspond to these patterns. In SuperEdit, you can modify patterns by double-clicking on the Brush tool on the Paint palette. In that case, the new pattern you create will replace one of the other patterns.

Color properties refer to numbered colors on the clut.

Fill Properties

Fill properties determine the pattern and color used to fill an object.

fillPat

get the fillPat [of object ¦ field ¦ buttonDescriptor]
set the fillPat [of object ¦ field ¦ buttonDescriptor] to integer

You can set the pattern of any selected object to a new pattern numbered 1 to 63 (SuperCard can only deal with 64 patterns). If you attempt to set the pattern to a value higher than 63, the pattern of the object will be set to 63; if you attempt to set it to a value less than 1, it will be set to 1.

This is both a global property and a property of specific objects. If you use the short form of the command (that is, do not specify an object), you will be setting the global property, and all new objects created will have that fill pattern.

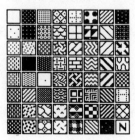

1	9	17	25	33	41	49	57
2	10	18	26	34	42	50	58
3	11	19	27	35	43	51	59
4	12	20	28	36	44	52	60
5	13	21	29	37	45	53	61
6	14	22	30	38	46	54	62
7	15	23	31	39	47	55	63
8	16	24	32	40	48	56	64

Figure 14-8.　SuperCard's patterns and their numbers

This property is synonymous with HyperCard's pattern property.

fillBack and fillFore

get the fillBack [of object | field | buttonDescriptor]
set the fillBack [of object | field | buttonDescriptor] to integer

get the fillFore [of object | field | buttonDescriptor]
set the fillFore [of object | field | buttonDescriptor] to integer

Patterns have two components: black pixels and white pixels. This is the way they appear on a Macintosh Plus or SE screen. They also appear this way when you have pattern palettes open in SuperCard. However, SuperCard allows you to set the actual colors that are used instead of black and white.

The fillBack property determines the color that will be used instead of white in a pattern. The fillFore property determines which color will be used instead of the black pixels.

Because cluts have 256 colors, it makes little sense to set either of these properties to values greater than 256. However, when you set one of these properties to such a value, it will be set to a new value that represents the remainder when that number is divided by 256; that is, if you set the value to 257, it will be set to 1; if you set it to 258, it will be set to 2, and so on.

Pen Properties

Pen properties determine which colors and patterns will be used for lines that define an object. For polygonal draw objects, these properties determine the line that defines the boundaries of the object. For lines, they determine the appearance of the object itself.

penPat

get the penPat [of object | field | buttonDescriptor]
set the penPat [of object | field | buttonDescriptor] to integer

You can set the pattern used to draw the line of any selected object to a new pattern from 1 to 64. If you attempt to set the pattern to a value higher than 64, the pattern will be set to 63; if you attempt to set it to a value less than 1, it will be set to 1.

This is both a global property and a property of specific objects. If you use the short form of the command (that is, do not specify an object), you will be setting the global property, and all new objects created will have that pen pattern.

penBack and penFore

get the penBack [of object | field | buttonDescriptor]
set the penBack [of object | field | buttonDescriptor] to integer

get the penFore [of object | field | buttonDescriptor]
set the penFore [of object | field | buttonDescriptor] to integer

These properties are counterparts to the fillBack and fillFore properties. The penBack property sets the color that will be used to replace white in the pattern; the penFore property sets the color that will replace the black color in the pen pattern.

penWidth and penHeight

get the penWidth [of object | field | buttonDescriptor]
set the penWidth [of object | field | buttonDescriptor] to integer

get the penHeight [of object | field | buttonDescriptor]
set the penHeight [ofobject | field | buttonDescriptor] to integer

In addition to patterns, pens have height and width. The height determines the vertical width of the line; the width determines the horizontal width of the line. As with the other pen and fill properties, you can specify this as either a global property (affecting new objects) or as a property of a specific object.

The maximum value for the penHeight and PenWidth is 1000. If you set it to a greater value, it will default to 1000. The minimum value is 0.

Color and Bitmap Objects

As mentioned earlier, you can only color bitmap objects *as you create them.* Coloring them after the fact involves painting over them in color, a difficult proposition that in essence requires recreating the original.

Converting Color Bitmaps to Black and White

Figure 14-9 shows the Object Info dialog box from SuperEdit for a paint object. Note that this dialog box contains two radio buttons that allow you to specify whether the object is a black-and-white or color object. If you are working in a color environment, all new bitmap objects you create are automatically color objects.

However, you can use this dialog box to convert a color painting to black and white. When you do so, SuperEdit creates a *dithered* version of the painting. Dithering is a process that simulates grey shades by using patterns of black dots and white dots (see Chapter Four). Darker areas of the painting will have more dots than lighter areas. Dithering is almost always used by painting programs on the Macintosh Plus and SE to simulate various shades of grey.

SuperEdit's dithering of color images is fairly good. It does not, however, substitute for other techniques for creating attractive graphics on black-and-white screens. If you are manipulating complex color graphics, it is best to use other programs that feature dithering. Silicon Beach's Digital Darkroom program features dithering superior to that

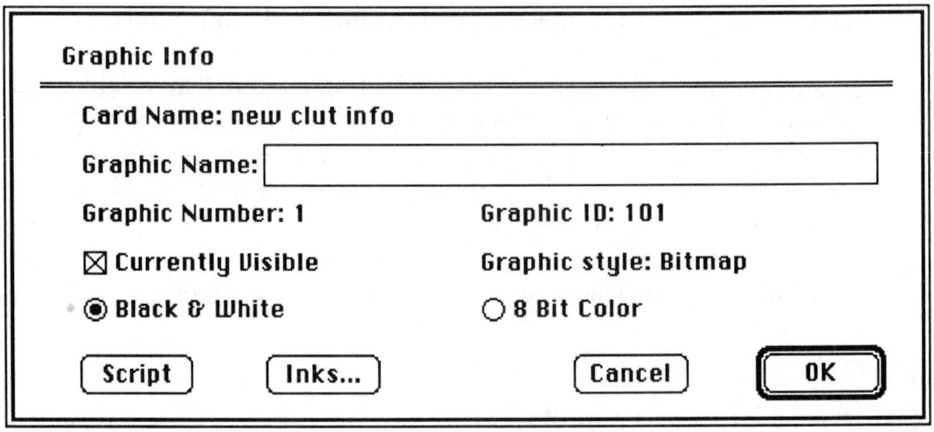

Graphic Info

Card Name: new clut info

Graphic Name:

Graphic Number: 1   Graphic ID: 101

☒ Currently Visible   Graphic style: Bitmap

◉ Black & White   ○ 8 Bit Color

(Script)   (Inks...)   (Cancel)   (OK)

Figure 14-9.   Graphic Info for bitmaps allows you to change them from color to black and white

of SuperEdit and gives you control over the process. If you are working with images that have been scanned or digitized, the software that you use to digitize the image usually has dithering capabilities.

It's important to note that converting a painting to black and white is a one-way street. While you can later change the painting back to color, the color information that was in the image will be lost. Keep backup copies of important images and use the Undo command to recover color information immediately after you have changed the painting to black and white.

Dithering is a complex process: large images, with a wide variety of colors or grey levels, can take several seconds to dither.

Optimizing Color

As mentioned at the beginning of this chapter, there are some catches to using color—the slower speed that results when working with large, color bitmap objects, and the visual effects that result, usually unintentionally, when you move from card to card.

Reducing Color Flashing

When you move between cards that have different colors associated with them, some "flashing" occurs as the transition is made. Before moving to the next card, SuperCard first loads the clut of the new card. If this new clut is significantly different from the previous clut, the effect can be quite disconcerting. You can handle this in a couple of ways. The first way to deal with color flashing was mentioned in the "Color Priority" section earlier in the chapter. This solution works, but has its drawbacks: the colors used on the new card might not match closely enough the colors in the current clut, which can sometimes cause a significant loss of color detail on the new card.

A second way to reduce color flashing is to interweave cards between two cards of very different colors. These cards can either be blank, or contain only noncolor objects. This approach is illustrated in the Tips and Techniques project included with SuperCard.

In this instance, when you leave the first card to go to the next card, you make a short stop at the intervening card 2. This card has nothing on it, so when you move from that card to card 3, nothing changes on card 2. Similarly, when you leave card 3 you go to card 4, which again has nothing on it. When you then leave card 4 to go to card 1, no colors are changed on card 4 and the transition time from card 3 to card 1 is very short.

This solution, however, has several problems, and you should use it with care. The first problem is that it creates a number of empty cards in windows, which can be a nuisance to manage. These blank cards do not take up much room on disk, however, so that penalty is not severe.

The second problem is due to the associated scripting requirements. If you create windows that tightly control how users navigate through the cards in a window, the problem is not serious. On the other hand, scripting problems can occur when creating windows that permit users to navigate at will using the Go Next Card or Go Previous Card commands.

Color and Palettes

When working with palette windows that have cluts associated with them, you need to take care when switching cards. Palettes work differently from other types of windows. When you move to a different card in a palette, the new clut for that card is not loaded automatically. Instead, the clut associated with the top window has priority and so is the one that is used. You can work around this with a script in your palette window such as

```
on openCard
  set the clut of topwindow() to the clut of this window
end openCard
```

One problem with this is that if bitmap images are on the card that is in the top window, the colors in that bitmap will be converted to the colors of the new clut. You can use the Revert command (discussed in Chapter Seven) to ensure that changes to the top window are not saved.

Another way around this problem is to change the style of the palette window, which will cause that window to quickly become the top window, thus forcing SuperCard to load the clut of the palette. A short script that accomplishes this goal is

```
on openCard
  set lockscreen to true
  set the style of this window to standard
  set the style of this window to palette
  set lockscreen to false
end openCard
```

This change happens fairly quickly and is barely noticeable as the new card appears.

Use Objects Where Possible

Using draw graphics instead of bitmaps in your card designs has several advantages. First, draw graphics require a great deal less room on disk and in RAM than do bitmaps, and this is especially true with regard to color. If you are not using complex drawings, draw graphics load from disk, and thus display, more quickly than do bitmaps.

Second, draw objects with color display much better on black-and-white screens. Dithering does not occur, and display is quicker and gives a more accurate screen representation of your design.

Remember that you can use SuperEdit's AutoTrace tool to do a lot of the work in converting a complex bitmap to a draw graphic or button.

Keep Bitmap Objects Small

Color bitmap objects can take up a lot of memory and disk space. Although SuperCard uses sophisticated techniques for compressing these bitmaps, these techniques can only do so much. The best solution is to work with only small bitmaps wherever possible.

Ink Effects

If graphics were always displayed against a white background, your job would be simple. You would not need to consider how the colors and patterns in one object interact with those of another object. However, you would not have many choices of how to display your images either.

Ink effects are rules determining how pixels in one object are displayed when they appear on top of pixels of a different color in a different object. You set the ink effect for the frontmost object; only the ink effect of the top object affects how the two objects appear when one is superimposed on another.

In the following discussion, the terms "black" and "white" are used in two ways depending on the type of object you are working with. With draw objects, the word "white" actually refers to the fillBack color—the one that is replacing white in the pattern design. The word "black" refers to the fillFore color—the one that replaces black pixels in the pattern design.

However, when applying ink effects to paint objects, the word "white" means pixels that are actually white in the painting. The word "black" then refers to all pixels that are not white.

Note that some of these ink effects—those that are "transparent"—can cause moiré effects on the screen when you are using various patterns of dots. The vast number of combinations of effects and patterns preclude a detailed examination of them here, but experimentation will allow you to determine how effects and patterns work together. You should test a number of effects and patterns when you are placing one object over another to make sure you achieve the effect you want.

The Ink Property

set the ink of graphicDescriptor to inkEffect
get the ink of graphicDescriptor

The ink property controls the ink effects used on the specified object. Black-and-white objects can have the following ink effects.

Mask	notSrcBic	notSrcCopy
notSrcOr	notSrcXor	srcBic
srcCopy	srcOr	srcXor

Color objects can have any of these effects:

addMax	addMin	addOver
addPin	Blend	subOver
subPin		

Ink effects are for appearance only; they do *not* actually modify any of the pixels in a bitmap object or the pattern or color of a draw graphic. You can always see the "real" colors of an object by setting its ink property to srcCopy.

Both Black and White and Color

These effects work when you are running on black and white as well as color Macintosh models. Refer to Figures 14-10 and 14-11 for illustrations of how these effects work. The "source" object is the one to which the effect is assigned, and this foremost or top object defines how objects are displayed.

SrcCopy

ScrCopy makes the source object opaque. A white box is visible around the object when it is on top of another object. This default ink effect for all new effects is useful for when you want one object to completely obscure objects that are underneath it and when you want to see the "real" colors or patterns in an object.

SrcOr

With ScrOr, black pixels on the top object remain black, while white pixels become transparent. In the example in Figure 14-10, it appears that the space shuttle is moving behind the black triangle.

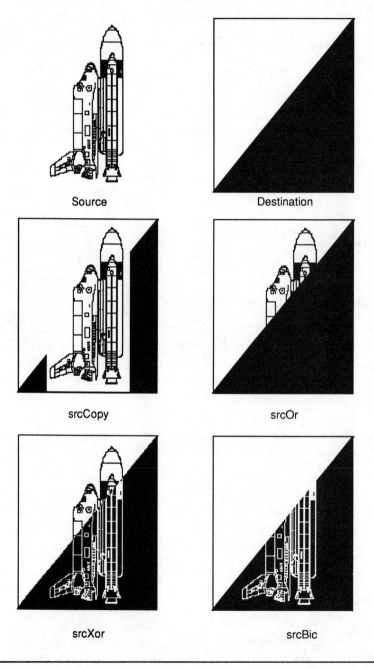

Source

Destination

srcCopy

srcOr

srcXor

srcBic

Figure 14-10. This figure illustrates four black-and-white ink effects

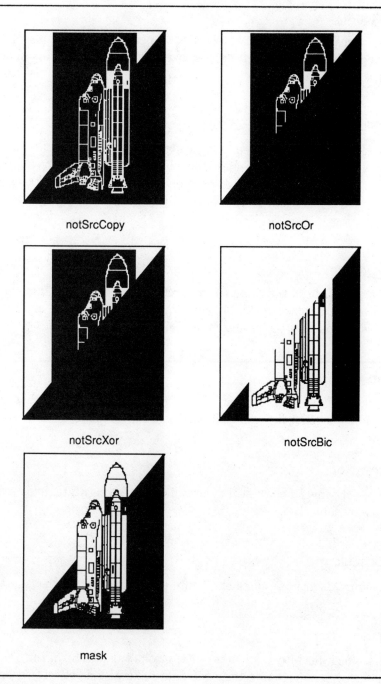

notSrcCopy

notSrcOr

notSrcXor

notSrcBic

mask

Figure 14-11.   Five more black-and-white ink effects

SrcXor

With ScrXor, any black pixels that appear over black pixels are inverted; black pixels that appear over white pixels in an underlying object appear as black.

SrcBic

Black pixels are inverted and white pixels are transparent. In the sample in the figure, because the black pixels at the top part of the space shuttle are over white space on the card, they seem to disappear. The black pixels that appear on the bottom of the rectangle have been inverted.

notSrcCopy

This effect works the same as the SrcCopy effect, except that the object is inverted. A black rectangle appears around the object, and any black pixels enclosed by it are shown as white.

notSrcOr

Black pixels remain black and white pixels become black; that is, areas of the object that lie over white areas are inverted.

notSrcXor

Pixels are inverted when they are displayed over white, but are always black over black.

notSrcBic

Black pixels are left alone and white pixels are white.

Mask

This effect, for bitmap objects only, "masks" an outline of the object as it passes over a dark object. As the figure shows, this effect preserves the original appearance of the object as it passes over another object.

Color Effects

The following effects appear in the Effects dialog box only if you are using a color Macintosh. These effects work by mixing the color values associated with a color on the clut. The numerical values are added or subtracted together, a new color is determined, and then SuperCard uses the color in the existing clut that most closely matches the color that would be produced by the effect.

All these effects are discussed in the context of two sample colors. The source color is a brownish color—its red value is 45000, green 30000, and blue 15000. The destination color is a light blue—its red component is 20000, green 40000, and blue 60000. Figure 14-12 shows an approximation of how these mixes appear on a color monitor.

You can produce this illustration in SuperEdit by creating two colors in a clut that have the values shown under the "Source" and "Dest" headings in the figure. Next create two draw-type objects and assign these colors to those objects. The "Source" object should be on top of the "Destination" object. Duplicate these objects across the card and assign to the Source object the color ink effects shown at the top of each column.

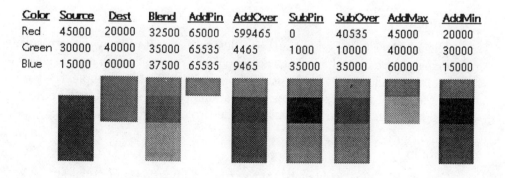

Color	Source	Dest	Blend	AddPin	AddOver	SubPin	SubOver	AddMax	AddMin
Red	45000	20000	32500	65000	599465	0	40535	45000	20000
Green	30000	40000	35000	65535	4465	1000	10000	40000	30000
Blue	15000	60000	37500	65535	9465	35000	35000	60000	15000

Figure 14-12.   Use this figure as a guide to exploring color ink effects in SuperEdit

Blend

This effect averages the source and destination color values. As its name implies, it blends the color of the source object with the color of the destination object. If the object is on top of a white card, for example, the blend effect makes that object brighter than it was originally.

When shown over the destination, a brown source becomes a bluish-grey, while it becomes light brown over the white card.

AddPin

The addPin effect adds source to destination and stops at white. In this case, the RGB values of the two colors in the top object are added to the RGB values in the color of the object it covers. When the values reach their maximum value—65535 or white—those pixels become white.

This effect causes any parts of an object that lie over a white area on the window to appear as white. In effect, it allows you to "mask" different parts of a bitmap object. Consider a large bitmap that lies on a white card. With the effect of this object set to AddPin, the object is invisible when it is on top of a white card, but the parts of the object that appear on top of dark objects are visible.

In the illustration, the entire source object becomes white for two reasons. The first is that both the green and the blue components "max out" at 65535, or full brightness, and the red component is very close to full brightness. The second reason is that the closest color to these values in the clut is a white color.

AddOver

The addOver effect adds source to destination and rolls over the result. Pixels that have values that exceed 65535 are also "rolled over" (meaning, if you added 4 to 65534, it would become 3). In the example, the part of the object that lies over the destination becomes a bright red, because red has by far the greater value of the three color components.

SubPin

The subPin effect subtracts source from destination and stops at black. In this case, the color values for the source pixel are subtracted from the color values of the destination pixel. If the result is less than 0, then 0 is used for that value.

In the example, the red color is eliminated entirely from the part of the object that overlaps the two, and the green value is very low, producing a deep purple.

SubOver

This effect subtracts source from destination and rolls over. This means that if the result of the subtraction is a number less than 0, that result is subtracted from 65535. You can see this in the example: instead of becoming 0, the red component of the color becomes 40535, making the resulting color a redder purple.

AddMax

The color mix displayed is composed of the colors that have the largest values in the color mix of the source and destination. In the example, the overlay becomes a purple with a large amount of red.

One use of this effect is to give color to a black and white bitmap. To do this, place a colored object over a black and white object, assign this effect to the object on top, and all black pixels in the destination take on that color; white pixels are left alone, since they are at the maximum value of 65535.

AddMin

This effect takes the minimum of source and destination. This colorizes only the white pixels of the destination. As you can see from Figure 14-12, this produces a deep green in the area where the colors overlap: the green value is the highest of the three values that comprise the color.

Importing PICT and TIFF Files

Bringing color images into SuperCard can be handled in a few ways. First, create the images yourself using the paint tools. This is useful if you are adept with paint tools and have used programs such as Pixel Paint or MacPaint.

You can also import most types of images into SuperCard. The first way is using the Macintosh Clipboard. SuperEdit accepts Clipboard images, using the Paste command. Virtually any object that can be placed on the Clipboard can be pasted into SuperEdit or SuperCard. Utilities such as Open It! from TenPoint0 are useful for placing images on the Clipboard.

SuperEdit also features an Import Graphics command, located on the File menu when you are editing a card or background. When you choose this command, you will be presented with the dialog box shown in Figure 14-13. Note that at the bottom of the dialog are three checkboxes that allow you to specify which types of files will be visible in the scrolling list field. These three types of files represent a very useful subset of the types of graphics you are likely to have on the Macintosh.

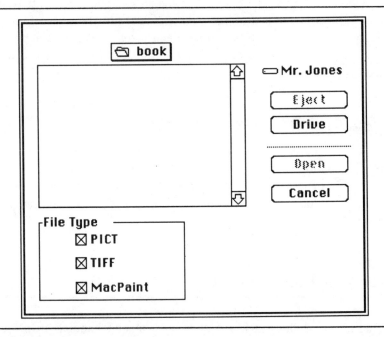

Figure 14-13. The Import Graphics dialog box

PICT   With the advent of the Macintosh II and color, Apple defined the PICT format as a standard way of storing color images on disk. Virtually every Macintosh graphics program can save to this format, and it is also the "native" format of a number of packages, such as Studio/8, Digital Darkroom, and others.

TIFF   "TIFF" stands for the Tag Image File Format that was developed for use by manufacturers of digitizers, scanners, and desktop publishing programs to represent a format for interchange of data between those programs. Unfortunately, TIFF as a standard is not as well defined as it might be. Enough room was left in the original definition to allow manufacturers to alter it to suit their own needs, and many users of this format have done so; not all TIFF files are created equal. SuperEdit supports 8-bit TIFF files.

MacPaint   MacPaint is the file format originally created by Bill Atkinson for his ground-breaking MacPaint program. Since MacPaint was the original graphics program for the Macintosh, many programs support this format. The problem with the MacPaint format is that it can only work with black-and-white pictures; it has no support for color or grey scales because they were not available on the early Macintoshes. Nevertheless, most users have fairly large libraries of MacPaint images, and a number of commercial clip-art programs that support this format are available.

When importing a MacPaint document, SuperEdit will create a graphic on the card that is the full size of the MacPaint document, regardless of how large the actual graphic is. Because MacPaint documents are the size of an 8″ X 10″ sheet of paper, you will need to select the bitmap with the pointer tool and resize it.

Animation

Card-Flipping
Animation with Objects
Animation with PICS Files
Animation with STEP Files

At the second annual CD-ROM conference, held in spring 1987 in Seattle, Bill Abel, of Abel and Associates, spoke of multimedia techniques. He showed a number of fascinating examples of mixing media—sound, text, pictures—to put across a point, or communicate an idea. If a picture is worth a thousand words, how many words is a moving picture worth? You can use moving objects in a number of ways. Bars on charts can grow dynamically to indicate rising sales. Pieces of a pie chart can appear magically from the side of the screen and gather to form a completed pie. Cartoon characters can lead the user through a complicated text, pointing out important highlights.

With SuperCard, you have several ways to present animation. Each has its own strengths and weaknesses. Depending on your goal and the context, one of these techniques will probably be right for you.

Card-Flipping

Card-flipping resembles the "flip books" you played with (and perhaps even created) as a child: a drawing is repeated on a number of cards, each slightly different than the previous one. By flipping through the cards quickly, you generate the appearance of movement. In Hyper-Card, card-flipping is used quite often for animation.

Card-flipping, however, is not the best way to do animation in SuperCard for a few reasons. First, SuperCard is not as fast as Hyper-Card at flipping through cards, especially when you are using color and large windows. Another major reason for eschewing card-flipping in SuperCard is that you have much better tools at your disposal.

Animation with Objects

Because all graphics are separate objects in SuperCard, you have a method of object animation that does not exist in HyperCard. There are several ways to manipulate the loc and rect properties of objects to move them across the screen in SuperCard. You can manipulate their properties explicitly, as was discussed in Chapter Ten, or you can use SuperCard's Move command to exert more control over object movement and use less coding.

The Move Command

SuperCard's Move command has three variations that allow you to specify two different types of movement: *relative* and *specific movement*. This chapter discusses graphic objects, but you should remember that all SuperCard objects — buttons, fields, draw and paint graphics — can be moved with this command.

Relative Movement

Move objectDescriptor rel[ative] distance [{nudge ¦ jump} number]

When you use the Relative option of the Move command, you tell SuperCard *how far* to move the object in each direction from its present location. The variable *distance* is a set of two integers, the first specifying the horizontal distance, the second specifying the vertical distance. For example, to move an object 10 pixels down and 10 pixels to the right, you would use a statement such as

```
move cd grc 1 rel 10,10
```

You can include more than two integers to specify a number of movements with one command. To create an oscillating effect in which the object bobs up and down, you would use a statement such as

```
move cd grc 1 rel 0,10,0,-10,0,10,0,-10
```

When you are building such a list, make sure to include an even number of comma-separated numbers or SuperCard will give you a "Can't Understand Arguments" alert. You can also store these numbers in a variable, and use that variable:

```
put "0,10,0,-10,0,10,0,-10" into bobIt
move cd grc 1 rel bobIt
```

The nudge and jump arguments to the Move command are discussed later in this section.

Movement to a Specific Location

Move objectDescriptor to location [{nudge ¦ jump} number]

This variation of the Move command moves the object to a specific location, which is specified by two integers separated by commas. Again, the first integer specifies the horizontal location; the second integer indicates the vertical location of the object.

As with relative movement, you can simultaneously specify several locations to move the object. For example, this statement

```
move cd grc 1 to 50,50,75,75
```

first moves the object to a point 50 pixels from the left edge of the card and 50 pixels from the top, and then moves it to a point 75 pixels from the left edge and 75 pixels from the top. Again, you can use a variable to contain the list of points to which you want to move the object. If you have a complex list of points, however, it is better to create a Polygonal

Draw graphic and use the points property of that object for the "route." This allows you to control and edit the movement more easily.

Movement to a Set of Points

Move objectDescriptor to points of objectDescriptor [{nudge ¦ jump} number]

This sort of movement is a variation on specific location movement. It uses the points property of a Polygonal Draw graphic or button (discussed in Chapter Ten) to get a list of locations to which it should move the object.

As shown in Figure 15-1, complex and even arbitrary shapes can be

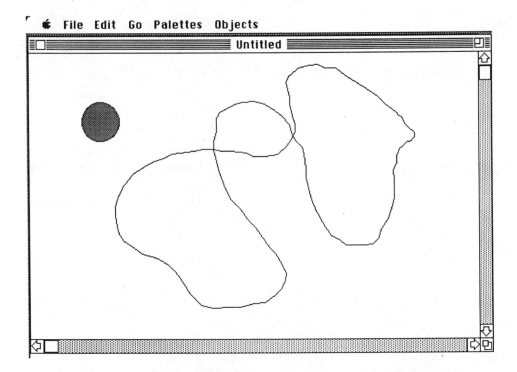

Figure 15-1.   The circular object will be moved along the path formed by the shape of the irregular object

created. In the figure, the circular graphic is the object to be moved (and is card graphic 1), and the irregular object is the path along which the object will be moved (and is card graphic 2). To move the circle along the points of the irregular object, the command is:

```
move cd grc 1 to the points of cd grc 2
```

One benefit of using the points property to move an object is that you can easily edit the movement of the object by using the Reshape Polygon command (discussed in Chapter Twelve) to edit the shape of the object that forms the path and fine-tune the movement of another object. In addition, the object that forms the path need not be visible on the screen. Referring to Figure 15-1, you can use the Hide command to make the path invisible, and the moving object will appear to move along an arbitrary route.

One disadvantage of this method is that only one object can be moved at a time, and no other Script can be executing while that movement is occurring. Instead of explicitly moving an object to the points of another object, you can place the points of the path object into a variable, and then move the moving object one step at a time along those points, while doing something else in a Script between moves. For example, Script 15-1 is a handler that moves two objects along the points of another object. One of the moving objects starts 180 degrees from the other, and they both orbit the path object.

```
on mouseUp
  put the points of cd grc "path" into thePoints
  --make 2 sets of points
  put (the number of items in thePoints / 2) into pointsCount
  put item pointsCount to the number of items in thepoints¬
  of thepoints into points2
  put "," & item 1 to pointsCount of thepoints after points2
  put 1 into x
  repeat pointsCount
    move cd grc 1 to item x of thePoints,¬
    item x + 1 of thePoints
    move cd grc 2 to item x of points2,¬
    item x + 1 of points2
    add 2 to x
  end repeat
end mouseUp
```

Script 15-1.   This handler orbits two ovals about the points of another object

As shown in Figure 15-2, the graphic called "path" in the Script is the rounded oval. (*Note:* Because draw ovals do not contain points, you need to create a polygon that is in the shape of an oval; this will be discussed later in this chapter.) The two circles are card graphics 1 and 2, respectively. The handler first gets the points of the path object, and then takes the second half of those points and places them into the variable *points2*. It then puts the first half of those points into the second half of that variable. This starts the movement of card graphic 2 halfway around the oval from the movement of card graphic 1. The repeat loop then moves each of the objects in turn. The variable *X* is used to give an incremental step value to the repeat loop, as points come in groups of two.

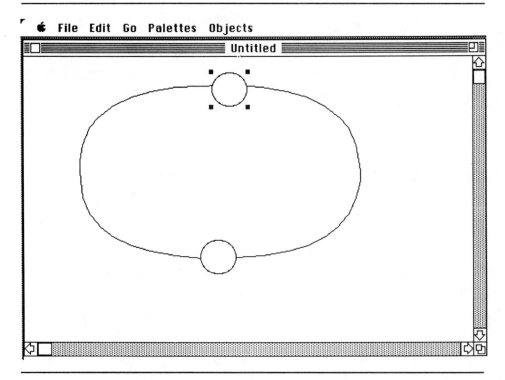

Figure 15-2.   The two circular objects will move along opposite sides of the oval path

Because draw graphics that are created with the Draw Oval, Draw Rectangle, Draw Line, and other tools do not have points, you cannot use those types of objects for paths of movement. The best way to get around this is to create a bitmap object that is square or circular with one of those tools and then use SuperEdit's AutoTrace tool to create a circular or square Draw polygon from that outline. The AutoTrace tool is discussed in Chapter Four.

Nudging and Jumping

Whatever method of movement you are using, you can specify *nudge* and *jump* factors. These factors allow you to control how fast the object moves between any two points.

The nudge option specifies how many pixels the object will move at one time between two locations. For example, if you are using relative movement to move an object 100 pixels to the right, the statement would read

```
move cd field 1 rel 100,0
```

If you want the object to move slower, you can nudge it in this manner:

```
move cd field 1 rel 100,0 nudge 1
```

The object will now move in 100 steps, each 1 pixel long. The smaller the nudge factor, the slower the movement of the object.

The jump option specifies the number of discrete steps in which the object moves. In the previous example where an object is being moved 100 pixels to the right, if you want to make that movement in two jumps, the command would be:

```
move cd field 1 rel 100,0 jump 2
```

In terms of numbers, jumping is the inverse of nudging: the larger the jump figure, the slower the movement.

Icon Switching with Buttons

You can also use button icons for animation, as many developers have done with HyperCard. The technique is to create several icons that compose the movement of your object, and use the Set command to change the icon property of your button in order to move from one icon to the next. Figure 15-3 illustrates this technique, showing four crude icons of a motion picture camera with a rotating handle. These illustrations were created in SuperEdit with the Paint tools, and then were pasted into icons using SuperEdit's Icon editor. The handler shown in Script 15-2 shows how these icons, named "Cam1" through "Cam4," are flipped quickly to produce animation.

As mentioned in the previous section, you can use the Move command to animate movement of all objects—including buttons—around the screen. Combined with icon switching, quick, sophisticated animation can be created.

The main problem in using icons for animation is the limited size of the icon. It is difficult to create sophisticated, textured illustrations within the 32-pixel by 32-pixel size of an icon. However, if you can work within that limitation, you can generate fast animation of even multiple objects on the screen.

Animation with PICS Files

A PICS file is a file containing a series of PICT II images. PICT II is the standard file format developed by Apple for storing and working with color images, though black and white images can also be stored in PICT II images. The PICS file constitutes a common format for animation files that can be used by a number of programs, such as MacroMind's Director, Silicon Beach's Super 3D, and Paracomp's Swivel 3D. For example, you can use a program such as Super 3D to create an animated spinning logo, and then use SuperCard to play that animation.

Figure 15-3.   Using the Set command, the rotating camera handle can be animated

```
on mouseUp
  repeat until the mouse is down
    set the icon of me to "cam1"
    set the icon of me to "cam2"
    set the icon of me to "cam3"
    set the icon of me to "cam4"
    set the icon of me to "cam3"
    set the icon of me to "cam2"
  end repeat
end mouseUp
```

Script 15-2.   This handler switches the icon of a button to animate the turning of a handle

Or you can use SuperCard to generate an animation that can be imported into Macro Mind's Director and then integrated with animation created by that program.

One benefit of using PICS animation (and STEP animation which is discussed later in this chapter) is that you do not need to worry about "real time" animation generation. You can use all the power of SuperCard's programming facilities to generate images that might take quite a while to generate between frames. Calculation-intensive animation might be slow to generate in real time, but you can put a lot of time into generating the PICS file, and then present the animation to others quickly.

PICS File Commands

The commands that allow you to open, close, play, and record PICS files are logical extensions to HyperCard's file commands.

The Open PICS Command

Open PICS [file] fileName [at Rectangle]

The Open PICS command creates a new PICS file on disk and prepares it for recording a new animation. You can only have one PICS or STEP file open at a time, and if you attempt to use this command with another PICS file open, you will get the dialog box shown in Figure 15-4.

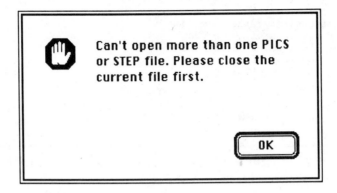

Figure 15-4. Attempting to open more than one PICS or STEP file causes this alert to appear

The fileName should be a *complete* pathname for the file in question, including the name of the disk and any folders into which you want to place the PICS file. If you specify only a filename, the PICS file will be placed into the same folder containing the SharedFile.

When recording a PICS file, the entire contents of the current window are normally saved into the file. You can, however, record an area *smaller* than the current window by specifying a rectangle as the last argument in the command. For example, if you want to open a PICS file named "PICS file" and record a rectangle occupying a square 100 pixels on a side at the upper-left corner of the current window, you would use this command:

```
open pics "pics file" at 0,0,100,100
```

After a PICS file has been opened, all the PICT images that comprise that file must be the same size. In the above example, all the images that are part of the PICS file would be 100 pixels on each side.

The Record PICS Command

Record PICS [file]

This command records the current window to the current PICS file. Because only one PICS file can be open at a time, you do not need to specify the filename. If you specify a rectangle as part of the Open PICS command, only the portion of the window that falls within that rectangle is recorded. If no PICS file is currently open, the alert shown in Figure 15-5 will appear.

The Close PICS Command

Close PICS [file]

This command closes the current PICS file, allowing you to play it. Because only one PICS file can be open at a time, you do not need to specify a filename. If you use this command when no PICS file is open, you get the alert shown in Figure 15-5.

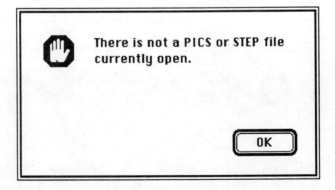

Figure 15-5.   Attempting to record or close when no PICS file is open
summons this alert

The Play PICS Command

Play PICS [file] fileName [frame number] [speed] [repeat number] [until event] [keep picture]

The Play PICS command plays the specified PICS animation file. If you specify a file that is not a PICS file or use an incorrect pathname, SuperCard will present the alert shown in Figure 15-6. If a PICS file has been opened for recording with the Open command, you will get the alert shown in Figure 15-7. This means that you cannot edit PICS files once they have been created. You cannot, for example, play up to frame 24 of a PICS file and then Record starting from that point.

PICS animations are played back at the same location, relative to the current window, at which they were recorded. If the current window is smaller than the window that recorded the animation, only that portion of the animation that fits within the window is visible.

PICS files recorded with SuperCard only occupy that portion of the window that they actually represent. Generally, PICS files created with other programs will take over the entire contents of the window, obscuring anything else that is in it.

You can use a number of variations when playing a PICS file.

Figure 15-6.   This alert appears if you attempt to play a PICS file that does not exist

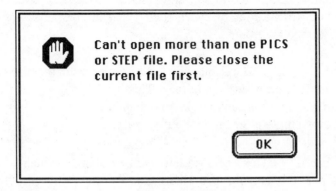

Figure 15-7.   This alert appears if you attempt to play a PICS file when you have one open for recording

Frame   The Play PICS command displays only the specified frame number. For example, if you want to play only frame 3 of a PICS file and keep the picture on the card (discussed in more detail later in this chapter) the command would be

```
play pics fileName frame 2 keep picture
```

You cannot specify a range of pictures to play; to do so, use a repeat loop. Here is a script fragment that plays only frames 3 to 10 of a PICS file:

```
repeat with x = 3 to 10
  play PICS fileName frame x
end repeat
```

If you specify a frame number that is greater than the number of frames that are actually in the PICS file, the command is ignored.

Speed   The speed option of the Play PICS command specifies the speed at which the animation is played. The allowable speed options are the same ones that HyperCard and SuperCard understand for visual effects: very fast, fast, slow(ly), and very slow(ly). PICS files can occupy a great deal of space on disk, and sometimes the constraints of loading them from disk might be more than you can compensate for by using the faster speed options.

Repeat   This option, followed by an integer, determines how many times the PICS animation will play. This is a good technique for creating a "rolling demo," or animation that repeats until it is stopped by the user. An example is given in the next section.

Until Event   This option allows you to specify which of two mouse events halt the playing of a PICS file. The allowable options are *until mouse* and *until click.* Both options stop the Play PICS command when you click the mouse; the difference is how SuperCard handles the clicking of the mouse once the animation is stopped.

If you use the until mouse structure, when the animation playback is stopped, SuperCard will absorb the mouse click rather than passing it to the card or object on which you click. If you use the until click structure, the animation is stopped and the mouse click is sent to the card on which you click. This structure is good for triggering an event that stops the animation and for executing a script in a floating palette.

As mentioned, you can create a "rolling demo" that repeats until the mouse is clicked. To do so, you would use a command such as

```
Play PICS fileName repeat forever until mouse
```

This animation would stop when the mouse is clicked, and the mouse-Click message would not be passed along to the card on which you clicked.

Keep Picture   When SuperCard stops playing the animation, this option can be used to "freeze" the last frame on the card. The screen is not updated, so any buttons, fields, or graphics that were obscured by the animation remain obscured by the last frame of the PICS file. The picture does not become part of the card, but rather an "artifact" of the animation process. With the picture on the card, you can use SuperCard as usual: clicking on buttons, selecting objects, and so on (though the objects remain hidden by the picture). The picture will disappear whenever any event that triggers an updateWindow message (discussed in Chapter Seven) is sent to the window. This includes selecting a menu item, resizing the window, and so on.

A PICS Animation Menu

It is not difficult to create a menu that handles all the basic PICS animation needs—for most uses a menu works better than does a floating palette or dialog box. For example, when using the Record PICS command, the current window is always used; you cannot have a Record PICS button in a palette. A minimal menu needs only four items.

Create, in SuperEdit, a new project called "PICS MENU." Then create a new menu called "PICS." The menu will have four items—Open, Record, Close, and Play. (For details on constructing menus, see Chapter Eight.)

Open. . .

This item allows you to open a new PICS animation file. You would insert Script 15-3 into this menu item. This handler uses the Ask command to present a dialog box (see Figure 15-8) asking you to name the new PICS file. Note the use of SuperCard's "at the screenLoc" feature, which always presents the Ask dialog box in the center of the screen. The Ask command places your response into the special variable *it*, and if you click on the Cancel button in this dialog box, then *it* is empty, and this handler exits. Otherwise, a PICS file with the name you specify is opened for recording.

Note that in keeping with Macintosh user interface standards, this menu item is followed by an ellipsis (. . .), which indicates that a dialog box will appear when you select the item.

Record

Once you have opened a PICS file, you can use the Record menu item to add new frames to the file. In the Menu Item Info dialog box for this

```
on itemSelect
  ask "Enter the complete name of the PICS file" ¬
  at the screenLoc
  if it is empty then exit itemSelect
  open PICS file it
end itemSelect
```

Script 15-3.   This handler prompts you for the name of a new PICS file, and then opens that file for recording

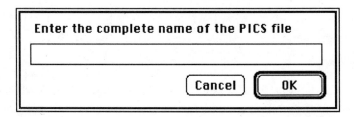

Figure 15-8. The Ask command presents this dialog box

item, shown in Figure 15-9, type **R** into the command key field. Adding frames to the PICS file will now become easier. The script you should type into this menu item is

```
on itemSelect
   record PICS
end itemSelect
```

Close

This menu item closes the current PICS animation so that you can play it. Its simple script is

```
on itemSelect
   close PICS file
end itemSelect
```

Play. . .

This menu item, which is followed by three periods to indicate a dialog box will appear, plays a selected PICS file from disk. Script 15-4 contains the itemSelect handler to put into this menu item.

GetFile is the name of an external function (XFCN) that is included in the SharedFile when SuperCard is shipped. This function allows you to display a standard file dialog box, as shown in Figure 15-10. The first argument of this function specifies the question the dialog box will ask. The second argument, "PICS," displays in the list of files only those files that have this file type. If you click on the Cancel button in this dialog box, the function returns nothing (or empty), and this handler exits. Otherwise, the specified PICS file is played.

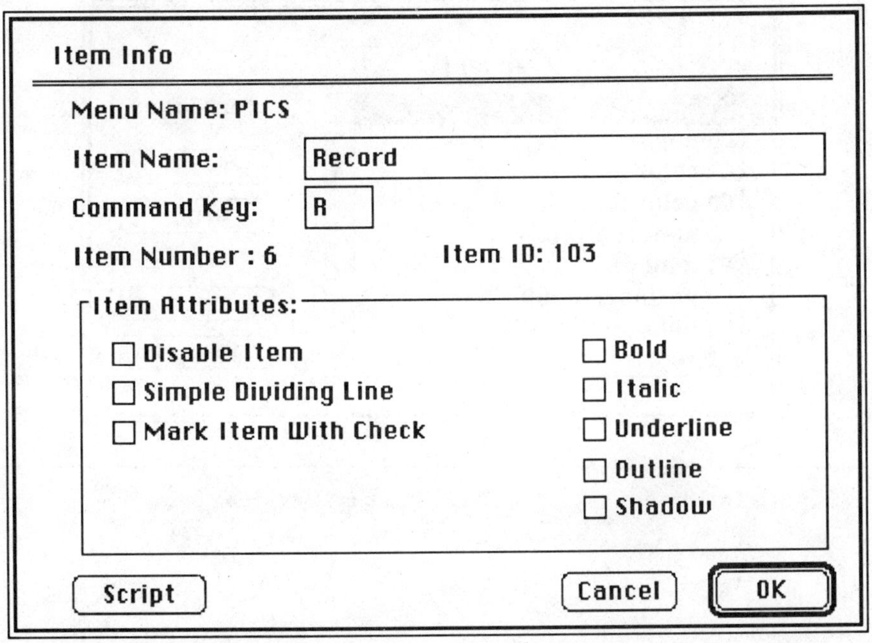

Item Info

Menu Name: PICS

Item Name: | Record |

Command Key: | R |

Item Number : 6   Item ID: 103

Item Attributes:
☐ Disable Item   ☐ Bold
☐ Simple Dividing Line   ☐ Italic
☐ Mark Item With Check   ☐ Underline
                            ☐ Outline
                            ☐ Shadow

(Script)   (Cancel)   (OK)

Figure 15-9.   In the Menu Item Info dialog box for the Record menu item, indicate that the keyboard shortcut for this item is COMMAND-R

If you have created a project called PICS MENU that contains this menu, you can install it by typing **Insert menu 1 of project "PICS MENU"** into the Message box. The menu will be added to the right of

```
on itemSelect
  put getFile("Choose a PICS file","PICS") into theFile
  if theFile is empty then exit itemselect
  --make sure the screen is restored after the dialog
  set lockscreen of topwindow() to false
  play pics theFile until mouse play pics theFile
end itemSelect
```

Script 15-4.   This handler prompts you to locate a PICS file on disk, and it then plays that PICS file

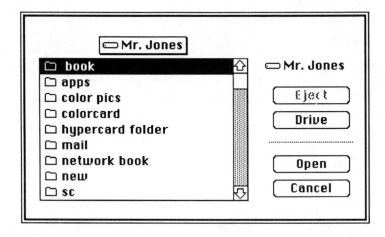

Figure 15-10.   The getFile XFCN summons this dialog box

existing menus. Next, use the Open ... item to create a new PICS file. You can then record a PICS file by changing the card, using the Record item (it is easiest to press COMMAND-R) to record the screen, make more changes, record those changes, and so on. You can see how this works by creating a small graphic and moving it around the screen, and recording that movement. When you are finished, use the Close menu item. To play the animation back, use the Play menu item, locate the PICS file you recorded, and it will play back.

This simple PICS menu can be enhanced in a number of ways. One way is to create a dialog box that allows you to specify different options when opening a file (namely the size of the rectangle you will be recording), and another for the Play command that lets you set different options for how the animation is played back. This might include speed options, certain frames, and the like. Remember, however, that if a dialog box is open when the Play command is issued, the animation will play within that dialog box.

Using PICS Files Created by Other Programs

Standard file formats offer a great deal of convenience, but you sometimes have to pay a price for it. In other words, there are few "gotchas" when using PICS files created by one program and used in another program.

Most programs that record PICS files save an entire window in the PICS file when you record to that format. In the interest of speed and disk space, then, you should size the window as small as you can before recording a PICS file. Complex animations in Super 3D, using a large window, can take up several megabytes of disk space, and consequently play back quite slowly.

MacroMind Director, however, does not record the entire window when exporting an animation to a PICS format. Instead, it saves a rectangle that is exactly small enough to contain the objects you are animating. If you have created a complex animation with SuperCard or Super 3D, you can import that animation into Director, and then export it again to a PICS file. The resulting PICS file will usually be smaller and play more quickly than it would otherwise.

Animation with STEP Files

Using PICS files for animations has several benefits, but it also has several drawbacks. One of the disadvantages of standard file formats is that they sometimes represent a lowest common denominator and might not include all the features of, or perform as well as, proprietary, customized formats. This is the case with PICS files: Because they include no picture compression, they take up more disk space, and play back more slowly than do other methods.

SuperCard's customized animation format is called the STEP format. It is a compressed format, which allows you to store larger animations in less space on disk. Additionally, because STEP files are smaller than PICS files, they generally play back more quickly.

Another key difference between STEP files and PICS files is that while PICS files only record the contents of a specific window (or a rectangle within that window), STEP files record the state of *the entire screen*. Therefore, when working with STEP animations, you need to remember that the entire screen will also be played back. Keep this in mind when you create your animations — the sudden appearance of a new environment on the screen might be disconcerting for your users. You can get around this by playing STEP animations only in conditions where you have total control over the environment.

You will also need to consider the effect of playing STEP animations on different size monitors.

STEP File Commands

SuperCard's STEP commands are much the same as its PICS commands. You can easily adapt the PICS menu discussed earlier in this chapter to work with STEP files.

Open STEP

Open STEP [file] fileName

This command opens a STEP file for recording. If another STEP file is already open, you will get an alert saying that only one STEP and PICS file can be open at a time (though a STEP file can be open while a PICS file is open, as long as only one file of each type is open). The "fileName" must be a complete pathname for the file. If a STEP file by that name exists, it will be overwritten by the new file.

Record STEP

Record STEP [file]

The Record STEP command records the contents of the screen to the current STEP file.

Close STEP

Close STEP [file]

The Close Step command closes the current STEP file, allowing you to play it.

Play STEP

**Play STEP [file] fileName [speed] [repeat number] [until event]
  [keep picture]**

This command works much the same way as does the Play PICS command. You have the same options as with the Play PICS command, with one exception: you cannot play specific frames of STEP files.

Speed   The speed option allows you to specify how fast the animation will be played. Allowable speeds are: very fast, fast, slow(ly), and very slow(ly). STEP animations play back very quickly, so you will most often use the slow or very slow speeds.

Repeat   This option, followed by an integer or the word "forever," tells SuperCard how many times to play the STEP animation file.

Until Event   As with the Play command, you can tell SuperCard to stop playing the animation when the mouse is clicked. If you use the "until mouse" option, the STEP animation will stop playing. If you use the "until click" option, the STEP animation will stop playing and the mouseClick message will be sent to the card on which you click.

Keep Picture   Using this option when playing a STEP file keeps the last frame of the animation on the screen. Use this option with care. As a screen is updated, it "kerchunks" depending on what areas of the screen you click on, and the appearance of the screen can be disconcerting when only parts of it are updated.

SIXTEEN

Building Applications

The Message Hierarchy of Stand-Alone Applications
Considerations
Assign an Icon to your Application
Stand-Alone Applications and Documents
Test the Application as an Application

One of SuperCard's unique features is that it allows you to transform a finished project into a stand-alone, double-clickable, standard Macintosh application. Others can then use it without actually having SuperCard. Indeed, others using your application do not even need to know that it was created with SuperCard.

Creating a stand-alone application requires more work than it first appears.

The Message Hierarchy of Stand-Alone Applications

When you are working in the standard SuperCard environment, the message hierarchy is similar to that of HyperCard, but when your project is working as a stand-alone application, the message hierarchy is quite different. Compare the stand-alone hierarchy shown in Figure 16-1 with the hierarchy shown in Figure 5-1 to see the differences.

The main difference is that your project becomes SuperCard itself and the SharedFile, and all message paths lead to your project. The standard SharedFile is not available, meaning you must include in your stand-alone project everything (including scripts and resources) that your project needs. Additionally, any projects you open from within a stand-alone project—whether they are standard SuperCard projects (which can be opened by stand-alones), or projects created by your stand-alone—use your stand-alone project as the final stop on their hierarchy as well.

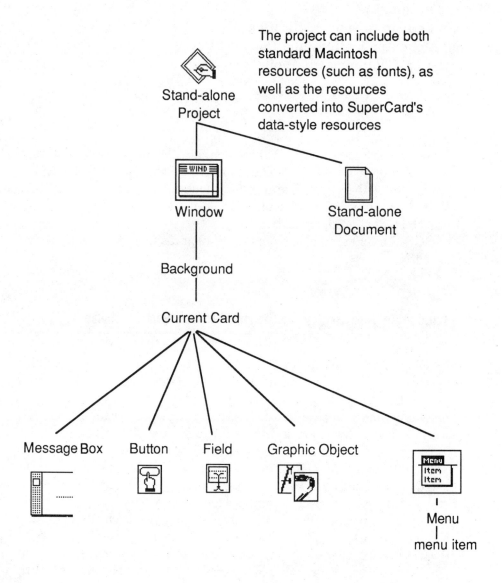

The project can include both standard Macintosh resources (such as fonts), as well as the resources converted into SuperCard's data-style resources

Stand-alone Project

Window

Stand-alone Document

Background

Current Card

Message Box

Button

Field

Graphic Object

Menu

menu item

Figure 16-1. This message hierarchy of a stand-alone application should be compared to the one shown in Figure 5-1

This requirement has both pleasant and unpleasant side effects when building stand-alone applications. In HyperCard, developers who were creating large applications faced a potentially serious problem when those applications spanned several stacks. Many of those stacks might need access to common handlers and resources. In HyperCard, you had two solutions to this problem. The first was to duplicate the necessary resources in all the stacks that needed them. The problem with this solution is that it sometimes made the stacks larger than they needed to be. Also, because a commonly-used handler could not be stored at a single location, changing that handler meant finding it in all the stacks that used it and then repeating the same changes in every instance.

The second solution was to install all the needed resources (including handlers) into the Home stack and provide a button that performed this installation into the user's Home stack. This solution is also problematic. After installing the resources of several different products into a Home stack, that Home stack could be quite crowded, and conflicts could result. It is also unprofessional to require users to customize their Home stacks to run your HyperCard stack.

You can solve this, however, with SuperCard's stand-alone capability. If you must deliver a SuperCard application as a collection of separate projects, you can include in your stand-alone everything needed by the other projects. To include handlers and functions that are needed by other projects, simply include them in the project script of the stand-alone. Because the resource fork of your stand-alone project is open, you can also include in the resource fork of that project any resources you need that cannot be imported into SuperCard's data fork resource handler.

Considerations

Aside from the revised hierarchy in effect when you work in the stand-alone environment, you need to consider a number of other aspects of these applications. First, you should plan ahead. If you decide to create a stand-alone project, during development you can make sure that your project includes everything it needs to run in the non-SharedFile environment. When you test your project in SuperCard, you will not have to rely on the tools of the Runtime Editor.

SuperEdit can edit projects even after you have turned them into stand-alone applications (provided you have not changed the creator ID of the file, as discussed later in this chapter). It is a good idea to turn your project into a stand-alone as soon in the development process as you can. This will help ensure that no surprises await you later in the development process.

Make Sure You Have the Correct Elements

The main thing to remember is that your stand-alone applications will *not* have access to any resources in a SharedFile. This means that handlers, functions, external commands and functions, sounds, icons, and other items will not be automatically available in your application unless you put them there. That is easy to remedy for resources that are part of SuperCard's resource structure, but it is not so easy for resources that are stored in the actual resource fork of the SharedFile. In the former case, you can easily use SuperEdit to open both the Shared-File and your project and copy those resources from the SharedFile into your project. However, if the resources you need are part of the Shared-File, you will need to use ResEdit or a similar program to copy the resources from the SharedFile into your project.

Build the Application with SuperEdit

To use SuperEdit to build a stand-alone application, simply make sure the project you want to convert is in the top project window in Super-Edit. It is usually a good idea to save a copy of your project under a different name before performing this step. Though you can edit stand-alone applications from within SuperEdit, some of the later steps in finishing the project can damage it. Saving a copy gives you a backup just in case.

Then, simply choose the Build Stand-Alone command from Super-Edit's File menu. At first, it will not seem that much has happened, but if you look at the Project Overview window, you will see that the project has grown by 350K on disk. This extra space is essentially occupied by all of SuperCard and SuperTalk, which has been added to your project.

Assign an Icon to Your Application

On the Macintosh, two items indicate the kind of file to the Finder: The file type, a four-character signature, indicates the contents of the file. For example, when you save a file as "text only" with most word processors, the file type will be "TEXT." That way, other programs can use the file type signature to open and edit the file.

The second signature is the *creator*, which tells the Macintosh what program created the file and allows the Finder to open a program when you double-click on a file created by that program. When you double-click on a file, the Finder looks at the file to determine the application it should open, consults its invisible Desktop file for the location of the program, opens that program, and instructs it to open the file on which you double-clicked.

SuperCard documents have a file type of MDOC and a creator of RUNT. SuperCard itself has a type of APPL (for application, telling the Finder it is a program that it can run) and a creator of RUNT. Super-Edit's type is APPL and its creator is MANP. Because SuperCard documents have a creator of RUNT, when you double-click on a project in the Finder, SuperCard is opened.

When you build a stand-alone application with SuperEdit, the file type of that application becomes APPL, and the creator of the file is STND, short for stand-alone. When the Finder is displaying this file on the Desktop, it consults the file itself to search for the icon it should use for the file.

The STND icon is satisfactory, but you may want to change it. How do you go about assigning your own icon to your stand-alone application? First, you need to get ResEdit 1.2 (or later), which allows you to edit the resources of a file. ResEdit is available from a number of sources. It can be licensed through the Apple Programmers and Developers Association, acquired from a user group, or downloaded from many on-line services, such as MacNet or CompuServe. Once you have ResEdit, you need to do the following.

1. Create your stand-alone application with SuperEdit. As mentioned earlier, use a copy of your project in case you make a mistake and damage or destroy the project.

2. Quit SuperEdit and start ResEdit.

3. When ResEdit opens, you will see a display like the one shown in Figure 16-2, showing all the files and folders on your disk. Navigate through these folders to find the one you want. In the example, the file called "TestApp" is being edited. Once you have found the file, select it by clicking on it, and then choose the Get Info command from ResEdit's File menu.

4. ResEdit's Info window for an application is shown in Figure 16-3.

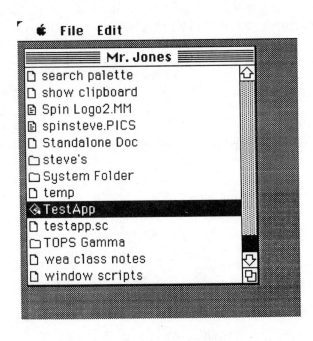

Figure 16-2.   ResEdit displays the files on your disk and allows you to modify the resource forks of those files

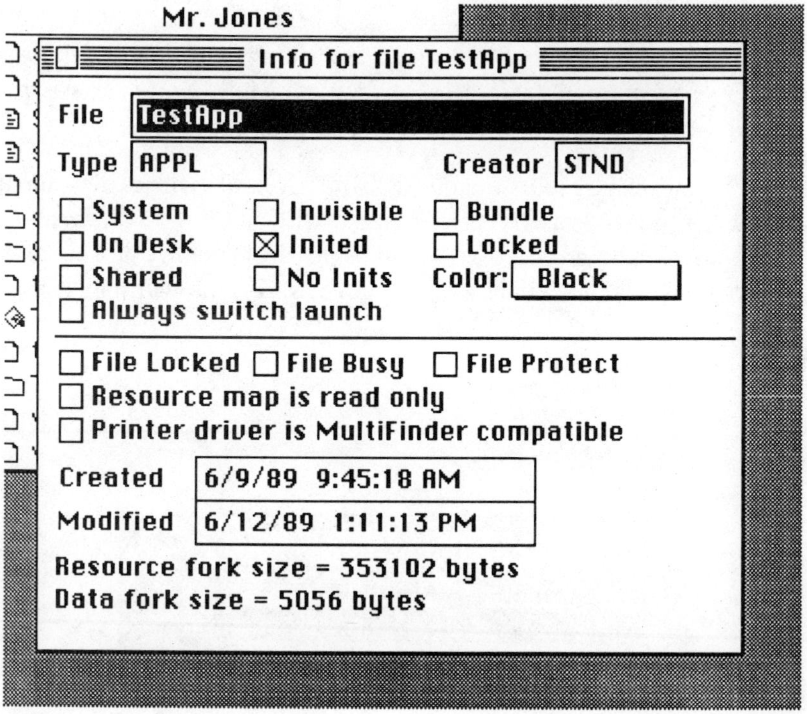

Mr. Jones

Info for file TestApp

File | **TestApp**

Type | **APPL**   Creator | **STND**

☐ System   ☐ Invisible   ☐ Bundle
☐ On Desk   ☒ Inited   ☐ Locked
☐ Shared   ☐ No Inits   Color: Black
☐ Always switch launch

☐ File Locked ☐ File Busy ☐ File Protect
☐ Resource map is read only
☐ Printer driver is MultiFinder compatible

Created | 6/9/89 9:45:18 AM
Modified | 6/12/89 1:11:13 PM

Resource fork size = 353102 bytes
Data fork size = 5056 bytes

Figure 16-3.   To change the creator of a stand-alone, change the creator field
and click on the checkbox labeled "Bundle"

You need to add two pieces of information to this window. First,
into the "creator" field, type the four-character signature of your
file. For example, if the creator is ABCD, you should type that into
the field. Next, click on the checkbox labeled "Bundle" to make sure
it is checked. This is called "setting the bundle bit." The bundle bit
tells the Finder that the resources are "bundled" together. After

You insert these two pieces of information, close the Get Info window. ResEdit will ask if you want to save the changes. Click on the Yes button.

5. Now, open your file by double-clicking on it (or by choosing the Open command from ResEdit's file menu). You will see a list of resources contained in the file, as shown in Figure 16-4.

6. Find the resource labeled "BNDL" and double-click on it. You will see a list of BNDL resources with only one resource showing; double-click on that resource. The first field you see is labeled "OwnerName," as shown in Figure 16-5. This will be set to STND.

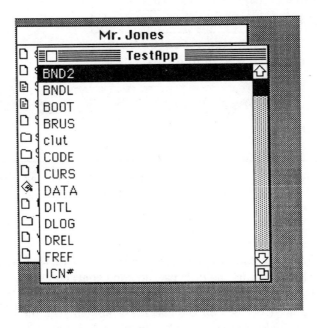

Figure 16-4.   Double-clicking on a file displays all the resource types that file contains

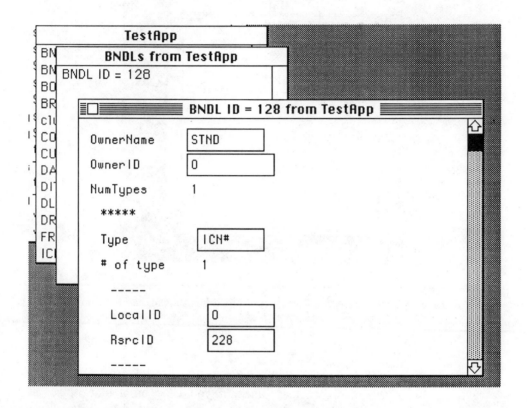

Figure 16-5.   The BNDL resource is another place in which you must type the creator signature

Double-click on this field and type your file signature (for example, **ABCD**). Close the BNDL resource windows.

7. Find the resource type ICN#, and open it by double-clicking. Find the application icon (the one bordered by a box in Figure 16-6). Double-click on it, and ResEdit will take you to the icon editor, shown in Figure 16-7. Editing an icon in ResEdit is like

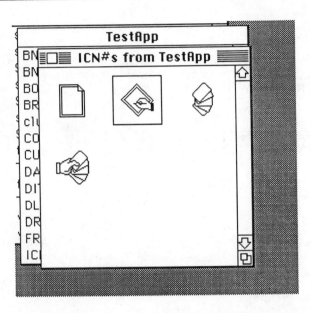

Figure 16-6. Select the icon bordered by a box to edit the file's icon

editing an icon in SuperEdit: if you click on a white pixel with the mouse, the pixel becomes black; if you click on a black pixel, it becomes white. In this example, a simple darkened triangle is created at the top of the icon. You can choose "Data → Mask" from ResEdit's ICN# menu to copy the contents of your changed icon to its mask. When you finish the icon, close the window and then close the window showing every ICN# in the file.

8. With the list of file resources open, choose "New" from the File menu to create a new type of resource. Type **ABCD** into this resource, as shown in Figure 16-8. An empty window will open. Choose "New" again, to create an actual resource. A window will appear, as shown in Figure 16-9. Do not type anything into this window; simply close it by clicking in its close box. With the new resource selected, choose "Get Info" from the File menu, and you will see a display such as the one shown in Figure 16-10. Type **0** (zero) into the field.

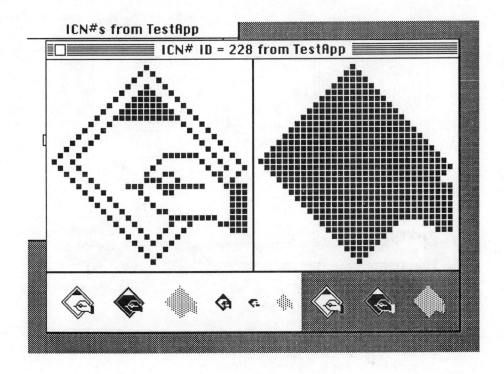

Figure 16-7.   ResEdit's Icon editor

9. Close the window. ResEdit will ask if you want to save changes to the file. Do so by clicking on the OK button in the dialog box.

10. Quit ResEdit. When you open the folder containing your stand-alone application, you will see the new icon for your file.

Stand-Alone Applications and Documents

Your applications can also create their own documents. These documents are created by using the New Project command in SuperTalk.

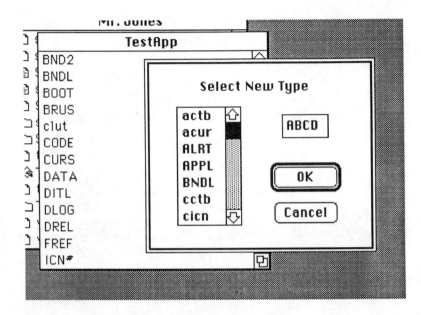

Figure 16-8.   The final step involves creating a new resource type of the same type as your creator signature

Test the Application as an Application

Before you distribute your application to others, you should thoroughly test it as an application. Testing accomplishes two goals. The first goal is to make sure that you have indeed installed all the necessary resources, especially handlers and functions. You should also make sure that any fonts or icons that you used in your project are available in the environments that will be used by others. This might include fonts that are not part of the standard set of Macintosh fonts: You can install those fonts or icons directly into your application using Apple's ResEdit or Font/DA Mover program.

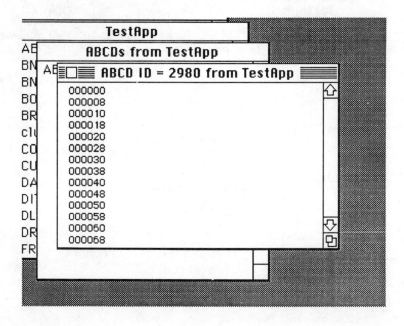

Figure 16-9.   Do not type anything into this window when creating a new resource type

The second goal is to make sure it is well-behaved as an application. Try to determine how well your application works both with the Multi-Finder and the regular Finder. Check the memory requirements of your program under MultiFinder. If you find that it can run in a small MultiFinder partition, use the Get Info command in the Finder to set the memory requirement as low as possible.

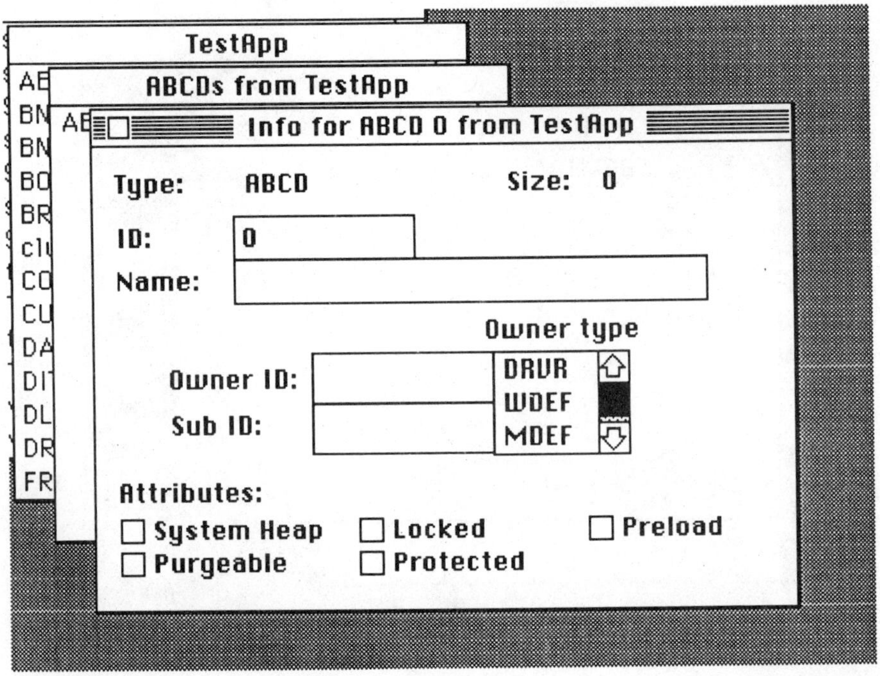

Figure 16-10. Set the ID of your new resource to 0

The HyperCard-SuperCard Transition

The Mental Transition
The HyperCard doMenu Command
Imported Stacks and Graphics
Some Tips

Although SuperCard incorporates many features of HyperCard, the two programs are not completely compatible. This appendix will examine some of the differences between the two programs. Other differences will become apparent after further evolution and usage of the product.

The Mental Transition

Although HyperCard and SuperCard are similar in the functions they provide and the means by which they provide them, you need to rethink some of your assumptions when creating projects in SuperCard.

Thinking in Projects and Windows

HyperCard stacks are composed of backgrounds and cards. The appearance of cards is determined by the appearance of the backgrounds that contain those cards. At this level, SuperCard is almost identical to HyperCard. Within a window, the appearance of individual cards is partly a result of the appearance of the backgrounds that contain the cards. However, a SuperCard project forms a new level above the HyperCard stack: a project contains one or more windows, which in turn contain backgrounds and cards. Working with projects takes some practice, but it has advantages.

Scripting around cards of different backgrounds in HyperCard can sometimes be a problem. If you have a script that checks every card in a stack for some characteristic (to pull a certain value out of a field, for example), you need to script around the occurrence of multiple backgrounds to make sure the same field is on every card.

In SuperCard, you can avoid this problem by constructing the project in a different way. Instead of using different backgrounds to contain the different kinds of cards, you can use different windows, each homogeneous in the kinds of cards it contains. You are then free from worry about backgrounds.

Free from Buttons

In HyperCard, only two kinds of card-level objects can have scripts: buttons and fields. The prime mover for scripts in HyperCard is the button, but in SuperCard "Anything can be a button." Yet another SuperCard slogan might be "Why use buttons at all?" In the standard Macintosh interface, most commands are given with the menu bar. Because SuperCard gives you control of the menu bar, you can use menus and menu items to drive your program; experienced Macintosh users will feel more comfortable with this mode.

In HyperCard, it is not always easy to create "universal" buttons—that is, buttons that can be used in different stacks and under different circumstances. To make a button available, that button must be copied to the actual card on which you want to use it. Later, then, if you change the button, you must change it in all its different locations, probably in many different stacks.

SuperCard provides a way around this with its floating palettes. Instead of creating a button that must be copied from card to card, you can create a floating palette that can be used with a variety of different projects, windows, and cards. Floating palettes give you the freedom to change the scripts of their buttons in only one location, instead of forcing you to search through a wide variety of stacks and cards to ferret out all instances of the button you want to change.

For examples of how to create floating palettes, consult the various palettes that are part of the Runtime Editor.

The HyperCard doMenu Command

One major difference between HyperCard and SuperCard is the content of the menus. HyperCard's menus contain many functions, and accessing some of those functions from within HyperTalk can only be done using the doMenu command, which executes a menu command. Because SuperCard has a "soft" user-definable menu, doMenu commands in SuperCard usually do not work in the same manner as doMenu commands in HyperCard.

If the checkbox labeled "Include Automatic Project Script with Converted Stacks" is checked in SuperEdit's Preferences dialog box, SuperEdit will automatically install a doMenu handler in the script of the new project that handles many of the incompatibilities between the menus of the two programs.

The following discussion is organized according to HyperCard menus. It examines how these menus and menu items are handled by SuperCard's doMenu handler.

The File Menu

As with most HyperCard menus, the File menu receives support in SuperCard. Some capabilities, such as Compact Stack, have been included as commands in SuperTalk, while other facilities are included as part of the Runtime Editor.

New Stack

Instead of using the New Stack menu item, SuperCard allows you to create a new project with the New Project command. When you issue this command, a Put File dialog box appears and asks you to name the new project and put it into a folder and disk. A new window is created in this project.

Open Stack

Using this menu item with the doMenu command is not often done in HyperCard. In SuperCard, you can replace it with a command such as

> open "The Project You Want"

and SuperCard (like HyperCard) will present a dialog box that asks you to locate the project you want to open.

Save A Copy

The Save A Copy menu item in HyperCard is useful for saving a copy of a stack under another name, to prevent loss of data when you are making big changes to a stack. Although SuperCard has no direct counterpart to this command, you can use the Save As item on the File menu in SuperEdit to save the current project under a different name.

Compact Stack

Compacting a stack, of course, removes extraneous free space generated in the stack. In SuperEdit, you can compact a project using the Compact item on the File menu. In SuperCard, you can simply use the Compact command, as discussed in Chapter Six.

Protect Stack

In HyperCard, you use the Protect Stack command to prevent others from making changes to the stack, or from using it at all if they do not know the correct password. In SuperEdit, you can assign a password to a project using the Password button from the Project Info dialog box.

The best way to prevent others from making unwanted changes to projects, however, is simply to not give them the tools to do so. If you build a stand-alone project, include only those tools others would absolutely need to use the project, and exclude those tools that could cause unwanted changes to the project. If you don't give others the tools to change the project, it will not be possible for them to change the project.

Delete Stack

In HyperCard, this menu item deletes the current stack from disk. SuperCard has no counterpart to this item.

Page Setup

Page Setup summons the dialog box that allows you to set certain printing parameters—paper orientation, paper size, and so on. Though SuperCard has direct counterpart for this command, whenever you issue the Print Card command, the Page Setup dialog is presented to you. You can also use the Open Printing With Dialog command.

Print Card

From within SuperTalk, you can use the Print Card command to print any card. As mentioned above, it first summons the Page Setup dialog box, to allow you to set certain printing parameters. The Runtime Editor includes a Print Card command.

Print Stack

In HyperCard, this menu item prints all the cards in the stack. In SuperCard's Runtime Editor, this is replaced with Print Window, which prints all the cards in the current window, and Print Project, which prints all the cards in all the windows in the current project.

Print Report

Included in the Runtime Editor is a menu item that works with the separate project called Print to give you control over printing fields. The ways to use this facility are discussed in Chapter Two.

Quit HyperCard

Using the statement

    doMenu "Quit HyperCard"

is the only way to quit HyperCard under script control. In SuperCard, you can quit with the Close all windows command.

The Edit Menu

Most of the HyperCard Edit menu items have directly compatible commands in SuperCard.

Undo

SuperCard has no Undo command. The doMenu handler included in converted stacks, however, uses the Revert command to undo the last action by recalling the current card from the last saved version on disk. The problem with this procedure is that any actions you performed since you last saved the card would be lost when the Revert command is used.

Cut

The Cut command removes the currently selected text or object and places it on the Clipboard. In SuperCard, you can simply use the Cut command instead of using the doMenu construct.

Copy

As with the Cut command, the Copy command is implemented directly in SuperCard, so you have no need for the doMenu construct.

Paste

The Paste command is implemented in SuperCard. There is no need to use the doMenu construct, which causes the program to paste the contents of the Clipboard onto the card.

Clear

SuperCard has no Clear command (which deletes the currently selected text or object without placing it on the Clipboard). The doMenu handler that is installed into converted stacks substitutes the Cut command for Clear when you use the doMenu Clear command. The problem with this is that the Cut command places the object or text you cut onto the Clipboard, which will remove anything that was already on the Clipboard.

New Card

SuperCard's New Card command is the counterpart of this menu item.

Delete Card

Use SuperCard's Delete Card command to delete the current card.

Cut Card

Use SuperCard's Cut Card command to delete the current card and place it on the Clipboard.

Copy Card

SuperCard's Copy Card command places a copy of the card on the Clipboard and leaves it in its current location. There is no need for the doMenu construct.

Text Style

SuperCard includes no built-in Text Style dialog box: instead of using a dialog box, at least in the Runtime Editor, you can use the separate Font, Style, and Size menus to style text within objects.

Background

In HyperCard, this menu item is a toggle: selecting it once turns background editing on; selecting it again turns it off. In SuperCard's Runtime Editor, this has been replaced by two menu items, which manipulate the editBackground property. In scripts, instead of using the doMenu construct, you can use the statements "set the editbkgnd to True" to turn background editing on, and "set the editbkgnd to false" to turn it off.

The Go Menu

In some ways, the Go command in SuperCard is quite different from the Go command in HyperCard. These differences are discussed in Chapter Seven.

Go Back

The Go Back command in SuperCard, as in HyperCard, takes you to the previous card.

Home

SuperCard does not includes an entity that is a direct counterpart to the Home Stack of HyperCard, so when you use the Go Home command in SuperCard, a dialog box asks you "Where is Home?" The doMenu handler installed in converted stacks beeps when you use this command.

Help

SuperCard does not include a standard Help stack, so when you use this menu command in a converted stack, the doMenu handler beeps.

Recent

In HyperCard, the Go Recent command presents a display showing miniature versions of the last 48 cards you opened. Because cards in SuperCard can be of radically different sizes, SuperCard has no similar Go Recent command. Instead, SuperCard's Go Recent command performs the same function as Go Back.

First, Prev, Next, Last

These four menu items are used for navigating among cards. As with HyperCard, there is no reason to use the doMenu construct to perform these actions. Instead, you can use Go First, Go Prev, and so on to go to these cards.

Find

In HyperCard, the Find menu item puts the word "Find" in the Message box and allows you to type in the text you want to find. The Find menu item in the Runtime Editor performs the same function.

Message

In HyperCard, this menu item toggles the visibility of the Message box. You can do the same thing with the Message menu item in the Runtime Editor, or you can use the statement "Show msg" to display the Message box, or "Hide msg" to hide it, as you can in HyperCard.

The Objects Menu

HyperCard's Objects menu contains items that let you access information about objects, cards, backgrounds, or stacks, and items that let you operate on some of those objects.

Info Menu Items

HyperCard's Info menu items present dialog boxes with information about selected objects. The Runtime Editor implements many of these functions using SuperTalk. You can either duplicate these scripts, or, if the Runtime Editor handlers are installed in your project, simply use the statement

    send doubleClickGraphic to graphicDescriptor

to get information on the graphic. See Chapter Ten for more information on the doubleClick message in SuperCard.

Bring Closer/Send Farther

HyperCard's Bring Closer and Send Farther commands are similar to the BringFront and SendBack commands in SuperCard. However, in HyperCard, the Bring Closer command brings the selected object one level closer, while in SuperCard, BringFront brings the selected object all the way to the front. The doMenu handler installed in converted stacks substitutes these commands, but that could cause a lot of problems with your scripts. See Chapter Ten for a discussion of these two SuperCard commands.

New Menu Items

In HyperCard, you can create new buttons, fields, and backgrounds. In SuperCard, you can use the New command to create a new card, background, window, or project. To create new objects on a card, you must manipulate the object tools from within SuperTalk, or manipulate them manually.

The Paint and Options Menus

Virtually none of HyperCard's Paint and Options Menu commands are directly supported in SuperCard. The doMenu handler installed in converted stacks beeps when a script attempts to use these menu items with the doMenu command. Only the Keep and Revert menu items on the Paint menu are converted to their SuperTalk rough equivalents (Save for Keep, Revert for Revert).

Imported Stacks and Graphics

When a HyperCard stack is converted to a SuperCard project, one key conversion is made to graphics. In SuperCard, of course, all paint graphics (the only kind available in HyperCard) are part of rectangular objects. When SuperCard imports a HyperCard stack, a graphic object 512 pixels wide and 342 pixels high is created on the card or background that contains that graphic. If the graphic is small, you can use SuperEdit's Pointer tool to resize the rectangle that encloses the graphic.

The fact that many, if not all, cards and backgrounds in HyperCard contain graphics led to Silicon Beach's decision not to send messages to unscripted graphics. If SuperCard did so, mouse messages generated by clicking on a card (not on a button or field) would never reach the card: the converted HyperCard graphic would intercept the message.

Some Tips

Part of the problem in switching from HyperCard to SuperCard may be mental: You can get used to certain features in HyperCard and become frustrated when those features are not implemented in SuperCard.

Implementing Script Peeking

In HyperCard, you can hold down the OPTION and COMMAND keys while clicking on a button to edit the script of that button (adding the SHIFT key to the combination allows you to edit the script of a field). When you hold down these keys, all the buttons are outlined, showing you where they are on the screen. You cannot easily simulate this feature in SuperTalk, but you can implement script peeking, with this script:

```
on mouseDown
  if the optionkey is down then
    if the commandKey is down then
      edit the script of the target
      if "button" is in the name of the target then
        set the hilite of the target to false
      end if
      exit to SuperCard
    end if
  end if
end mouseDown
```

If you place this handler in the script of your SharedFile, you can edit the script of any object by holding down the OPTION and COMMAND keys and clicking on that object. This mouseDown handler receives the messages, checks the status of the two keys, and then edits the script of the object that received the message.

When you have finished editing the script, the "exit to SuperCard" line stops execution of the handler and prevents the mouseUp message from being sent to the object on which you clicked. The "If" test (to see if you clicked on a button) is due to a bug in the first release of SuperCard. This bug causes the highlight of a button to be set to true when the button receives the mouseDown message. When you are using this handler, the button never receives the mouseUp message, so the line "set the hilite of the target to false" dehighlights the button.

Importing your Home Stack

Another thing that you can do to adapt to the SuperCard environment is import the resources and scripts in your Home stack into SuperCard's SharedFile. If you have been using HyperCard a great deal, you have probably customized the script of your Home stack fairly heavily and have added sounds, icons, and other resources to it.

To make these available in SuperCard, use SuperEdit to convert your Home stack to a SuperCard project. To move the resources from your Home stack into the SharedFile, open the converted SuperCard project, click on the Resources icon in the Project Overview window, and select "Copy" from the File menu. Next, click on your SharedFile Project Overview window, click on its Resources icon, and select "Paste" from the File menu. All your HyperCard resources should now be available to SuperCard. This is especially appealing with button icons; though SuperCard provides a counterpart to each HyperCard icon, the design is a little different. If you want to see the familiar HyperCard icons, this conversion is the way to do it.

When SuperEdit converts a Hypercard stack, the scripts that were in your stack script become part of the window script of the first window of the converted project. To copy these handlers into the SharedFile, open the window script of the converted Home stack, select the handlers you want to copy, and choose "Copy" from the File menu. Open the script of the SharedFile *Project* (not a window script) and paste in the handlers you copied. You will probably need to do some testing in SuperCard to see if your scripts work in the same manner as they do in HyperCard.

In the final analysis, the best tip for making the transition from HyperCard to SuperCard is to spend a lot of time working with Super-Card, particularly its wide range of tools, such as windows (including dialog boxes and palettes), menus, and graphic objects.

The Runtime Editor Scripts

Installing the Runtime Editor
Modifying What Is Installed
Optimizing the Editor Scripts

The Runtime Editor provides an environment that reproduces much, if not all, of what is available in HyperCard or SuperEdit and at the same time gives you capabilities that neither of these two programs offers.

The fact that the Runtime Editor is written entirely in SuperTalk has advantages as well as drawbacks. One advantage is that you can entirely customize the SoftEditor to suit your particular needs or habits; you can even abandon it entirely and write your own editor. One major drawback is that features written in SuperTalk simply do not execute as quickly as those hardcoded into the language.

This appendix will examine some of the Runtime Editor scripts and give you some ideas about how you can change them to suit your habits, and perhaps increase their performance. By studying these scripts, you will learn some of the ways various functions can, and should, be handled in SuperCard.

Installing the Runtime Editor

Before your project can use the facilities of the Runtime Editor, you must install the Runtime Editor. There are two ways to do this.

In SuperCard

If you are running the Runtime Editor in SuperCard and want to install its scripts into your project, choose the Install Editor menu item from the Runtime Editor's File menu. You will be presented with a dialog box that asks if you want to install the scripts.

The editor is installed into your project by getting the script of a window called "Boot Script" from the Runtime Editor project. The handlers in this script are then installed into the script of the current project. You can modify these handlers, then, by modifying the script of the Boot Script window, as will be discussed later in this appendix.

In SuperEdit

In SuperEdit, you do not have to do anything to install the Runtime Editor scripts. Instead, if the "Include Automatic Project Scripts W/New Project" checkbox of SuperEdit's Preferences dialog box is checked, the Runtime Editor scripts are installed automatically whenever you create a new project.

SuperEdit, however, does *not* take the Runtime Editor scripts from the same source as does SuperCard. Instead, the scripts are read in from a resource that is part of the SuperEdit program itself. The resource is one of two "BOOT" type resources in SuperEdit. Unfortunately, this makes changing the scripts installed automatically by SuperEdit very difficult to modify. The best solution is to make sure the Preferences box is *not* checked, and only use SuperCard to install the Runtime Editor scripts.

What Is Installed Into Your Project?

When you install the Runtime Editor into your project, eight handlers are installed.

The Startup Handler

The first handler installed into your project is for the startUp message, which is sent to the first project started when running SuperCard (that is, if you double-click on the project in the Finder, or if you open this project when presented with the dialog box after you start SuperCard). An annotated version of this handler is shown in Script B-1.

```
On startUp
  -- declare the global variables
  Global SE_MENUS -- how many menus to install?
  Global SE_PALETTES -- which palettes?
  Global SE_STACK -- the name of this project
  Global SE_AUTOLOAD -- automatically load the editor?
  Global SE_MENUBAR -- display the menubar?
  Global SE_MESSAGEBOX -- display the message box?
  Global SE_AUTOLOADBOX -- tell you SC is autoloading editor?

  -- these lines hold the preferences for this stack
  Put the name of this project into SE_STACK
  Put 6 into SE_MENUS
  Put "0,0,0,0,0" into SE_PALETTES
  Put "AutoLoad" into SE_AUTOLOAD
  Put true into SE_MENUBAR
  Put false into SE_MESSAGEBOX
  Put false into SE_AUTOLOADBOX

  -- these lines handle loading the editor
  -- automatically load the editor?
  If SE_AUTOLOAD is "AutoLoad" then
    If SE_AUTOLOADBOX is true then -- display the notice?
      -- if yes, at center of screen
      Put the screenloc into POS
    Else
      Put "-1000,-1000" into POS -- way off the upper left
    End if
    Set loc of wd "Auto Load" of project ¬
    "Runtime Editor" to POS
    Open wd "Auto Load" of project "Runtime Editor"
    Show wd "Auto Load" of project "Runtime Editor"
    -- this "Runtime Editor" handler, in the Runtime Editor,
    -- does the dirty work of opening the editor.
    -- it uses the global variables already declared
    Send "RuntimeEditor" to project "Runtime Editor"
    -- keeps this window open for later use, but hides it
    Hide wd "Auto Load" of project "Runtime Editor"
  End if
  If SE_AUTOLOAD is "Option" then -- ask to load the editor
    Set the loc of wd "Option" of ¬
    project "Runtime Editor" to the screenloc
    Open wd "Option" of project "Runtime Editor"
  End if
End startUp
```

Script B-1.   The startUp handler installed into your project for using the Runtime Editor

The purpose of the startUp handler is to reflect and store the status of the Preferences dialog box that you reach from the Project Info menu item in the Runtime Editor. This dialog box is shown in Figure B-1. As you can see, the Runtime Editor Preferences allow you to determine which menus and palettes are opened automatically when you start up, as well as allowing you to automatically show or hide the Message box, the menu bar, and the AutoLoad alert (which tells you that the Runtime Editor is loading). These settings are stored on disk in the script of the project. This script is modified when you click on the OK button in the Preferences dialog box.

The first group of radio buttons on the Preferences dialog box lets you specify the menus to be installed when the Runtime Editor is launched. Your choice is reflected in the script, in the variable *SE_Menus*, which contains the number of menus you want to install.

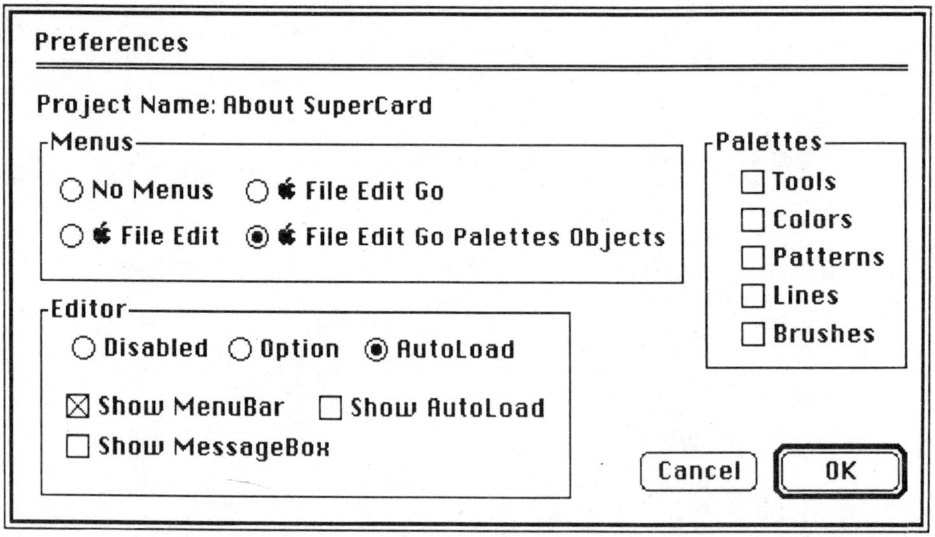

Preferences

Project Name: About SuperCard

Menus
- ○ No Menus   ○ ⚫ File Edit Go
- ○ ⚫ File Edit   ● ⚫ File Edit Go Palettes Objects

Palettes
- ☐ Tools
- ☐ Colors
- ☐ Patterns
- ☐ Lines
- ☐ Brushes

Editor
- ○ Disabled ○ Option ● AutoLoad
- ☒ Show MenuBar   ☐ Show AutoLoad
- ☐ Show MessageBox

[Cancel]   [OK]

Figure B-1   The Preferences dialog box in the Runtime Editor

The Editor section of the Preferences dialog box allows you to specify whether the Runtime Editor is disabled, loaded as an option, or is automatically loaded. If you check the Disabled radio button, the Runtime Editor is not loaded when the project starts. If you click on the Option radio button, you are presented with a dialog box asking if you want to load the Editor. If you click on the AutoLoad radio button, the Runtime Editor is loaded automatically. Your setting is stored in the script in the global variable *SE_Autoload*.

The checkboxes below these radio buttons let you specify whether you want to have the menu bar, Message box, or the AutoLoad alert window visible on startup. These settings are stored in the appropriate variables.

The final group of checkboxes allows you to specify the palettes that you want displayed automatically. Your choices are stored in the global variable *SE_Palettes* as a set of numbers that can be either "true" (1) or "false" (0) for each palette.

When your project starts, the startUp handler first declares these variables and then inserts values that reflect your Preferences settings. After doing so, if the *SE_Autoload* variable is "true" (that is, if you have checked the AutoLoad radio button in the Preferences dialog box), the Runtime Editor will be installed. This is handled by the first If test in the script. If you set the Runtime Editor to AutoLoad, the handler checks the *SE_AutoloadBox* variable, to see if you want to be notified that the Runtime Editor is loading. If so, the center of the screen is stored in the variable *POS*; otherwise, a location on the left and top of the screen is stored in this variable, and the window "Auto Load" of the Runtime Editor is opened at this location.

The message "Runtime Editor" is sent to the Runtime Editor project. The handler for this message uses the global variables initialized in the startUp handler, and then opens the appropriate menus and palettes.

The MenuKey Handler

Also installed into your project is a handler for the message menuKey, which is sent whenever you hold down the COMMAND key and type another key. This handler provides support for standard functions, including displaying the Message box, quitting SuperCard, and editing, no matter which card is visible. One of the primary benefits of this handler is that it allows you to quit SuperCard, or bring up the Message box, even if a dialog box is visible that might otherwise prevent you from carrying out these actions.

The DoubleClick Handlers

Finally, a series of handlers for various doubleClick messages are included in your project. As discussed in Chapter Ten, these messages are sent to objects when you double-click on them with the Pointer tool. The purpose of these handlers is to present the Info dialog box for an object when you click on that object. The basic functions of these scripts are the same, so this discussion will focus on the doubleClickGraphic handler, which responds to the message that is sent when you double-click on a graphic object with the Pointer tool.

Script B-2 shows the handler for this message that is installed into your project. This handler has two functions. Its first function is to initialize the global variable *SE_TARGET*, which contains the name of the object on which you double-clicked. This is handled by the line "Put the target into SE_TARGET." This would contain a complete descriptor of the graphic on which you double-click, such as:

```
card graphic ID 101 of card ID 153 of window ID 100 of Project
''hard disk: sc project''
```

```
On doubleClickGraphic

  Global SE_RUNTIME_EDITOR
  Global SE_TARGET

  Put the target into SE_TARGET
  If SE_RUNTIME_EDITOR is "Installed" then
  Send doubleClickGraphic to project "Runtime Editor"

End doubleClickGraphic
```

Script B-2.   The doubleClickGraphic handler installed by the Runtime Editor

The handler's second function is to check the global variable *SE_Runtime_Editor*, which tells it whether the Runtime Editor is running. If the editor is running, the message doubleClickGraphic is sent to the Runtime Editor. This message is handled by the handler shown in Script B-3.

The purpose of this handler is to display a complete Info window for the object on which you double-click. As you can see from the script, this task entails a fair amount of work, which accounts for some of the sluggishness of the Runtime Editor.

The first thing this handler does is declare a series of global variables. The variables *SE_Color_Palette*, *SE_Pattern_Palette*, and *SE_Line_Palette* tell the handler whether or not these palettes are visible. These variables are controlled by the items on the Palettes menu in the Runtime Editor, and the buttons on those palettes.

The first If test in the handler determines if the OPTION key is being held down. If so, the various palettes are updated to show the color, pattern, and line settings by sending messages to these palettes if they are open.

If you are not holding down the OPTION key, the handler checks the SHIFT key. If it is down, the script of the object is opened.

If you are not holding down any key, the Info dialog box about the graphic is displayed. The window is first displayed off the screen to make for clean screen updating as its items are filled in. The handler then simply cycles through each of the items in the dialog box and fills them in with the relevant information about the object on which you double-clicked. Once all the information is filled in, the location of the window is set to the middle of the screen.

Many of the particulars of this handler relate only to graphic objects, but the same process is handled by the relevant handlers for fields, buttons, cards, backgrounds, and projects.

Modifying What Is Installed

The Runtime Editor handlers total about 2500 characters. Although this is not a great deal of overhead, you can reduce it by moving some of the scripts into the SharedFile, where they can be used by all your projects.

```
On doubleClickGraphic -- displays info box about a graphic

   Global SE_OBJECT_NAME
   -- is color palette showing?
   Global SE_COLOR_PALETTE
   -- is pattern palette showing?
   Global SE_PATTERN_PALETTE
   -- is line palette showing?
   Global SE_LINE_PALETTE
   -- an objectDescriptor, set by the calling handler
   Global SE_TARGET

   -- Indicate a wait.
   Set the cursor to watch

   -- Get the long id of the selected object.
   Put the long id of SE_TARGET into SE_OBJECT_NAME

   -- Determine if a special key was pressed.
   -- these keys allow you to update the palette information
   -- for a selected object.

   If the optionKey is down then

      -- update colors in color palette
      If SE_COLOR_PALETTE is "Open" then send CopyColors ¬
   to window "Color Palette" of stack "Runtime Editor"

      -- update pattern palette
      If SE_PATTERN_PALETTE is "Open" then send CopyPatterns ¬
   to window "Pattern Palette" of stack "Runtime Editor"

      -- update the line palette
      If SE_LINE_PALETTE is "Open" then send CopyLines ¬
   to window "Line Palette" of stack "Runtime Editor"

      Exit doubleClickGraphic
   End if

   -- allows you to edit script of an object, by holding down
   -- the Shift key and double-clicking on it.
   If the shiftkey is down then
      Edit script of SE_OBJECT_NAME
      Exit doubleClickGraphic
   End if
   -- Open the window, to contain the graphic info
   -- off screen, while it's being updated.
   Set loc of window "Graphic Info" of ¬
   stack "Runtime Editor" to -1000,-1000
   Open window "Graphic Info" of stack "Runtime Editor"
   Set lockscreen to true
```

Script B-3.   The doubleClickGraphic handler in the Runtime Editor itself

```
-- Fill the dialog with info.
Put the short name of SE_OBJECT_NAME into SHORT_NAME
If SHORT_NAME contains "Graphic ID" then
   Put empty into cd field "Name" of window ¬
   "Graphic Info" of stack "Runtime Editor"
Else
   Put SHORT_NAME into cd field "Name" of window ¬
   "Graphic Info" of stack "Runtime Editor"
End if
Set textfont of cd fld "Name" of wd "Graphic Info" ¬
of stack "Runtime Editor" to Chicago
Put number of SE_OBJECT_NAME into cd field "Number" of ¬
window "Graphic Info" of stack "Runtime Editor"
Put short ID of SE_OBJECT_NAME into cd field "ID" of ¬
window "Graphic Info" of stack "Runtime Editor"
Put the style of SE_OBJECT_NAME into card field "Style" ¬
of window "Graphic Info" of stack "Runtime Editor"
If visible of SE_OBJECT_NAME is true then
   Set hilite of cd btn "Currently Visible" of wind ¬
   "Graphic Info" of stack "Runtime Editor" to true
End if
Select text of cd fld "Name"
Set lockscreen to false

-- Center the window.
Set loc of window "Graphic Info" of ¬
stack "Runtime Editor" to the screenloc

End doubleClickGraphic
```

Script B-3.   The doubleClickGraphic handler in the Runtime Editor itself
    (continued)

As mentioned earlier, you cannot easily change the scripts that are installed automatically by SuperEdit, because they are contained in a resource that is part of SuperEdit itself. You can, however, change the scripts that are installed by SuperCard. If you choose to do this, make sure that SuperEdit is instructed *not* to automatically install scripts, by not checking that option in its Preferences dialog box.

Prime candidates for inclusion in the SharedFile are the various doubleClick handlers that are contained in the Boot Script window of the Runtime Editor. To move these from the Boot Script window, first, save backup copies of both the Runtime Editor and the SharedFile. Then open the script of the Boot Script window in SuperEdit, select these doubleClick handlers, and choose Cut from the Edit menu. Next, open the SharedFile, open the script of the SharedFile project, and paste the doubleClick handlers into that script. The menuKey handler is also a good candidate for moving. Note that moving these handlers into the SharedFile means that the messages they respond to must travel through many more layers of the hierarchy, so their performance will suffer as well.

You could also move the startUp handler from the Boot Script window of the Runtime Editor into the SharedFile, but since the Preferences settings for each project are stored in this handler itself, moving the handler would mean that you could not change the Preferences for any individual project.

Making drastic modifications to the Runtime Editor handlers that are installed in your project also means that you might have some problems should these handlers be modified in future releases of Super-Card. Regardless of where you put them, you should not *change* these handlers unless you remember to adapt your changes to future versions of the Runtime Editor.

Optimizing the Editor Scripts

As mentioned at the outset of this appendix, the main penalty for having the Runtime Editor implemented as SuperTalk code is its performance. An example is the Tool palette on the Runtime Editor's Palettes menu. Using this palette, switching between the Draw and Paint palettes can take several seconds, even on a Mac IIX. If you examine the script of this window (open the Tool Palettes window of the Runtime Editor in SuperEdit and then open the script of that window), you can see that this script is occupied to a great extent with resetting the various buttons on the card to highlight the tool you have selected. The same is true of most of the scripts in the Runtime Editor. The difference between the performance of SuperCard's Runtime Editor, SuperEdit, and HyperCard is that the user interfaces of the latter two programs are written in speedy compile languages, whereas the Runtime Editor is written in SuperTalk.

Besides buying faster (and more expensive) Macintoshes, you have a couple of solutions to this problem. One solution is to do most of your development with SuperEdit instead of SuperCard. SuperEdit has many advantages over SuperCard: it is less modal (especially when editing scripts), has more tools (such as the AutoTrace and Draw Text tools), and is much faster than SuperCard. SuperEdit was made to edit projects and is very fast at doing it. The disadvantage of working extensively in SuperEdit, however, is significant—your scripts do not work. A better solution is to use SuperEdit for drawing, sorting windows and cards, and copying and pasting between scripts, and then use SuperCard to debug and fine-tune the scripts of your project. Appendix A includes a short script that you can include in your SharedFile that makes it easier to open scripts of objects.

A third solution is simply to work without the Runtime Editor, or not use all its features. You can lean on the Runtime Editor while you are learning SuperCard, but it is not as necessary once you become familiar with SuperTalk. As mentioned, much of the code of the palettes is dedicated to enhancing the user interface. While user interfaces are very important, and you should be sure to include complete user interfaces in projects you develop, you might not need to have the palettes constantly updated when you are developing them. Explore the scripts of these palettes, and try to reduce them to their bare necessities. If you write a better, faster Runtime Editor, be sure to make it available to others!

Suggested Reading

Creating stacks or projects with such applications as HyperCard or SuperCard breaks the traditional programming mold. Only part of your work with these programs can correctly be called "programming." These programs are designed, at least in part, as publishing tools: media to present ideas, to teach, and to excite.

This bibliography, then, is intended as a source for ideas about such topics as interface design, presentation techniques, graphic design, and more. It is not meant to be a complete listing but rather a starting point that might lead you to other tools and sources.

The Human Interface Guidelines: The Apple Desktop Interface. Reading, Mass.: Addison-Wesley, 1987.

The "official" definition of how programs on the Macintosh are supposed to work.

Technical Introduction to the Macintosh Family. Reading, Mass.: Addison-Wesley, 1987.

In nontechnical language, this book explains how software works on the Macintosh.

Dewdney, A.K. *The Touring Omnibus: 61 Excursions in Computer Science.* Rockville, Md.: Computer Science Press, 1989.

A popularization of computer science, by the author of *Scientific American's* "Computer Recreations" column. If you are starting to program without an education in computer science (as are many users of HyperCard and SuperCard), this book helps you understand some of the underlying theories of programming. Dewdney's algorithms are clear and not too difficult to translate into HyperTalk or SuperTalk. His other book, *The Armchair Universe* (New York: W.H. Freeman & Co., 1988) is also recommended.

Dreyfuss, Henry. *Symbol Sourcebook.* New York: Van Nostrand Reinhold, 1984.

A codified collection of graphical symbols from throughout the world. A great source of ideas for icon and graphic designs.

Heckel, Paul. *The Elements of Friendly Software Design.* New York: Warner, 1984.

An excellent examination of what makes software useful. Somewhat dated—he discusses Visicalc and WordStar—but still very helpful. Heckel's book contains a superb bibliography.

Kelly, Kevin, ed. *Signal: Communication Tools for the Information Age.* New York: Harmony Books, 1988.

A catalog of books, information, devices, and other tools relating to communication. The book is a good place to look for ideas and other sources.

Macaulay, David. *The Way Things Work.* Boston, Mass.: Houghton Mifflin, 1988.

Some books guide by example as well as their content. This is an entertaining and informative reference describing how many types of tools work. Both Macaulay's text and illustrations are clear, informative, and humorous.

Norman, Don. *The Psychology of Everyday Things.* New York: Basic Books, 1988.

This book is an examination of what goes wrong in product design, why it goes wrong, and how to avoid these errors. Designers of products of all types would profit from a close reading. The book contains numerous principles that creators of computer software should remember, and a section called "The Foibles of Computer Systems" is especially helpful.

Tufte, Edward R. *The Visual Display of Quantitative Information.* Cheshire, Conn.: Graphics Press, 1983.

This book examines the use of visual means (charts and graphs) to express numerical data.

Apple®	Apple Computer, Inc.
Canvas™	Deneba Software
CompileIt!™	Itty Bitty Computers
Digital Darkroom™	Silicon Beach Software, Inc.
Director™	Macromind, Inc.
HyperCard®	Apple Computer, Inc.
HyperSound™	Farallon Computing
HyperTalk™	Apple Computer, Inc.
MacDraw™	Apple Computer, Inc.
Macintosh®	Apple Computer, Inc.
MacPaint™	Apple Computer, Inc.
MacRecorder™	Farallon Computing
MultiFinder™	Apple Computer, Inc.
Open It!™	Tenpoint0
PageMaker®	Aldus Corporation
Pixel Paint™	Pixel Resources, Inc.
QuickDraw™	Apple Computers, Inc.
Red Ryder®	The FreeSoft Company
ResEdit™	Electronic Arts
SoundEdit™	Farallon Company
Studio/1™	Electronic Arts
Studio/8™	Electronic Arts
Suitcase II	Software Supply
Super 3D™	Silicon Beach Software, Inc.
SuperCard™	Silicon Beach Software, Inc.
SuperEdit™	Silicon Beach Software, Inc.
SuperPaint™	Silicon Beach Software, Inc.
SuperTalk™	Silicon Beach Software, Inc.
Swivel 3D™	Paracomp, Inc.

INDEX

The manuscript for this book was prepared and submitted to Osborne/McGraw-Hill in electronic form. The acquisitions editor for this project was Jeffrey Pepper, the technical reviewer was Ric Ford, and the project editor was Nancy Beckus.

Century Expanded was used for the text body and Eras DemiBold was used for display.

Cover art by Bay Graphics Design, Inc. Color separation and cover supplier, Phoenix Color Corporation. Book printed and bound by R.R. Donnelley & Sons Company, Crawfordsville, Indiana.